**Leos Carax**

D1591114

MANCHESTER
UNIVERSITY PRESS

FRENCH FILM DIRECTORS

DIANA HOLMES and ROBERT INGRAM *series editors*
DUDLEY ANDREW *series consultant*

**Jean-Jacques Beineix**   PHIL POWRIE

**Luc Besson**   SUSAN HAYWARD

**Bertrand Blier**   SUE HARRIS

**Robert Bresson**   KEITH READER

**Claude Chabrol**   GUY AUSTIN

**Marguerite Duras**   RENATE GÜNTHER

**Diane Kurys**   CARRIE TARR

**Georges Méliès**   ELIZABETH EZRA

**Jean Renoir**   MARTIN O'SHAUGHNESSY

**Coline Serreau**   BRIGITTE ROLLET

**François Truffaut**   DIANA HOLMES AND ROBERT INGRAM

**Agnès Varda**   ALISON SMITH

FRENCH FILM DIRECTORS

# Leos Carax

FERGUS DALY AND GARIN DOWD

**Manchester University Press**
MANCHESTER AND NEW YORK

distributed exclusively in the USA by Palgrave

*Published by* Manchester University Press
Oxford Road, Manchester M13 9NR, UK
*and* Room 400, 175 Fifth Avenue, New York, NY 10010, USA
www.manchesteruniversitypress.co.uk

*Distributed exclusively in the USA by*
Palgrave, 175 Fifth Avenue, New York, NY 10010, USA

*Distributed exclusively in Canada by*
UBC Press, University of British Columbia, 2029 West Mall, Vancouver, BC, Canada V6T 1Z2

*British Library Cataloguing-in-Publication Data*
A catalogue record for this book is available from the British Library

*Library of Congress Cataloging-in-Publication Data applied for*

ISBN 0 7190 6314 0 *hardback*
     0 7190 6315 9 *paperback*

First published 2003

11 10 09 08 07 06 05 04 03     10 9 8 7 6 5 4 3 2 1

Typeset in Scala with Meta display
by Koinonia, Manchester
Printed in Great Britain
by Biddles Ltd, Guildford and King's Lynn

# Contents

LIST OF PLATES                                                          page vi
SERIES EDITORS' FOREWORD                                                    vii
ACKNOWLEDGEMENTS                                                             ix

Introduction: genesis of Carax's system                                       1

1  *Boy Meets Girl*, *Mauvais Sang* and the *nouvelle vague*
   inheritance                                                               30

2  *Feux d'artifice*: *Les Amants du Pont-Neuf* and the spectacle
   of vagrancy                                                              103

3  *Pola X* or Carax's ambiguities                                          137

FILMOGRAPHY                                                                 177
SELECT BIBLIOGRAPHY                                                         179
INDEX                                                                       183

# List of plates

1   The planes occupied by Alex and Mireille seem to be
    set in motion in *Boy Meets Girl.* © Mercure Distribution   *page* 27
2   Alex's own fireworks in *Les Amants du Pont-Neuf.* © Roissy
    Films                                                                27
3   Anna ascends into a 'pure image' in *Mauvais Sang.*
    © Mercure Distribution                                               28
4   Alex and Anna play in *Mauvais Sang.* © Mercure Distribution         28
5   Pierre and Isabelle in *Pola X.* © Arena Films                       29
6   Alex and Anna arrive at the airfield in *Mauvais Sang.*
    © Mercure Distribution                                               29

# Series editors' foreword

To an anglophone audience, the combination of the words 'French' and 'cinema' evokes a particular kind of film: elegant and wordy, sexy but serious – an image as dependent on national stereotypes as is that of the crudely commercial Hollywood blockbuster, which is not to say that either image is without foundation. Over the past two decades, this generalised sense of a significant relationship between French identity and film has been explored in scholarly books and articles, and has entered the curriculum at university level and, in Britain, at A level. The study of film as an art-form and (to a lesser extent) as industry, has become a popular and widespread element of French Studies, and French cinema has acquired an important place within Film Studies. Meanwhile, the growth in multi-screen and 'art-house' cinemas, together with the development of the video industry, has led to the greater availability of foreign-language films to an English-speaking audience. Responding to these developments, this series is designed for students and teachers seeking information and accessible but rigorous critical study of French cinema, and for the enthusiastic filmgoer who wants to know more.

The adoption of a director-based approach raises questions about *auteurism*. A series that categorises films not according to period or to genre (for example), but to the person who directed them, runs the risk of espousing a romantic view of film as the product of solitary inspiration. On this model, the critic's role might seem to be that of discovering continuities, revealing a necessarily coherent set of themes and motifs which correspond to the particular genius of the individual. This is not our aim: the *auteur* perspective on film, itself most clearly articulated in France in the early 1950s, will be interrogated in certain volumes of the series, and, throughout, the director will be treated as one highly significant element in a complex process of film production and reception which includes socio-economic and political determinants, the work of a large and highly skilled team of artists and technicians, the mechanisms of production and distribution, and the complex and multiply determined responses of spectators.

The work of some of the directors in the series is already known outside France, that of others is less so – the aim is both to provide informative and original English-language studies of established figures, and to extend the range of French directors known to anglophone students of cinema. We intend the series to contribute to the promotion of the informal and formal study of French films, and to the pleasure of those who watch them.

DIANA HOLMES
ROBERT INGRAM

# Acknowledgements

GARIN DOWD   I am grateful to Robert Ingram, Diana Holmes and the anonymous readers of the manuscript, staff at the BFI and at Manchester University Press, Alex Raja at Artificial Eye for assistance and information, Claire Marchandise, Arena Films and Leos Carax for enabling us to view 'sans titre'. The Faculty Research Committee of the London College of Music and Media at Thames Valley University gave me valuable research time to devote to the final typescript. Finally, I must thank Anne Scallan and our daughter Eva for being there and thereabouts respectively throughout the development of the book

FERGUS DALY   I would like to thank (for references, tapes, e-mail addresses, etc.): Nicole Brenez, Jean-Michel Frodon, John Gianvito, Marie-Pierre Richard, Jonathan Rosenbaum, Brad Stevens. Very special thanks (for assistance that went way beyond the call of duty) to: Lili le Cain, Max le Cain, Garin Dowd, Adrian Martin, Tony McKibbin. What can I say except to express my love and thanks to Katherine Waugh and our 4-year-old son, sorry pirate, Lucien Waugh-Daly, who were my daily companions during the book's composition; Katherine a superb critic in her own right and constant source of inspiration, who has loved and analysed films with me for a greater number of years than Lucien can calculate; Lucien, living as he does in a world of sailing ships and treasure, of capture and flight, and with a smile that pierces like the blade of a cutlass, often brought a tangible mood of 'ontological lightness' to the proceedings. Here's hoping that traces of his improbable rationality remain in the book. I would like to dedicate this book to Bill and Maureen, my father and mother.

# Introduction: genesis of Carax's system

Moi je crée un chaos dans lequel j'essaie de m'en sortir, et ça fait un film. (Leos Carax 1999)[1]

## Some biographical co-ordinates

Leos Carax's early career was in two complementary ways conducted under the scrutiny of the French film journal *Cahiers du Cinéma*. Hired in his teens as a reviewer by its then editor Serge Daney, Carax, in writing a glowing review of Sylvester Stallone's directorial debut *Paradise Alley* (1978) was already, in 1979, adopting an idiosyncratic approach to film appreciation, Stallone being, either at the time or since, rarely championed as a model auteur. At the age of 20, Carax's first short film won a prestigious award at the Hyères festival and garnered column inches in *Cahiers*. His first feature-length film at the age of 23 drew praise from Daney, this time from within the influential culture pages of *Libération*. In 1991, in the same year in which he would be given *carte blanche* for a *numéro hors série* of the magazine, Carax's name featured in a *Cahiers* list of 'cinéastes pour l'an 2001'. In his 1988 film, and on the basis of the evidence provided by Carax's first two feature films, Philippe Garrel was confident enough to include Carax in his list of so-called *Ministères de l'art* (1988), along with already fêted directors such as Chantal Akerman, Jacques Doillon and André Téchiné. In 1988 a fledgling project supposedly destined to be shot on super 8 film began to outgrow its intended

1 'I create a chaos out of which I try to find an exit, and that makes a film.'

confines. Three years later, after a total of just eighteen weeks' shooting and three stoppages totalling 144 weeks, the construction, collapse and reconstruction of a vast Pont-Neuf film-set in the south of France, illness, a death, and general despair among cast, crew and producers, the film which almost ruined Carax's career finally made it to cinema screens. Eight years intervened between the infamous *Les Amants du Pont-Neuf* (1991) and *Pola X* (1999). Carax's critical reputation, however, remains relatively intact among a certain sector of French critics – notably those associated or once associated with *Cahiers*. The distinguished director Jacques Rivette, a former editor of the journal, for example, in 1999 nominated *Pola X* 'le plus beau film français des dix dernières années' ('the most beautiful French film in the last ten years').

In his 1999 television interview with Pierre-André Boutang, Carax touches on many of the qualities of a still developing personal mythology (Carax 1999).[2] He speaks of his withdrawal from the world, of his need for self-protection, first within the 'bande à part' of artists and technicians of the first three features, then of his period of fear, illness and anxiety between *Les Amants* and *Pola X*, of the fact that he claims to have met only a handful of fellow filmmakers (Garrel and Godard are notable for their inclusion in this short list), of regarding himself as an impostor (he would be a writer, he says, but it is easier to pass oneself off in cinema), of failure (good failures he adds), of being ill-schooled (not museums for him but photographs of paintings of which, after all, he actually knows nothing), of books he devoured at the prompting of others (Céline, Melville and Musil most notably).

From a French point of view, Carax was returning from a lengthy absence. On the other side of the Atlantic, however, the gap between the two films was felt somewhat less forcefully by viewers coming to *Pola X* on its US release in December 2000, since *Les Amants du Pont-Neuf* had initially and repeatedly failed to secure a theatrical release there, only receiving a limited release in the preceding year. In between, several enticements to take on US projects failed to yield any offers that sufficiently interested him. However, despite his invisibility as

2 A transcription of this interview can be accessed via a website devoted to Carax (see *www.patoche.org/carax*). This indispensable resource for those interested in Carax provides the text of several other interviews. When quoting from these versions, the parenthetical reference does not include a page number.

far as US cinema audiences were concerned, the critic Stuart Klawans notes that Hollywood film directors had absorbed some Caraxian influences, citing the scene in *The English Patient* (1996) where Juliette Binoche is lifted to view a painting and the entwined lovers as ship's figurehead in *Titanic* (Klawans 1999), to which we might add the bunjee-jumping scene featuring Julie Delpy in *An American Werewolf in Paris* (1997), with its strong visual echoes of the parachute scene in *Mauvais Sang* (1986).

## A band apart: Carax as auteur

Carax's first finished film, *Strangulation Blues* (1979) is in the director's own words the student film he never made. In high-contrast mono-chrome, two semi-volitional beings co-ordinate a strained relation-ship, wherein they appear to function primarily as images for each other. In particular, the male character has ambitions to make a film: in a nightmare, he tries to strangle his female companion because she has failed to inspire 'un foutu plan de cinéma' ('single damn shot'). When he awakes, he believes he has killed her and flees. With hind-sight, then, the film announces certain Caraxian elements: a set-up to which Carax would return is the interplay of chance and destiny, in the form specifically of the chance encounter, allied to the idea of making a film about 'that moment', within the context of that specific falling together of conditions for an encounter to have taken place. In terms of set and setting, the Paris revealed in the film announces the emptied oneiric space of the first three features – emptied by means of specified artificial coincidences in the case of *Mauvais Sang* and *Les Amants du Pont-Neuf*. Also characteristic of what is to come, here the mumbled voiceover remains below the threshold of clarity in order to complement the absence of clear signification in the sequence of unmotivated events within the images.

In his early work, then, Carax would inaugurate a number of procedures which were to endure in the subsequent career. The Carax of the short films (*La fille rêvée* was abandoned in 1977) is already amassing the elements designed to authenticate his claims to auteur-ism. By the time of the release of his first feature *Boy Meets Girl* (1984) the mission will be accomplished. These are: a common band of artists and technicians; thematic consistency; credible intertextual references. Part of the auteurist aspirations of the young Carax involves the acquisition of certain indices that make his world an immediately identifiable one. The character of Alex is absolutely central to the development of this personal mythology. There are both biographical and aesthetic factors involved in Carax's self-generated personal mythology and in the key characteristics of its leading personae. Indeed when the first two films are viewed together the personae demand a new idiom; *Boy Meets Girl* and *Mauvais Sang* foreground three principal types: the orphan of chaos, the *autiste-bavarde* and the *enfant-vieillard* ('autistic man-chatterbox', 'elderly child').

The idea of Alex as 'orphan of chaos' is intimately linked to Carax's own 'auto-creation' via his anagrammatic, Scrabble-like renaming of himself (he was born Alexandre Oscar Dupont – thus conjuring his name anagrammatically from 'Alex Oscar'). Casting himself adrift from the filial structure and making himself an 'orphan', Carax inserts himself into an alternative 'family'. The co-ordinates of this family lie in the realm of cinema, and film history. '*Mauvais Sang* est un film qui a une espèce de relation d'enfant avec le papa–cinéma. Le cinéma était là pour me rassurer' (Carax 1991).[3] Alex, Carax's alter ego, in each of the first three films, is detached, or in the process of detaching himself, from filial lineage, and engages with the social body in an increasingly precipitous and risky series of operations presided over by chaos and chance.[4] Alex's persistent seeking out of limit experiences[5] might invite theorisation in terms of transgression; in this study, however, this aspect is linked to terminology less inflected by a psychoanalytic idiom: hence its placement within the typology with its three parts, of which 'orphan of chaos' is merely one element.

The two further categories – 'autiste-bavarde' and 'enfant-vieillard' – derive elements from stock characters traceable back to silent

---

3  '*Mauvais Sang* is a film that has a sort of a child–father relationship with cinema. Cinema was there to reassure me.'

4  Denis Lavant in being both Alex and inseparable from Alex's exploits and feats produces, in the view of Jousse (Jousse 1991: 23), a marvellous two-headed creature: Alex–Lavant, 'Car les risques pris par l'un sont aussi pris par l'autre' ('Because risks taken by the one are also taken by the other').

5  As indicated by Michel Foucault in his study of Georges Bataille, such experiences may be said to amount to an 'interrogation of the limit replac[ing] the search for totality and the act of transgression replaces the movement of contradictions' (Foucault 1977: 50).

cinema. When asked in an interview about an 'autism' specific to his films, the term is employed by the interviewer as a metaphor aiming to describe certain solipsistic and self-reflexive strategies in contemporary culture (Carax 1991). The 'autistic' part of 'autiste-bavarde' as this persona populates the films of Carax must be differentiated from this metaphorical usage. Carax's characters, it will be suggested – especially in Chapter 1 – always fall short or are somewhat in excess of 'character'. The typology developed by Carax contributes to the characters' withdrawal from verisimilitude – they are presented to us less as formed, reified types, or exemplars, than as 'supple individuals':

> A supple individual lies between the molecular and the molar both in time and in mode of composition. Its particles are correlated, but not rigidly so. It has boundaries, but fluctuating ones. It is the threshold leading from one state to another. (Massumi 1992: 55)

All of Carax's characterisation is tending toward this threshold state, a state of being inbetween, occupying a point on a scale that is ever shifting. The term 'autiste-bavarde', then, serves to emphasise the fact that Carax gives us very clear indications that Alex, and by extension Carax's world, is not fixed within a gridded, polarised and hierarchised system of values that would see the 'autistic' as a quality to be (unproblematically) celebrated. Rather Alex, and Carax's world, is characterised by its oscillation between poles, and by its penchant for 'ambiguities'. Alex has qualities which make him both 'autistic', or cataleptic, and *bavarde*. 'Langue pendue' is his paradoxical nickname. To someone unversed in French idioms it would seem a reasonable guess that this would translate into the English 'tongue-tied', whereas on the contrary the term means one gifted in the art of speech, someone with the 'gift of the gab' – a chatterbox.

As for the third category – that of 'enfant-vieillard' – that Alex occupies a temporality that takes him beyond mere youth is indicated by the special relationship between him and Caroll Brooks's character in *Boy Meets Girl*, and by his capacity to care for the room full of babies at the party. Alex, then, as supple individual is a force of destabilisation vis-à-vis several loci of coalescence and coagulation according to social norms. This supple aspect links Carax to the 'vor-da' characters of the baroque worlds of Raoul Ruiz: 'Un vor-da que perpétue l'enfant devenu trop vite adulte, à jamais immature ... apparitions-disparitions, morts-vivants, adultes puérils et enfants vieillards' (Revault-d'Allonnes 1987: 64).[6] By virtue of being an 'orphan of chaos' he represents a challenge to social order grounded in the family; his status as *autiste-bavarde* means that he renders communication subject to aberrant reconfiguration; because he is also *enfant-vieillard* time is thrown out of joint by his visionary propensities.

The need to propose the above typology is testament to the fact that Carax is thinking and working within a relatively circumscribed body of thought – one that sees him develop a thoroughgoing personal signature. For example when he declares 'On fait des films pour des morts ou des fantômes' ('we make films for dead people or phantoms', Carax 1999: 14–15) it is quite some distance from the sort of pronouncement one might expect of, say, a Steven Spielberg. However, within the context of French literary and cinema culture it is a perfectly acceptable and coherent declaration. Compare, for example, this statement by *nouvelle vague* film director Jacques Rivette: 'les hommes n'ont aucun sens des forces cosmiques qui les dépassent' ('men have no awareness of the cosmic forces that outstrip them': Rivette cited in Frappat 2001: 199), or the question posed to Rivette by Serge Daney in *Jacques Rivette, le veilleur* (Claire Denis, 1990): 'does art exclude sanctity?'. The notion of cinema as concerned with rendering unseen forces visible is a staple not just of criticism in France but also a cinematic theme and formal approach. Think of Cocteau's declaration: 'J'étais le véhicule d'une force qui veut vivre à ma place' ('I was the vehicle of a force wanting to live in my place'), or the relentless evocation in his films of Orphic states and processes of mediation. Yet when it comes to Carax the patience of certain English-language critics no longer holds. It is as if the notion of unseen forces – that is, experience as *only* sensed and not experience as the mere correlate of common sense or the merely empirical – finds no purchase in the critical response. Perhaps, one is tempted to speculate, it only ever worked when these strange ghosts could be corralled into compartments with names like 'memory' or 'God' (hence the acceptability to critics of Resnais and Bergman), the images remaining psychologically or transcendentally motivated. Carax's world is devoid of grounding either in the psyche or in a transcendent God; and when it comes to

6  'A *vor-da* perpetuated by the child who's too quickly grown into an adult, forever immature ... apparitions-spectres, living-dead, puerile adults and elderly children.'

those aspects of his films owing something to the more abstract realms of ontology, metaphysics or cosmogony many critics lose patience and go on the offensive. However, from Bazin to Deleuze and beyond, for French thinkers, the cinema explores the multidimensional entity that we call reality or the universe. Not to take this into account, especially when analysing French films embedded in the tradition to which we refer, is to miss something essential to the proper understanding of what has been created. What lies beneath the diverse strategies and formal experimentation of a given director is invariably a philosophy of life – one which might be, in the case of Bresson, for example, religiously or transcendentally inspired, or which might in the case of Ruiz be powered by baroque *puissances*.[7]

## First times and debuts

In order fully to comprehend a body of work, it is necessary to isolate the will or belief that colours the variety of an auteur's inventions. Beyond the mere listing off of a director's stylistic traits or techniques, one needs to be attentive to the 'system' of which these are at the service. The French tradition of film analysis out of which Carax emerges is very much animated in this way. If a critic like Fabrice Revault d'Allonnes does attempt such a list it is only as a point of departure in the search for the problematic a film or body of work explores:

> Ces travellings fous, ces ellipses osées, ces changements d'axes 'cut', ces arrêts nets du son, ces dialogues en amorce de plans, ces bords-cadres et gros-plans 'limites': ce ne sont pas ici des effets de style, c'est l'enfance de l'art retrouvée. (Revault-d'Allonnes 1986: 4)[8]

---

7 When the term 'baroque' is used in a way which marks it as detached from its historical context, it is in lower case, whereas when the sense in which it is intended implies a strong link to the way in which the term is used in connection with a historical context 'Baroque' will be employed. The same is true of the terms 'mannerism' and 'Mannerism'.

8 'These demented tracking shots, these audacious ellipses, these "cuts" that shift the axis, these clean break-offs/dead-stops of sound, these dialogues that initiate shots/dialogues in fragmented shots, these edge-framings/edged frames, these "limit" close-ups. These are not stylistic effects but the rediscovery of the infancy of art.'

Another French commentator on cinema provides a further instance of this type of engagement. In his account of Godard's preoccupations (in the 1980s) as a filmmaker Jean Douchet writes:

> ses films sont plus contemplatifs, reposant sur un système d'images à contempler, dont la raison profonde est le plaisir qu'elles procurent à être associées. L'action consistant à combler intellectuellement ou émotionnellement la distance qui les sépare. Distance de plus en plus cosmique, macro et micro, galaxie et atome. Godard filme directement la lumière et son énergie. Son écriture est passée du mode narratif au mode poétique. (Douchet 1989: 51)[9]

Carax is no different in this respect. From a set of basic conceptual operators, his film worlds are built up stage by stage. Therefore in *Boy Meets Girl*, for example, Alex's obsession with 'first times' has as its more general correlate his creator's penchant for an originary purity of the image. This is an obsession that somewhat inevitably led Carax to a confrontation with the work of Herman Melville, the author who wrote that 'an overpowering sense of the world's downright positive falsity comes over him; the world seems to lie saturated and soaking with lies' (Melville [1852] 1996: 208). Carax's fourth feature film *Pola X* – which is adapted from Melville's novel, *Pierre, or The Ambiguities* (1852) – will not only make this its theme and constructive premise but will bring to a peak Carax's concerns with falsity and with the task of exploring its potential as a key to the richness and multi-dimensionality of the world. In this respect, there is a point of comparison with the work of Raoul Ruiz, whose greatest films come precisely from the early to mid-1980s (when Carax was beginning his career) and about whom it has been written: 'pour Ruiz, la vérité ne peut être dans l'image, qui ment toujours, qui ment nécessairement ... mais il n'y a pas plus de vérité dans le monde que dans l'image: "le monde est mensonge" est-il encore dit dans *Les Trois Couronnes*' (Revault d'Allonnes 1987: 53).[10]

9 'his films are more contemplative, built on a series of images to be contemplated, and whose profound reason is the pleasure that they procure in being associated. The task consists in intellectually or emotionally filling in the distance separating them. A distance that has become more and more cosmic, micro and macro, atom and galaxy. Godard directly films the light and its energy. His writing [*écriture*] has passed from a narrative mode to a poetic one.'
10 'for Ruiz, the truth can't be in the image which always lies, which lies of necessity ... but there's no more truth in the world than in the image: "the world is a lie" is furthermore what's said in *Three Crowns of the Sailor*.'

The 'powers of the false' as somehow the key to much that was interesting in 1980s cinema was already a given in *Cahiers du Cinéma* debates as Carax shot his first feature in 1983. Carax the critic and defender of early Stallone films will have recalled that line from Stallone's debut *Paradise Alley*: 'everyone in the whole stupid, stinking world is faking everything'. Historically speaking, Carax arrives in the middle of the 'powers of the false' debate, and takes a particular position in relation to it. If, in the words of Jacques Aumont, 'tout dans cette vie est mensonge et fausseté ... comme dans un jeu de glaces ... la vie n'est qu'illusion, songe ou mensonge d'un reflet' (Aumont 1996: 17), then Carax will answer that to create is to embrace whatever forces the false allows us to glimpse.[11] This is an idea of cinema that goes back to Bazin, whose (less radical) calls for a cinema of ambiguity have haunted French cinema since the *nouvelle vague*. As Dudley Andrew has argued, an ambiguous 'give and take between the image and the real' has characterised this cinema since *A bout de souffle* (Godard 1959). Andrew seizes on the image of the mirror as signifying 'the problematic and the *dispositif* I take to be central to Modernism in cinema' (Andrew 1998). The simultaneous search for the beautiful image and its critique, a tension between images of frozen eternity and temporal decay, unites auteurs from early Godard to Carax. Andrew could be specifically describing Carax's universe when he defines fifty years of French film as 'the cinematic struggle between life and death, image and flow, beauty and decay' (Andrew 1998). This is also a cinema of ambiguous tone and mood. Take for instance the scene in *Boy Meets Girl* where Alex strides along the quays in desolate mood, having just learned about an affair between his best friend and girlfriend. As Bowie's song 'When I Live My Dream' strikes up on the soundtrack, he stops to watch a couple's highly mannered dance. It is an ambiguous moment. On the one hand there is the expression of cynicism exemplified by the woman's distracted gazing at Alex and by the money he throws at the performing couple. But the same scene is also an image of the birth of love expressed in the song and in the superimposed and cross-cut visions of the new woman in his life (Mireille Perrier). Chapter 1 will argue that Carax's specific take on doubling, reflexivity and ambiguity is distinct from that associated with modernism in cinema and bears

11 'life is nothing but lies and falsity ... as in a play of mirrors ... life is only the illusion, dream or lie of a reflection.'

a relation to a set of problems and questions more properly identified as Baroque. This book attempts to show that for Carax the powers of the false are precisely the baroque powers of the cinema, the baroque being the 'other' of western reason and baroque cinema the medium's 'ever-tested limit' (Bellour cited in Martin 2001).

Suffice it to say here that when Carax talks about desiring orphanhood ('at last I'm an orphan' is Alex's response on hearing of his father's death in *Mauvais Sang*) he is speaking on a metaphysical or cosmological level – 'on ne vient pas seulement de nos parents, heureusement, on vient de bien plus loin' (Carax 1999).[12]

As opposed to attempting to reproduce events in as realistic a manner as possible, the kind of cinema to which Carax adheres seeks to capture the intensity of events before they become fully real or actualised. Few have spoken more eloquently or precisely about a cinema that seeks to capture the event *en puissance*:

> *Mauvais Sang* est un film qui ressemble à une rencontre. Vous rencontrez une fille dans un café. Vous commandez une boisson, les sentiments viennent ... Vous commandez une seconde boisson, puis une troisième ... Alors au bout d'un moment, vous avez envie de pisser, vous descendez aux toilettes. Vous vous retrouvez seul, la fille est en haut ... vous sentez qu'il y a une chose sentimentale qui s'installe. Et ce moment, seul dans les toilettes ... vous êtes en train de pisser, de vous laver les mains. C'est un moment extrêmement fort, j'ai toujours eu envie de filmer ça. C'est à dire la naissance des sentiments, le moment où on sait que la fille est en haut, qu'on va la retrouver ... Cet instant-là est tres pointu. *Mauvais Sang* est un film tourné dans ces toilettes-là. Donc très émotif et naïf. (Carax 1991)[13]

In his brief time as *Cahiers* critic, Carax had sought out such intensity, believing he had found it in Stallone's directorial debut *Paradise Alley*.

12 'happily, we don't only come from our parents, we come from much further away.'
13 '*Mauvais Sang* is a film which resembles an encounter. You meet a girl in a café. You order a drink, feelings grow ... you order another drink, then a third ... then after a while you need to piss and you go down to the toilet. You're alone down there, the girl is above ... you feel that something emotional is happening between you. At this moment, alone in the toilet ... in the middle of a piss, then washing your hands – it's an extremely powerful moment. I've always wanted to film this. The birth of feelings, the moment when you know the girl is upstairs and that she'll still be there, waiting ... This is a very acute moment. *Mauvais Sang* is a film shot in this toilet. For this reason, it's very emotional and naive.'

Reviewing the film in his first published piece, Carax is very impressed with the way in which through still shots Stallone creates a sense of compressed intensity, the characters almost bursting out of their frames. *Paradise Alley* is 'un cauchemar d'orphelin' ('an orphan's nightmare') in the manner of *The Night of the Hunter* (1955). There are many elements in Carax's review which will find an echo in his first films (indeed scenes from *The Night of the Hunter* also feature in Carax's 1997 short unreleased film *Sans titre*). Like the children in Laughton's film, Stallone's brothers have grown old before their time; they are true 'enfants-vieillards' in the manner of Alex, who can only repeat 'comme dans un mauvais rêve' ('as in a bad dream': 'I never tried to fulfil my best dreams. Only to re-dream them' will be *Boy meets Girl*'s variation on this). Revealingly, as far as the course that his filmmaking career would take is concerned, Carax reads American cinema through the most recent and innovative developments in French cinema. 'Comme les Enfants – demi-orphelins – du Placard ils partagent des *secrets de famille* ou *d'enfance*'.[14] Furthermore, Jonathan Rosenbaum points out how Carax finds in Stallone's film the 'physicality and *nostalgie de la boue* of his subsequent movies' (Rosenbaum 1994: 18). In later contributions to *Cahiers*, he will consistently pinpoint innovations in the areas of ethology, communication and young love, noting 'qu'il est difficile pour deux jeunes amants de garder la cadence entre le temps de vivre, le temps d'aimer et le temps de mourir' and proclaiming that 'le noir-et-blanc est la couleur fondamentale du cinéma'.[15] From Zanussi's *Camouflage* (1976), he draws his concept of le 'film bavard muet' ('silent talkative film'), an idea that will contribute to Alex's character traits as an 'autiste bavarde'. Like Alex, *Camouflage* 'parle trop mais il est aussi trop *mime*' ('speaks too much but it also mimes too much': Carax 1980: 56). And in a striking first draft of his later 'manifesto' of filmmaking, spread throughout the various interviews, he ends his review of a Polish retrospective by asking: 'les metteurs en scène qui comptent aujourd'hui ne seraient-ils pas ceux qui interrogent le cinéma muet *par l'absurde*, en cherchant comment le cinéma parlant parle (ou vice-

---

14 'Like the semi-orphan children of the closet, they share family and childhood secrets' – a likely reference to Benoit Jacquot's film *Les Enfants du placard* (1977).

15 'that it's difficult for two young lovers to maintain the rhythm they've established between the time to live, the time to love and the time to die'; 'black and white is the fundamental colour of the cinema.'

versa)?' (Carax 1980: 56).[16] He will later describe the genesis of his
films as advancing by way of the absurd. In his piece on the Hyères
film festival he singles out for praise Robert Kramer's *The Edge* (1976)
and the director's skill in portraying the 'rapports de force entre les
personnages' ('relations of force between the characters'), and in
demonstrating how to film 'la relation amoureuse' ('the amorous
relationship'), or simply 'filmer des gens qui parlent' ('to film people
speaking'). In Kramer he also admires in the acting 'l'impression
qu'ils jouent leur *histoire* en même temps que leur rôle' ('the
impression that they act out their story at the same time as their role')
as well as the *actualité* of the film he describes as 'un cinéma de
l'urgence' ('a cinema of urgency': Carax 1979a: 40–1). Finally, in the
Hyères review, in what amounts to an *avant la lettre* defence of his
own filmmaking practice, Carax asserts that 'On partait d'un amour
fou du cinéma, on *retournait* cet amour pour arriver (au bout des
comptes à régler avec ce cinéma) à des films tout à fait autres, neufs'
(Carax 1979a: 41).[17]

## *Cahiers* and criticism as a way of making films

The *Cahiers* context is informative in other ways too. If, by examining
the annual end-of-year critics' top ten film lists, one considers the
kinds of films that *Cahiers* critics enthused about in the years coming
up to 1983 – the year *Boy Meets Girl* was shot – one finds films by such
directors as Oliveira, Rivette, Téchiné, Godard, Schroeter, Ruiz and
Syberberg – in short, a whole range of filmmakers with what Chapter
1 will call 'mannerist' tendencies. Therefore, not only to film analysis,
but to filmmakers themselves the pressing problems were to do with
dealing with the ambient 'crisis of representation' – in particular as
manifested in the 'incredulity towards Grand Narratives' and rise of
the 'new images' flooding the culture and society of the 1980s. Since
Carax is so immersed in *Cahiers* culture (particularly of the late 1970s

16 'aren't the directors who count today those who interrogate the silent cinema by
way of the absurd, through asking how the talking cinema speaks (or vice
versa)?'
17 'You began with a mad love for the cinema, you turned this love inside out in
order (having settled your accounts with this cinema) to arrive at films that are
totally different and new.'

and 1980s) it is necessary to undertake a detailed examination – in the course of Chapter 1 – of his first two feature films against the backdrop of the *Cahiers* scene and the debates conducted in its pages during the encompassing period.

There is also the issue of parallel evolution to consider. To put this in context let us consider how more recently the 'Caraxian' issue of ontological lightness versus heaviness has also become a problem for Jean-Luc Godard. *Eloge de l'amour* (2001), as Olivier Séguret has noted, expresses 'sa manière de voir dans l'âge adulte le point mort de la vie, tenu en suspension par l'énergie de l'enfance et les forces de la vieillesse' (Séguret 2001).[18] In this film, Godard returns to the problem treated by Carax in his first films, now staged in terms of history, more specifically the history of the French resistance. In this context, Godard examines the way in which memory is transmitted from old to young people and the role of cinema in that transmission. Here Godard continues his search for a specifically cinematic ethics that would also say something philosophically about the present's relation to the past. The film suggests that there is a certain lightness that passes straight from childhood to old age (from liberty to wisdom) thereby bypassing heavy adulthood. (In this respect it is important to note that Alain Bergala once asked 'Godard a-t-il été petit?' ('Was Godard ever little?': Bergala 1990)).

Carax from the outset sought such a lightness through the figure of the couple: 'L'idéal, c'est de trouver la plus grande vitesse possible à deux' (Carax 1984).[19] Later he adds:

> Sur ma tombe, je mettrai 'Que n'étais-je fougère?' ... La pesanteur, la lourdeur, ça commence avec le premier pied qu'on pose au bas du lit le matin. C'est effroyable ... Oui, j'ai toujours été à la recherche de la légèreté ... [à 20 ans] je confondais mon propre poids avec le poids du monde ... la lourdeur des autres m'insupportait [sic], mais elle était peut-être tout simplement en moi ... Je ne suis pas encore un papillon, mais je me sens beaucoup plus léger qu'avant.[20]

18 'his way of seeing adulthood as the neutral gear of life, held in suspension by the energy of childhood and the forces of old age'
19 'The ideal is to find the greatest possible speed together.'
20 'On my tomb, I would put 'That I would be like a fern' ... weight, heaviness, begins with the first step out of the bed in the morning. It's appalling ... Yes, I've always looked for lightness ... [at 20] I confused my own weight with the weight of the world ... I found the heaviness of others unbearable, but perhaps it was simply all in me ... I'm not a butterfly yet, but I feel much lighter than I was.'

In this he shares the baroque philosophy of a Raoul Ruiz: 'Les personnages de Ruiz évoluent quelque part entre la vie et la mort, leurs corps suspendus entre la pesanteur et la légèreté, l'incarnation et la désincarnation, l'existence et l'évanescence' (Revault d'Allonnes 1987: 65).[21]

## A note on methodology

The concepts and distinctions introduced here will form a frame of reference to be returned to in subsequent chapters – more generally, the typology outlined above is aligned, at another level in Carax's work, to its tendency to invoke consistently two poles, those of move-ment and stasis. The interplay between drift (*dérive*) and flight (*vol*), evident in *Boy Meets Girl* is but one example of the type of oscillation between states that will come to characterise the subsequent work, which manifests oppositions such as acceleration versus catatonia, exhilaration versus hieratic posturing, weightlessness versus gravity, the city's movement and flows versus the congealed private sphere, neo-baroque giddiness versus naturalist abjection. In each film, Carax will set up complex tensions between stasis and flux through editing and *mise en scène*. In the course of this study, definitions of the 'neo-baroque' and 'naturalism' are deployed because it will be shown that, when the films are viewed chronologically, the guiding aesthetic of Carax's work moves from a neo-baroque to a naturalist one. These concepts will be clearly articulated in the relevant chapters. Both concepts offer distinct ways of discussing what Chapter 1 will call 'the powers of the false'. Carax's work lies at the node of a whole series of problems being dealt with in filmmaking, theory and criticism and it is incumbent on any serious analysis to disentangle these. Differ-entiation necessitates a genealogical approach; to specify originality one must place an artist in her or his correct genealogical line and particular problematic. Take, for example, the influence on Carax of the work of post-new wave director Philippe Garrel. Despite the fact that almost every French critic writing on Carax has discussed it, of all the secondary literature on Carax in English, only Jonathan Rosen-

21 'Ruiz's characters move between life and death, their bodies suspended between heaviness and lightness, incarnation and disembodiment.'

baum's exemplary introduction to Carax's work (Rosenbaum 1994) alludes to this important link. Indeed this was immediately recognised by the older filmmaker who saw in *Boy Meets Girl* echoes of his own 1967 film *Marie pour Mémoire*, and even read a tribute to the film in poem form when the two filmmakers shared a platform in Montreal in 1984.[22]

The foregoing statements about Carax's genealogy underline the importance of furnishing an alternative to the caricature – with several notable exceptions – that has often passed for commentary on Carax in the English-speaking world. For, in the case of his films as of those of comparable directors, it can often seem that the more complex are the ideas involved, the more it is considered excusable for the critic to ignore the aesthetic, even thematic, construction of the work in question. Take for instance Tom Charity's dismissal of Garrel's intricate existential study *Le Vent de la Nuit* (1999) as 'unconscionable pretentious tosh' (Charity 2001), or Paul Willemen claiming that von Trier's world is one 'emptied of all traces of a world other than that of the film maker's idiotic, sorry: idiosyncratic "personal perspective", replete with pompous kitsch' (Willemen 2000). One of the tasks of criticism, if it is to avoid mere caricature hiding highly personal and subjective expressions of preference or taste, or highly prejudiced forms of exclusion, is that of identifying, at the very least, the specific problem or problems the artist has set herself or himself to explore in a particular work.

The challenge which Carax presents to certain enduring orthodoxies can be summed up by considering some exemplary scenes. In *Boy Meets Girl*, Alex stands on the pavement outside a building eavesdropping as a stranger seems to break from a lover over an intercom, yet the movement of whose lips bears no relation to what we hear him say; in a scene from *Mauvais Sang*, a song on the radio makes Alex bound, run and stagger at speed along a pavement while punching himself; in the same film, when the gang is driving to the airfield escaping from both the police and the imminent threat of a rival gang, one of them – Hans – recites in English a quatrain borrowed from a Prince Hal monologue in Shakespeare's *Henry IV Part 1*. These scenes do not exist for no other reason than that they are

22 Note from correspondence between John Gianvito of the Harvard Film Archive and Fergus Daly.

visually and/or aurally arresting or striking. They express, rather, a
state of being in the world and a set of aesthetic principles seeking to
capture that state at whatever cost to conventions of verisimilitude or
even to the limits of the rationally acceptable. It is an unwillingness to
negotiate with the material that can lead critics to dismiss or more
often ignore such scenes, dwelling instead on at best problematic
generalisations about pop-promo aesthetics, about wilful obscurity or
about the artificiality of the lighting or the resemblance of the image's
texture to that used in advertising. The character of Alex is a very
complex creation, and in many respects he is the answer to a set of
aesthetic and philosophical problems (or such a problem in itself).
His body is the key to a new mode of *mise en scène*. In Carax's radical
experiment, several complex questions are being asked both of the
viewer and of the medium, much in the same way as Godard, of
whom one commentator writes: 'le cinéma est pour lui la grande
question et ses films, des éléments de réponse' (Flot 2001).[23]

In order to assist in the isolation of the problems posed by and
explored in Carax's films, works of philosophy have been an especially
rich resource in yielding a vocabulary to account for their articulation,
resolution or exploration.[24] Aside from the richness of the philosophical concepts which Gilles Deleuze has brought to film criticism
and appraisal, the reader will encounter in this volume, brief and it is
hoped illuminating references to Lucretius (the ancient father of
modern dynamics according to Prigogine and Stengers [1979] (1984)),
to the seventeenth-century philosopher Leibniz, and to a contemporary
of Deleuze, Michel Serres.

The assessments of the work of Carax which you are about to read
are the result of the development of a series of disparate viewing
experiences of Carax's films shared and spread out between the two
authors. If we came to Carax separately, we both did so, however,
partly through the pages of *Cahiers du Cinéma*. It was within the pages
of *Cahiers* in particular in the 1980s that one encountered a commitment to philosophical reflection on film. Carax apparently reads the
work of Deleuze, which may explain why *Pola X* lists 'Gilles D' as one
of the individuals who needs to be thanked. The same film features an
epigraph which is perhaps as much from Deleuze (who devotes an

23 'The cinema is the big question for him, films are the elements of a response.'
24 As they were for Phil Powrie in his study of Beneix in this series (Powrie 2001).

essay to the theme of 'time out of joint') as it is from *Hamlet* and Melville. In challenging the viewer to reconsider certain preconceptions regarding cinema, narrative and the image, Carax's films on occasion create the conditions for something like thinking *otherwise*. 'L'essence du cinema, qui n'est pas la généralité des films,' Deleuze has remarked, 'a pour objectif plus élevé la pensée, rien d'autre que la pensée et son fonctionnement' (Deleuze 1985: 219).[25] One of the aims of this book is to find a critical language that registers this aspect of Carax's oeuvre. To this end, we attempted to come to the work ready to receive the shocks it could produce afresh. With the release of *Pola X* both authors had to suffer the disturbance of what seemed at first a radical break with the three first features. On reflection, however, it was clear that we were locked in a petrified hermeneutic landscape of our own configuration, since on further inspection there is an inexorable logic to *Pola X* in relation to the preceding work, offering as it does another perspective on the problem of 'the powers of the false'. It is our hope that the account of Carax's career to date – which gives us a mannerist, a baroque, a neo-baroque and a naturalist Carax respectively in the space of his four films – does more than provide a convenient narrative thread. The following pages aim to show how these paradigms assist in teasing out the specificity of each of the films, and emphasise those continuities and discontinuities that so fascinate in the four-film career to date. It is hoped that the philosophical reflections and parallels which are elucidated track as closely as possible the thought which Carax's films at once inhabit and summon forth.

As a result of our emphasis on Carax's mannerist and baroque tendencies, when his work is related to other filmmakers it will almost invariably be to those which it is felt have had a profound influence on these aspects of his work. One could search at length for correspondences between Carax's films and those silent and early sound directors he so admires. Therefore, rather than Epstein, Vidor, Gance or Griffith, when Carax is thought of in relation to film history, it will be to its more recent history in the shape of Godard and Garrel, Rivette and Ruiz, Téchiné and Robbe-Grillet. Moreover, in most cases, comparisons will highlight more a shared set of problems and interests than any direct influence.

25 'The essence of cinema – which is not the majority of films – has thought as its higher purpose, nothing but thought and its functioning' (Deleuze 1989: 168).

## Cinematic and non-cinematic intertexts: music, *tableaux parisiens*, Melville

As in the 'Blues' of the title of his 1979 short, the musical reference will remain an ever-present one in Carax's work. Carax's soundtrack, here as elsewhere, shows his aesthetic allegiance to certain performers, all of whom have at some point been noted innovators or maverick talents: Barbara, Bowie, Dead Kennedys, Les Rita Mitsouko and Sonic Youth to name but a few. In *Mauvais Sang* the veteran singer and actor Serge Reggiani plays Charlie, while Carax had the singers Léo Ferré, Jacques Dutronc and Serge Gainsbourg in mind for the role of Hans in *Les Amants* (Carax 1991), and the legendary Scott Walker composes the soundtrack for *Pola X*. Carax's use of music on the soundtrack will be dealt with in some detail in the following chapters, a use which rarely if ever entails a merely decorative or purely supplementary (in the sense of reinforcing) employment. For example, as the analysis of *Les Amants* will suggest, the bridge during the fireworks sequence becomes a vast radio dial: as the lovers move back and forth the 'channel' changes. In the latter case the music emerges from distinct spaces in the city and its intrusion into the soundtrack is thus 'motivated' and anchored in an ostensibly diegetic space. This, however, is not the case with the other songs which emerge from a non-diegetic space. If motivation is sometimes provided, however, by the song being played on a cassette player – as in the 'deaf-blind-flâneur' moment in *Boy Meets Girl* – that is often only a brief anchoring before the song explodes free of that mooring. The support is overburdened and the song takes on a life of its own. This is especially true of the song–dance sequences of each film until *Pola X* (Pierre's karaoke attempt to mimic Barbara's incomparable rendition of the song 'Sans bagages' in the television cut of *Pola X* (2001) is the closest that film comes).

These ruptures in what an audience might expect in terms of rational transitions are of course neither new nor especially challenging, since in part they are already familiar from musical comedy. But when combined by Carax with his innovations in gesture, movement and exploration of the multiple planes of the cinematic image, there is a subversive lack of grounded rationality more profound than the mere visibility of artifice associated with that genre.

The milieu of these films is another constant which facilitates a maximum of diversity. Paris forms the setting for the first three films; it also acts as the setting for the second half of *Pola X*. Each of Carax's *tableaux parisens* depicts locations of particular significance to the director. Each of the chapters which follow will seek to show in which respects the locations enable Carax to establish a fresh perspective on the capital. The Paris of *Boy Meets Girl* is a nocturnal one, with the lighted banks of the Seine much in evidence, and the *bateaux mouches* visibly indexical of its Parisian setting. *Mauvais Sang* offers a nocturnal studio-set Paris populated by somnambulants and thrown out of joint by the impending Halley's comet and by an escalating 'plague' STBO. *Les Amants* returns to the bridge which had featured in the earlier films. *Pola X* has scenes set in the centre, and even one which features the Pont-Neuf as a backdrop, but its Paris is one largely deprived of either tourist or Caraxian landmarks. But Paris for Carax is more than a convenient backdrop – and clearly, as *Les Amants* was to prove, it can be a less than convenient film set. The Paris we witness over the course of the four feature films which Carax has made to date is one of multiple temporalities. Often these layers are provided by means of the felt resonance of other films, songs and works of literature: Prévert, Céline, Godard, Zola, Cocteau, Vigo, Baudelaire, Reggiani, Ferré, Barbara. But there is also the layer provided by history and politics, especially in *Les Amants* and *Pola X*.

The Seine, so omnipresent in the first three features, is the liquid thoroughfare upon which so many of the characters will at various stages throw themselves or immerse themselves. While both the bridge and the Seine operate metonymically as signifiers of the city of Paris, in their respective metaphorical senses they may be, at least initially, distinct, the bridge being a metaphor for exchange and the river a metaphor for traversing and transcending Paris. The Seine seems to operate as pure trajectory without terminus. Le Havre in *Les Amants* is a terminus without terminality, being the river's port, and therefore an opening. Yet within the space of the bridge there is room for experimentation, both for Carax and for his protagonist. Hence when Alex stops to applaud and tip the lovers in *Boy Meets Girl* he immediately signals his alternative use of the bridge as vector rather than organiser of co-ordinated exchange. Mireille on the other hand is housebound while her lover, being incapable of loving (a refrain in the next film) leaves to the soundtrack of 'Holiday in Cambodia' by the Dead Kennedys – which conjunction also prevents her and the viewer from hearing his parting monologue on the intercom. By contrast to this closure, the dance routine, at which she becomes comically adept over a short period, is a modality of transport and flight *sur place*. In this cumulative energy dissipated through the dance which engenders it, we locate a uniquely Caraxian sumptuary arrangement.

The protagonists live alone, Alex in a monadic garret, Mireille in an entirely open space which is all window and no wall. The cinematic allusion is of course Hitchcock's *Rear Window* (1954), but there is also a hint of Rivette's *La Religieuse* (1967), and – more obliquely – Falconnetti in Dreyer's *La Passion de Jeanne d'Arc* (1928) when Perrier, freshly shorn of her long hair, dons the coif-like hood. The young Carax amasses these constituent parts with an infectious energy. However, there is a wealth of difference between this undeniable cinephilia and that of a Tarantino – and it is in the modality of appropriation that the difference is to be located, not only from Tarantino and Hartley, but also Beineix and Besson. Carax does not neutralise through comedy or parody. The absence of such neutralisation however does not mean that the results are pious. While it is indisputable that Carax feels a sense of apprenticeship, the process does not end as mere homage. There is always something else at work: the images culled are located and reanimated in a new Caraxian series. The extent to which Carax seems to be able to animate the culled image, severed from its context, is matched by his ability to return cliché from the dead. In this respect, his use of music as narrative can be contrasted sharply with that of David Lynch for example. In Lynch there is a literalism which one does not find in Carax – the preposterous 'lust in the dust' scene in the headlights of *Lost Highway* (1996), as aurally decorated by This Mortal Coil's version of Tim Buckley's 'Song to the Siren' is a good example.

That Carax should 'arrive' at Melville in his film *Pola X* shows once more how much his personal preoccupations have always been in tune with more general cultural concerns and aesthetic experiments. Melville is also a resource for other like-minded filmmakers, among them Claire Denis ('Billy Budd' forming the basis of her *Beau Travail* (1999)), while naturalism – with which later tradition Melville has a clear link in *Pierre* – is, it can be argued, present also in certain films by Thomas Vinterberg and Lars von Trier. In the films of von Trier especially, the naturalist elements are at the forefront. Just as in

Carax, in the Danish director's work, there has been a parallel development from mannerist/neo-baroque concerns to a fully developed naturalism. Whereas *Element of Crime* (1984) is a prime example of a mannerist film, in *Breaking the Waves* (1996), *The Kingdom* (1994), *The Idiots* (1998) and *Dancer in the Dark* (2000) von Trier is firmly in the world of naturalism as it will be defined in Chapter 3. The kirk of *Breaking the Waves* is a 'derived milieu' troubled by the strength of Bess's sexual desire and by her unconscious and unintended force of deformation; *The Kingdom* interrogates all sorts of *heimlich* spaces (the hospital, the native land, the lodge), which are subjected in every case to anamorphic transversal forces and spectral becomings (ghosts, melting walls, zones of indiscernibility, aborted foetuses); *The Idiots* is von Trier's most comprehensive attempt to present an entirely naturalist utopia, albeit one which is in this case emphatically entropic; while the much misunderstood *Dancer in the Dark* is a further reflection on 'affects' and forces, rather than affections and characters (which suggests an explanation as to why the film required Björk rather than a professional actor in the lead role).

## Carax as 'visionary'

Carax is often described by his supporters as a visionary. This is tied to his baroque tendencies, while his use of allegory – as Chapter 2 will show – will help account for the passage in his work from baroque to naturalism. Allegory is often linked to a visionary impulse or trope. The visionary, the seer, or one with enhanced powers of perception: these are never far away in Carax, even if the seer is impaired. Alex, the alter ego of Carax, was always a kind of mutated Orphic figure in the trilogy of films beginning with *Boy Meets Girl* and culminating inadvertently with *Les Amants*. The presentation of character as amanuensis – with the attendant *mise en abyme* of the figure of the filmmaker as amanuensis – finds its principal roots in Cocteau. For Carax, Lavant is a mutant Jean Marais: where for Cocteau Marais is indexed most succinctly in the narcissus image of the miraculous face reflected back from the puddle, the Lavant face is more Echo than Narcissus (and the astronaut figure Jerry in *Boy Meets Girl* is very reminiscent of Marais). If Marais was the (ultimately) eloquent Orpheus of Cocteau, lying face down outside the poet's café in

Cocteau's film (*Orphée* 1950), Lavant occupies the mute pole of the Orphic myth as he is found lying in disarray and transported off to the suburbs for a hosing down in the exemplary hand-held documentary sequence at the beginning of *Les Amants*. Lavant is Orphic in another emblematic manner, namely as the mouthpiece of Carax.[26] The acting style, verging on a kind of automatism, of Lavant throughout the trilogy, from somnambulant wanderings, to ventriloquised speeches, to risky acrobatics and abject self-mutilation, is central to the elaboration of this aspect of Carax's oeuvre: a reflection on mediation – on how it injures and wounds its vehicle. This suggests another related issue: it is expected of a good inheritor of the *nouvelle vague* tradition that they explore the question of mediation, both the question of the mediation of a cinematic and literary heritage (Godard, Melville) and the question of passing on to a character a role (Truffaut). Carax is part of this lineage in that he reflects through a complex interplay of homage and allusion his relationship with precursors and influences, occasionally the better to free himself of the stranglehold these latter can effect upon the filmmaker. Partly through a novel approach to character, and partly through *mise en scène*, Carax co-ordinates an idiosyncratic relationship with his characters and with their models. Rivette, Godard, Ruiz and Carax all to different degrees and with distinct emphases adhere to the dictum, coined by Deleuze in homage to Nietzsche, 'powers of the false'.

In *Boy Meets Girl*, in *Mauvais Sang* and in *Les Amants* Alex alternates between quest, finding and losing, the three films all presenting stages in the development of *amour fou*. Indeed, on a related point, something else to be kept in mind as we enter the possible and 'incompossible' worlds of Leos Carax is the problem of communication. It is in part Carax's distinct perspective on this notion that separates him from the so-called *cinéma du look* school. It is true that as, Fabrice Revault d'Allonnes states, 'entre l'axe Beineix–Besson et la démarche de Carax, il y a un univers'.[27] Rather than style for its own sake, for Carax 'l'invention formelle va intrinsèquement de paire avec le sujet: l'enfance retrouvée, le regard premier, neuf, l'émotion intacte de "la première fois"' (Revault d'Allonnes 1986:

26 There is in fact a host of Cocteau 'clones' in *Mauvais Sang*: the train-driver, the man – supposedly Alex's father – who leaps under the métro train, the man in the café who is taken for Cocteau.

27 'there's a universe separating Carax's approach from the Beineix–Besson axis'

4).[28] For Carax (and for Alex who veers from autistic silence to logorrhoeac prolixity), the question of the image is tied to that of communication. To communicate is to circulate an image. For example politics as articulated via the contemporary media is an affair of images, of marketing. The *cinéma de l'image/du look* was both attracted and repulsed by the powers of communication. In films by Beineix and Besson, this complex issue becomes levelled on to a horizontal plane, a mode of linkage enthralled to the *mot d'ordre* (or to the command): communicate! The only difference is that now through images rather than words the call is to 'make conversation'! Express yourself! This is why Carax's Alex is of necessity an *autiste-bavard*. Silence and logorrhoea are the two extremes that resist dominant discourse; refusing to submit to the already said or taking language to the limits of sense – this is Carax's approach to both language and the image. Carax thereby aligns himself with the *Cahiers* project in the 1980s, its return to the image 'comme une chose plastique', especially by way of its rethinking its relationship to painting: to give new breath to the image is to save it from the leaden discourse of communication.

## Conclusion

Carax comes to cinema laden with a weighty ambition. It has been a career marked by daring, innovation and constant surprise. In his first feature, there is already a finely developed cinematic sensibility. However, it is one imbued with a deep sense of melancholy. The manner in which Carax inflects the sundering of image and meaning with a studied intertextuality marks his first full-length film with the features described in Chapter 1 as mannerist in inclination. Amid the proliferating image reservoir of the mid-1980s, *Mauvais Sang* amounts to a dizzying and frenetic neo-baroque work. *Les Amants du Pont-Neuf* is a further exploration of neo-baroque elements, as Chapter 2 will suggest. In *Pola X* – to which Chapter 3 turns – with the anxiety of influence evident in the 1980s films now gone, Carax turns to literature to sustain a set of problematics already there in embryo in

28 'The formal inventiveness is intrinsically inseparable from the subject matter: childhood rediscovered, the first, new gaze, the emotion of "the first time" remaining intact.'

the other films. In the version of naturalism which is emergent in *Pierre, or The Ambiguities*, Carax finds a way of engaging with political, social and economic assemblages of our time.

In order on the one hand to introduce and on the other to enhance an existing audience's experience of the films of Carax, part of this book's purpose – especially in the case of a director so concerned to negotiate a relation with film and literary history – entails a serious negotiation of all of the above-mentioned elements – typology, setting, decor, acting, philosophical aspects, influences, intertexts and innovations. It is also intended to bring to the exegesis of the audio-visual dynamics and narrative components a strong sense of intellectual and cultural context. The vertiginous entry on Carax's interests provided by Mazabrard serves to underline the extent to which such a commitment is demanded by Carax's work:

> Mon amour du cinéma, mon amour du cinéma muet, mes amours à Paris, 'dans les rues de la ville il y a mon amour', mon amour de Char, mon amour de Rimbaud, mon amour de la poésie, mon amour de Cocteau, mon amour de Godard. Je prends Denis Lavant, je reprends Denis Lavant. Il y aussi Anna, Thomas, Alex. Et il y aura les films à venir pour ceux que j'oublie. Et 'j'ai plus de souvenirs que si j'avais mille ans' (Baudelaire). Leos Carax, croulant sous le poids des références, comme déjà si ridé, sorte d'Amour fripé, inventant le cinéma emblématique et fétichiste, faisant des films comme autant de hiéroglyphes de la nostalgie. (Mazabrard 1990)[29]

The task of this book, which will be to find 'Leos Carax', continues with an encounter between a boy and a girl, followed by a measure of bad blood.

29  'My love of cinema, my love of silent cinema, my loves in Paris, "my love is to be found in the streets of the town", my love of Char, my love of Rimbaud, my love of poetry, my love of Cocteau, my love of Godard. I take Denis Lavant with me, I take him again. There is also Anna, Thomas, Alex. There will be films to come for those I forget. And "I have more memories than I would have if I were a thousand years old" (Baudelaire). Leos Carax, buckling under the weight of references, as if already so wrinkled, a sort of worn-out Cupid, inventing an emblematic and fetishist cinema, making films like so many hieroglyphs of nostalgia.'

## References

Andrew, Dudley (1998), 'French film at the mirror: the cultivation and defacement of the look', in *Premises: Invested Spaces in Visual Arts, Architecture and Design from France: 1958–1998*, New York, Guggenheim Museum Publications.

Aumont, Jacques (1996), *A Quoi pensent les films?*, Paris, Seguier.

Bergala, Alain (1990), 'Godard a-t-il été petit?', *Cahiers du Cinéma*, 'Special Godard: trente ans depuis'.

Carax, Leos (1979), 'La taverne de l'enfer' *Cahiers du Cinéma*, no. 303, September, 98–9.

—— (1979a), 'Festivals: "Hyères"' *Cahiers du Cinéma*, no. 304, October, 40–2.

—— (1980), 'Semaine officielle et retrospective du cinéma polonais', *Cahiers du Cinéma*, no. 307, January, 55–6.

—— (1984), 'Entretien' on France-Culture, November.
Available online at: *www.patoche.org/carax/interviews*

—— (1991), 'A l'impossible on est tenu', *Les Inrockuptibles*, no. 32, December.
Available online at: *www.patoche.org/carax/interviews/inrocks.htm*

—— (1999), 'Interview FNAC', Interview with Pierre-Andre Boutang, CanalWeb, 15 May.
Available online at: *www.patoche.org/carax/interviews/fnac.htm*

Charity, Tom (2001), '*Le Vent de la Nuit*', in *Time Out Film Guide*, John Pym ed., 9th edition, Harmondsworth, Penguin.

Daney, Serge (1984), 'Libé meets Carax', *Libération*, 17 May.
Available online at: *www.liberation.fr/cinema/cine25/carax.html*

Deleuze, Gilles (1983), *Cinéma 1. L'Image-mouvement*, Paris, Minuit .

—— (1985), *Cinéma 2. L'Image-temps*, Paris, Minuit.

—— (1986), *Cinema 1: The Movement-Image*, trans. Hugh Tomlinson and Barbara Habberjam, London, Athlone Press.

—— (1989), *Cinema 2: The Time-Image*, trans. Hugh Tomlinson and Robert Galeta, London, Athlone Press.

Douchet, Jean (1989), 'La rue et le studio', *Cahiers du Cinéma*, no. 419/420, May–June.

Flot, Yonnick (2001), 'Eloge de l'amour', *essai.org/groupactionfilms/elogeamour.htm* (accessed 14 February 2002).

Foucault, Michel (1977) 'A preface to transgression', *Language, Counter-Memory, Practice*, in Donald F. Bouchard (ed.), pp. 29–52.

Frappat, Hélène (2001), *Jacques Rivette, secret compris*, Paris, Editions Cahiers du cinéma.

Jousse, Thierry (1991), 'Argent', short entry in 'L'alphabet des amants', *Cahiers du Cinéma*, no. 448, 22.

Martin, Adrian (2001), 'The ever-tested limit', in Stuart Koop ed., *Value Added Goods*, Melbourne, Centre for Contemporary Photography.

Massumi, Brian (1992), *A User's Guide to Capitalism and Schizophrenia: Deviations from Deleuze and Guattari*, Cambridge, MA, MIT.

Mazabrard, Collette (1989), 'Leos Carax', in 'Dictionnaire: 80 Cinéastes des Années 80', *Cahiers du Cinéma*, no. 419/20, May–June, 43–9.

Melville, Herman ([1852] 1996), *Pierre, or the Ambiguities*, Harmondsworth, Penguin.

Powrie, Phil (2001), *Jean-Jacques Beineix*, Manchester, Manchester University Press.

Prigogine, Ilya and Stengers, Isabelle ([1979] 1984), *Order out of Chaos: Man's New Dialogue with Nature*, London, Flamingo.

Revault d'Allonnes, Fabrice (1986), 'Le grand-méchant look' and 'Céline, Cocteau, Carax', *Cinéma* 86.

—— (1987), 'Pour R. R., Il y a réel et réel', in Buci-Glucksmann, Christine and Revault d'Allonnes, Fabrice, *Raoul Ruiz*, Paris, Dis Voir.

Rosenbaum, Jonathan (1994), 'Leos Carax: the problem with poetry', *Film Comment* 30:3, May–June, 2–18, 22–3.

Séguret, Olivier (2001), 'A propos du film ...', *Libération*, 16 May.

*Vertigo* (Paris), 2001, numéro spécial hors-série, 'Projections baroques'.

Willemen, Paul (2000), 'Note on Dancer in the Dark', *Framework: Journal of Cinema and Media* 42, *frameworkonline.com*.

1 The planes occupied by Alex and Mireille seem to be set in motion in *Boy Meets Girl*

2 Alex's own fireworks in *Les Amants du Pont-Neuf*

**3** Anna ascends into a 'pure image' in *Mauvais Sang*

**4** Alex and Anna play in *Mauvais Sang*

5 Pierre and Isabelle in *Pola X*

6 Alex and Anna arrive at the airfield in *Mauvais Sang*

# 1

## *Boy Meets Girl*, *Mauvais Sang* and the *nouvelle vague* inheritance

[A] method designed to break down not only conventional dramatic techniques but also the more recent conventions of improvisation with all the prolixities and clichés it entails ... and to establish an *écriture* based on actions, movements, attitudes, the actor's 'gestural', in other words. The ambition ... is to discover a new approach to acting in the cinema, where speech ... would play a role of 'poetic' punctuation. Not a return to the silent cinema, neither pantomime nor choreography: something else, where the movement of bodies, their counterpoint, their inscription within the screen space, would be the basis of the mise-en-scène. (Rivette in Rosenbaum 1977: 89)

When in 1984 Carax first brought to the screen his alter ego Alex (played by Denis Lavant), the then 23-year-old director became an overnight sensation in certain highly influential quarters of the French cinema intelligentsia. 'Un frêle fantôme hante tout le festival' ('A fragile phantom haunts the Cannes Festival'), the critic Serge Daney would write. For the *Cahiers* critics Carax was exceptional: his youth belied a great maturity in terms of cinematic and literary erudition, while his 'innocence' was offset by the cinematic paean to lost innocence which was his debut feature, *Boy Meets Girl*. In many respects, Carax seemed to 'cristallise tous les enjeux esthétiques et économiques du cinéma en ce milieu des années 80' ('crystallise all the aesthetic and economic stakes of mid–1980s cinema', Chévrie 1986: 25). Carax's project was said to be an 'aventure de la beauté et des méandres par lesquels elle advient' ('adventure of beauty and of the meanders through which you find it', Chévrie 1986: 25). In addition to the fulsome praise, they respected the aggression of Carax's approach to the press and to other filmmakers; in particular they were drawn to that manner in which this antipathy was associated with a larger creative strategy. For Carax, the genesis of a film involves not only 'l'envie de filmer telle ou telle chose ... [mais] aussi un dégout du cinéma des autres' (Carax 1986: 26).[1] This belligerence is born not out of malice towards other filmmakers but out of devotion to the cinema, as the same interview makes clear: 'je trouve important de dire que je n'aime pas les autres films ... pour qu'il soit vu comme tel par les gens qui l'aimeront' (Carax 1986: 32).[2] Invoking an idiom that led many to dismiss Carax as pretentious, for him a film is a 'un miracle à accomplir' ('a miracle you must accomplish', Chévrie 1986: 28). Such lyrical descriptions of the process of filmmaking are relatively rare. Love, beauty, fear, impotence, disgust and a procedure defined by Carax as 'd'avancer par l'absurde' ('advancing by way of the absurd', Chévrie 1986: 26), 'la panique de ne pas arriver à la légèreté dont on rêve' ('the panic of not attaining the lightness you've dreamed of', Chévrie 1986: 26): such were the raw materials with which Carax aspired to work. It seemed that French cinema had found its Céline.

Daney ends the aforementioned review with the words 'Godard est un dieu pour Carax' ('Godard is a god for Carax'), thereby inadvertently contributing to the persistent misunderstandings and misjudgements that have dogged the reception of Carax's films. The consensus is clear: either Carax is a pale imitator of Godard or, even worse, he, along with Besson, Beineix, Annaud and others, has merely married ticks and tropes stolen from Godard to the worst form of advertising imagery. Those who have deviated from the consensus, like his erstwhile colleagues at *Cahiers* or Raphaël Bassan in his well-known essay 'Trois néobaroques français', claim that Carax (but in Bassan's case also Beineix and Besson) represented a new 1980s film aesthetic, one whose foregrounding of ornament and decor, taste for gestural reinvention, and reliance on lighting to create mood and *trompe l'œil* effects, would seem to have more than a little in common with those episodes in art history known as Mannerism and the Baroque.

In a wider cine-historical perspective it can be seen what was at stake for these filmmakers. In the eyes of many film viewers, French

1 'the desire to film such and such a thing, but also disgust with the cinema of others'
2 'it's important to say that I don't like those other films ... so that people who love the cinema can see that it matters'

cinema is often thought to be 'cut off from reality', its intellectual and aesthetic concerns believed to have little relation to everyday life or the concerns of real people. When French auteurs speak of the ambitions of their work they are often met with calls of pretentiousness, self-obsession and irrelevance. Philip French, in his caricature of Rivette's *Va Savoir* for the *Observer* provides a good example of such a response: 'vapid, high-flown dialogue about love and art conducted by cool, confident French narcissists' (French 2002). The logical correlate of such dismissals is that only blunt realism can fulfil the demand for representations of the lives of the average person. Since the birth of the *nouvelle vague*, the tides of French cinema have ebbed and flowed between these two poles of naturalism and aestheticism. This caricature would have it that at one extreme there lie auteurist films expressing the ecstatic or paranoid visions of egotists, while at the other are found populist true-to-life representations of quotidian ups and downs. More often than not, financially successful French films will come from somewhere in the middle, everyday concerns peppered with stylistic flair, be it by way of the milieu and beautiful stars (*Jean de Florette* and *Manon des Sources* (Berri 1986) for example), or the application of state-of-the-art technology to the dreams and aspirations of the common person (*Amélie* (Jeunet 2002)) Now the first thing that must be said is that, as David Russell argued in his *Sight and Sound* essay on Beineix, 'it *is* impossible to talk about modern innovative French cinema without talking about style' (Russell 1989–90: 43). Whether the emphasis has been on character, form, theme or narrative structure, since the *nouvelle vague* it has come to be expected of French auteurs that they will set the agenda. 'The politique des auteurs was founded on the concept of style (*mise en scène*) as vision or interpretation of the world' (Russell 1989–90: 43). Style no longer meaning (only) fashion but metaphysics. Style can of course, as Russell points out, end in indulgent work, in overelaboration, hence cliché, even burlesque (Godard is often singled out for criticism in this respect). For this reason, the French films of the early 1980s that are in question here are often dismissed as empty, style driven, derivative and pretentious, and there is no doubt that the name of Carax tends to figure prominently in this debate.

While it must be admitted that the 1980s gave us little that was not a hybridisation of images and styles from bygone eras, this was necessarily so since it was a time in which the proliferation of images of every type was occurring on a massive scale. Nevertheless, there has been a general flattening by critics of heterogeneous forms, problems, concerns and types of filmmaking from the period. For this reason many diverse and disparate strands of filmmaking need disentangling. It is the intention of this chapter to undertake such a task. Only a minute dissection of the heterogeneous elements shaped by Carax into works of great complexity and *élan* will permit us to isolate the true singularity and originality of his 1980s films, *Boy Meets Girl* (1984) and *Mauvais Sang* (1986).

The first of these is shot in a now celebrated reinvention of monochrome: 'On redécouvre dans *Boy meets Girl* un travail du rapport visage/fond largement perdu au fil de l'âge classique, visage-masques sur fonds sombres' (Revault d'Allonnes 1991: 120).[3] There remains in the Carax of the 1980s an 'atteinte à la figuration du monde et de soi dans le monde' (Revault d'Allonnes 1991: 120).[4] The second draws luxurious reds, blues and yellows out of a neutral impasto surface and sends a now more aggressive but still schizoid Alex into previously uncharted spheres of existence: 'une inquiétude sur le lien entre homme et monde qui renvoie la brutale discontinuité lumineuse du ou des plans, ruptures ou sautes lumineuses' (Revault d'Allonnes 1991: 131),[5] a series of concerns which find their correlates in the film. These include a seeking out of limit points, pure sensations, radical experience beyond sense and beyond co-ordinates, co-ordination, orientation (*sens*) and signification (*sens*).

### *Boy Meets Girl* (synopsis)

On the banks of the Seine, young Alex enacts revenge on his girlfriend Florence's lover and returns futilely to seek solace in his fridge-illuminated room. Forced onto the streets again, a nocturnal *flânêrie* takes him, and he becomes the invisible link in a chain of events that will end in disaster. Set in motion by his eavesdropping on an intercom breakup of lovers Bernard and Mireille, what appears to

3 'One rediscovers in *Boy Meets Girl* an emphasis on face–ground relations lost during the classical age, a preference for mask-faces on dark backgrounds.'

4 'suffering from [the question of] figuration in the world and of self in the world'

5 'the brutal discontinuities of light in a shot or shots refers to an anxiety about the man–world link'

be a destiny sees Alex pursue the new object of his romantic longing by way of a series of detours and bizarre encounters. Having almost botched an attempt to steal Barbara records to leave at the home of Florence, he descends into the subway where his path crosses that of a put-upon Arab boy, eventually coming face to face with Mireille at a high-society party he has gatecrashed. Alone in the kitchen they speak at length, and mainly in monologue, of their dreams and fears. Alex suddenly declares his love to Mireille and begs for hers. They go out into the night, unknowingly crossing the path of Bernard, but are separated. The next day Alex, with a sense of foreboding, rushes to Mireille's flat. Approaching her from behind, but unaware that she is holding a pair of scissors, he embraces her, (hence) accidentally occasioning her death.

### *Mauvais Sang (The Night is Young)* (synopsis)

Marc and Hans, a couple of middle-aged down-at-heel crooks, based in an old horse-butcher's shop, discuss the recent death of their colleague Jean and consider using his son Alex as his replacement in a job they have planned. They intend to steal a virus that has been isolated at the Darley Wilkinson laboratory, in the hope of producing a vaccine against STBO, a syndrome contracted by those who have sex without being in love. In this, Marc and Hans face competition from a rival gang of criminals led by a woman known only as the American, a former colleague of Marc's and lover of Jean. Alex at first refuses but is mesmerised by a mysterious woman he sees on a bus who turns out to be Marc's girlfriend Anna. As plans for the robbery continue, Alex attempts to seduce Anna away from Marc producing aggressive tension between the two men. At an airfield owned by a friend Charlie, Marc forces agrophobic Anna into a parachute jump and when she faints in mid air it is Alex who rescues her. Later, Alex and Marc fight and, while the injured Marc sleeps, Alex performs tricks for Anna. But the world is under a spell: 'Nothing's moving' Anna tells Alex. Then comes the 'Modern Love' sequence in which Alex runs, dances and performs acrobatics in an attempt to lose the heaviness within; he succeeds and is summoned back by Anna's humming to a kind of spectral coupling between them. They talk at length, he tells her of his time in prison and of how it left him with a feeling of great heaviness he cannot shake off, about Lise's suicidal tendencies and speculates about father–daughter relations. Anna recounts the story of her first love Julien. At one point, Alex becomes aggressive, and forces a bright lamplight onto Anna's face. She must sleep but Marc has taken over the bed so she decides to use the hotel opposite. The passing of Halley's comet has made the tarmac hot and Alex carries Anna over it. From her window, Anna sends Alex a note pleading that they must save Marc. This puts an end to their night of possible love. There follows a series of scenes featuring the gang members, as well as Anna and Lise that are variations on silent-cinema conventions. The next morning Anna arrives back at the shop and there is a flirtatious scene with Alex which Marc's arrival breaks up. Alex receives a phone call from Lise telling him she has slept with Thomas but does not love him. Thomas overhears. While Alex is doing a three-card trick on the street he is dragged off by Boris, the American's henchman and is forced to play ball with them. We see a clip from Gremillon's *La Petite Lise* as Alex chides Anna about Marc's true contempt for her. Attempting to retrieve one of his own books from storage, Alex badly cuts his hand and has it dressed by Hans. Tensions mount with Marc about their mutual competence as the time of the big heist approaches. Alex meets Thomas who has contracted STBO. Lise receives a call from Thomas, Anna tells Marc 'I want infinite love'. The men leave for the job tailed by Thomas. Inside the Darley Wilkinson building, Alex steals the virus. Tipped off by Thomas, the police arrive. Through a combination of holding himself hostage and assistance from Lise, Alex escapes, killing a police inspector in the process. He injects the virus into an egg and hides it at the airport. That night, as snow falls, he sleeps beside Lise. Outside the butcher's shop, he is shot by Boris. Marc and Hans plan an escape for the four of them and drive to Charlie's airfield. Pursued by the American and her henchmen, a gun battle ensues and the American's car plunges into a river. Alex rejoices that the bullet in his gut has relieved him of the awful heaviness inside. At the airfield he ventriloquises his last words congratulating Lise on attaining the 'smile of speed'. In a repeat of Alex's 'Modern Love' turn, Anna races across the airfield and appears, by means of camera angle alteration and accelerated film, to float upwards.

## A band apart?

In terms of Carax's allegiance to the *nouvelle vague*, there is little doubt that he drew great stylistic inspiration from Godard in particular, as well as a taste for flamboyance, an arrogant faith in one's cinephilia, including the creation of a personal lineage in which to insert one's work, and a recognition of the need for a regular team of collaborators. If the Carax–Godard link is examined in detail, it is possible to isolate the following overt influences of Godard on Carax's first films, for the purposes of illustration placing particular emphasis on how *Bande à part* resonates in *Boy Meets Girl*.

1  Following the example of Godard, Carax in his first two features begins to amass a common band of associates, most notably cinematographer Jean-Yves Escoffier, editor Nelly Quettier (beginning with *Mauvais Sang*), producer Alain Dahan and actors Denis Lavant, Mireille Perrier and Juliette Binoche – the disbanding of which it seems in part (although other factors also ultimately contributed) to have been imposed on Carax only following the commercial failure of *Les Amants du Pont-Neuf*.

2  In *Boy Meets Girl*, Alex is something of a latter-day 'pierrot', while the party scene evokes the similar scene in *Pierrot le fou*, right down to the echo of Sam Fuller's famous definition in that film of cinema as 'Love ... hate ... action ... violence ... death ... in one word ... emotion'. This receives a Caraxian update as 'first came love ... no, emotion'. The deliberate reprise and reformulation is revealing not only of what has changed in the cinema and in the concerns of filmmakers from the 1960s to the 1980s, but about the fundamental novelty of Carax vis-à-vis Godard. For example, Godard would never have said 'L'histoire [du cinéma], c'est le couple ... tous les mouvements, toutes les vagues, ce sont simplement des gens qui ont été amoureux au même moment' (Carax 1986: 28–9).[6] It is useful to recall Rivette's claims that during the 1970s – 'les années Giscard' – he could not force himself to film the reality around him, a reluctance that lasted a decade and led him to take refuge in fantasies such as *Céline et Julie vont en bateau* (1973), *Duelle* and *Noroit* (both 1976). Only when the 'blocked society' was

6  'The history [of cinema] is the couple ... all the movements, all the waves, simply people who've been in love at the same time.'

replaced with the euphoria of the 1980s, and a mood that was 'exciting, euphoric and playful' could he return to *l'actualité* with his 1980 film *Pont du Nord*. The macro-level corollary of this change is that destiny and chance replace politics as the major exterior force moving us. But less is not necessarily less important or interesting, merely different. Carax seeks a new image–reality relationship, one that, in line with the widespread critique of representation, which was a feature of the 1980s, is not content with a mimetic or analogical model, but rather thinks in terms of powers or dimensions. Therefore, if he can pinpoint the origin of the amorous affect, Carax feels he might be led to crack the secret of those dimensions of reality whence turbulent movement and shafts of light originate and come to meet the senses. Carax sought to distil Godard's question 'What is cinema?' in order that it becomes 'What is an Image?'. Or, in other words, what is the image that I am and that she is? That I am to her and she is to me?

3   There is the centrality of fashionable records and music such as Jean Ferrat in *Bande à part*, Dead Kennedys in *Boy Meets Girl*, while the famous 'Madison' dance scene in *Bande à part* has its counterpart in Perrier's exuberant tap-dancing in *Boy Meets Girl*. In addition, we could cite a correlation between Karina's song which moves from deigetic to non-deigetic space in Godard's film and Mireille's decidedly *nouvelle-vague*-like song at the party.

4   Clothing likewise provides a series of visual echoes of the *nouvelle vague*. Where Karina has her pleated check skirt, Perrier has her check trousers. Also notable is the check scarf passed from hand to hand, which Alex wraps around his face in the manner of Belmondo – whose 'scarf' of course is made of dynamite – in *Pierrot le fou*.

5   In terms of decor and lighting there are also clear affinities. The two directors share, for example, a taste for non-diegetically justified light changes. In Carax, this strategy is usually deployed in two-shots, helping him to push the close-up to the point of facial indeterminacy.

6   Poetry and citation should also be mentioned. Carax continues Godard's search for poetic dialogue and monologue. Of course Cocteau is the main other precursor here, but while Cocteau goes very far in this respect and is also a clear influence on Carax, Godard more than Cocteau provides a model for generating the

   text. This is because in Godard one finds a combination of citation
   and of self-penned words (often without a clear distinction between
   levels), while, in addition, the referenced authors are often the
   same: notably, Rimbaud, Ramuz and Céline.
7  Carax takes Godard's search for new kinds of bodies and
   behaviour into a new dimension. Not only do characters often act
   as if they are barely concerned by what happens to them, they also
   stand outside themselves. Examples of this arise in *Boy Meets Girl*
   when Alex's violent neighbour screams 'I'm gonna hit, watch',
   when Mireille takes her gestures from an instruction book, and in
   the deliberate artificiality of the security guards.

Carax brings to the screen a new sort of character. In order to begin to
flesh out the contours of these new personae, let us first consider
what one might call 'normative' characterisation: a character has a
goal, a motivation pushes her/him forward in a specific direction, and
the goal pulls her/him towards a climax. In *Pierrot*, however, Ferdinand
is a split subject; more generally, in this film, characters defy development. Ferdinand's diary serves less and less to confer an identity on
this disordered collage of sense(less) experiences. He is a fragment in
a world of scraps without cohesion, a cog plaintively boasting 'I've a
mechanism for seeing'. These characters are not so much individual
beings as a collection of traits lying somewhere between beings.
Godard can be said to be approaching a neo-baroque formulation,
along the lines of Ruiz's description of 'le corps dispersé' ('the
dispersed body'): 'cette idée m'attire, mon corps éparpillé dans le
monde' (Ruiz 1987: 98).[7] Carax pushes this sense of incompletion
and of *personnages morcelés* further by severing it from Godard's
obsessional reflections on the cinematic medium. There is nothing in
Carax's work remotely like the famous Godardian references to his
films *as films* – no 'an attempt at a film' (*Pierrot*) or 'a film found on a
scrapheap' (*Weekend*), no thoroughgoing *mise en abyme*, as in *Le
Mépris*. What we get instead is the persistence of duplicating devices
that call attention to the image *as image* and not to the cinematic
medium per se. There is a sense of artifice, combined with a mannerism engaged with via the mediation of silent-film conventions.
Arguably, this combination very often brings Carax closer to the world
of a Pasolini than to that of a Godard, let alone to Besson or Beineix.

7 'this idea appeals to me, my body scattered around the world'

Another differentiating factor is that, instead of manipulating the chronology of sequences, such as in Godard's handling of the getaway scenes in *Pierrot*, Carax sometimes gives us an indeterminacy of events vis-à-vis one another, since what primarily concerns him in these sequences is movement. He wants to explore movement in all its forms but more particularly those will later be discussed in terms of the set of principles identified as neo-baroque. As he said in a 1984 interview:

> [il y a] deux mouvements dans le cinéma, qui sont un mouvement où on va vers ce qu'on ne sait absolument pas faire, ou ce qu'on ne connaît pas, c'est à dire les étoiles, la lune, et puis un mouvement où on rentre très fort à l'intérieur, mais à toute vitesse, quoi, y'a autant de distance, et on cherche la partie la plus mystérieuse qui est en soi. (Carax 1984)[8]

Another major difference between Carax and Godard is in the way that the exploration of the dimensions of the image replaces the medium as focal point of the new cinema. It is in this context that Alex's 'map of firsts' is to be understood. It replaces the notebooks and diaries of Godard's films. That an image of a life is an ongoing imaging of affects, seems to be Carax's point. It gives rise to the question, posed more generally by the film, of 'What sense of self does that map imply/construct?'. Alex's attributes are laid out cartographically as a series of points, not flows, mapping both the world and the self. What, then, of the space between these forms/points? The first conclusion we can draw about the Caraxian character (Alex) is this: he is like an acrobat who walks on two tightropes simultaneously, one soaring to giddy levels while the other drags close to the ground. This is one of the major factors that makes Carax neo-baroque. Substituting for the Baroque combat between good and evil, light and dark, Carax's neo-baroque plays out a struggle between fate and chance, heaviness and lightness. As Carax said to David Thompson on the British release of *Les Amants du Pont-Neuf*, life and love are, for him, concerned with the 'irredeemable' and the *inespéré* (what you

8 'two movements in the cinema, one whereby you go towards what you absolutely don't know how to do, or which you don't even know, i.e. the stars, the moon, the other a movement where there's an intense return to the interior but at top speed, like, there is so much distance and you search for the most mysterious part of yourself.'

dare not hope for) (Carax 1992:a 11). Fate creates irredeemable lives and heavy bodies but a mere throw of the dice can bring the 'unhoped for' or the passage to a lighter, more ecstatic level of existence: 'à l'impossible on est tenu' ('we are bound to the impossible', Carax 1991a). The connection between this idea and the 'naturalism' (understood in a very specific sense) of *Pola X* will be explored in Chapter 3.

## Body double

As with those of Godard, Carax's characters often act as if they are barely linked in any common sense manner to the actions they perform. In this connection, we have already mentioned the 'I'm gonna hit, watch' moment in *Boy Meets Girl*. This kind of auto-duplication of experience is one of the traits that have been identified as an instance of Carax's mannerism. It should be noted that this doubling does not resemble that of a great modernist like Antonioni where the camera seems to have a life of its own and does not always oversee the narrative or identify with a character's point of view, but 'in its freedom simply to look, "objectively", doubles over for the spectator, equally free, positioned in a place of objectivity and non-necessity' (Rohdie 1990: 150). Carax's camera seeks out the pure, the *enfance d'image*, but finds it intrinsically folded over, a delayed mirror reflection of itself, as Bazin liked to say.

Therefore, when Perrier has difficulties in occupying the space of the flat once left alone, she submits her body and its gestures to the commands of a tap-dancing instruction book. This whole magnificent sequence concerns the idea of occupying space (thereby rendering it a place) and time, the exigencies of being in the here and now. Being there, being present is impossible since one's thoughts are dictated by external forces: Alex's at first by Bernard, and then by his nextdoor neighbour who literally commands him to 'hit' the wall; Bernard's himself by an impersonal voice that has floated free of him; Mireille's by Bernard, and then by the book; the neighbour by some extremely aggressive and misogynistic forces that have seized hold of him. Alex walks along by the river and seeks to control his movements in the face of all the aberrant movements around him, and struggles with the question of how to occupy space or inhabit the world. This fundamental question is tied to another: what belongs to me? In a world of cliché, of clichéd discourse, gestures and sentiments, in a world in which 'I' am one image among the rest (not only is each couple around Alex and Mireille an image before anything else but Mireille herself dancing at the window is an image for others), the question arises: how can I build a self out of all this cliché? This is the neo-baroque formulation of a question that Deleuze isolated as 'Baroque par excellence', and as a reply to which the Baroque philosopher Leibniz's inventory had included 'd'abord la pensée du moi, le cogito, mais aussi le fait que j'ai des pensées diverses ... enfin, c'est le corps, c'est un corps ... un corps organique auquel je suis immédiatement "présent", dont je dispose d'une façon immédiate et auquel je coordonne du perçu' (Deleuze 1988: 143).[9] By the 1980s the response will have changed. In the decade which saw the term 'postmodern' become so fashionable one could no longer lay claim to possessing any of the above: not a *cogito*; not the world as perceived; perhaps not even a (unified) body. In this context, it is interesting to note that there are scenes in *Boy Meets Girl* that resemble Samuel Beckett's *Film*, which was directed by Alan Schneider in 1965 and starred Buster Keaton.[10] In Beckett's film, as in Carax's, the character alone in his room desperately seeks the ground of (his) being, but it can no longer be found in self-perception, since cliché has taken the place of one's interior as much as of the world outside. In place of such grounding, Alex constructs a cartography of affects – we watch him adding a new property (that of 'attempted murderer') to the affective map hidden in his room. Carax hereby brings to the screen a new sort of character for whom it is not perception that is primary as in the 'optical dramas' of an Antonioni. Nor is the emotion of action cinema, to which Fuller referred in *Pierrot*, his goal, but, rather, impersonal affects of which he may form part, what Carax might term 'First Times' or Events – the moment of birth of each new affect or depersonalised emotion. This is why anomalous decor, irregular lighting and aberrant movement rule Carax's world – they free up bodies from stasis, depicting characters in the middle or mi-lieu of events. While Mireille finds the rhythm of her emotion through the body, Alex discovers his on a deaf-

9  'First of all the thought of the self, the cogito, but also the fact that I have diverse thoughts ... finally, the body ... an organic body with which I am immediately "present" ... and with which I coordinate what is perceived' (Deleuze 1993: 107).
10 For more on Beckett's *Film*, see Waugh and Daly (1995).

blind stroll through a world of strangely dehumanised movements. On the bridge, the lovers dance like mannequins. They seem to defy gravity, and in this drifting space a few flashes of superimposed simultaneity (Mireille's face is superimposed on the scene) succeed in creating a single impersonal affect and a moment of inflection as defined by Cache: co-ordinates and co-ordination fail (Cache 1995: 151). This is then carried through to the next morning when Alex is seen to repeat Mireille's posture on his bed, until his father's call restores the world of duplication. 'I had a déjà vu experience, a memory of the present,' he tells his caller. In this duplicated present, it is appropriate and/or inevitable that Alex goes out to the Xerox machines where he encounters what looks like a pair of identical twins. Intensifying the doubling motif, the twins are themselves reflected in a mirror as they use one particular duplicating machine.

Such dizzying layers of reflexivity contributed to the appellation of Baroque and/or neo-baroque being applied to Carax's cinema. In order to grasp Carax's specificity and originality it is perhaps in the area of baroque *puissances* that one should look, rather than in Godard and the new wave. For although these were an undeniable inspiration to Carax as a novice filmmaker, his citing of these models has more to do with wanting to situate and carefully delineate (yet ultimately differentiate) his own set of problems and concerns from them, than it has with any direct mimicking of them.

## Mannerism and the neo-baroque

Two connected but finally distinct sixteenth- and seventeenth-century artistic categories were invoked in the 1980s by critics trying to come to terms with the new French cinema of the image: Mannerism (the *Cahiers du Cinéma* group) and the Baroque (most succinctly formulated by Bassan from the vantage point of 1989). There are elements of both tendencies in Carax's first two films, *Boy meets Girl* tending more to a Mannerist aesthetic, *Mauvais Sang* to the Baroque as revisited with a neo-baroque sensibility.

Mannerism can perhaps be most succinctly defined as an aesthetic that foregrounds awareness of a revered style yet is not content to mimic that style. The ensuing clash between loyalty to a master's work and the desire for individual statement gives rise to artificiality, fake elegance, exaggerations of style, contrived postures and gestures, scalar (as in Pontormo's visitation in Carmignano) and thematic imbalances (often the main incident pushed into the background or swamped in irrelevant detail) and so on, in short the *manner* of an art form at the height of its perfection is pushed over the edge producing a generalised deformation. Historically, Mannerism is associated with the sixteenth-century late Renaissance where new philosophical and scientific thought produced a crisis of truth and an ensuing crisis of religious belief. Aesthetically, what followed was the disintegration of the rigid order of High Renaissance art whereby its forms and manners are still being copied but by artists without the luxury of believing in them in quite the same way. Baroque art will soon follow like a mad and excessive invention of forms intent on sealing up the cracks in the world that had shone through Mannerist art. In the classical thought underpinning the High Renaissance, everything had an assigned place in a representational order ruled by geometric perspective with the spectator at its centre. Come the Baroque, this system is shattered: there is no longer any centre, merely a multi-plication of viewpoints, which phenomenon gives rise to works of great complexity, to obscure treatments of familiar themes. Of course, one of the most identifiable traits is the rise of decoration to a place of new and often equal importance to the figures it contains. As Raoul Ruiz so eloquently put it 'in the baroque system there is not a statement [plus the secondary ornaments], there are only ornaments but any ornament is the way the statement is divided into many pieces, into infinite pieces, and inside each of these pieces there are others' (Ruiz 1993: 51). This gives rise to art, especially cinema, which is often accused of formal and technical virtuosity 'for its own sake' when fundamentally there is an entire metaphysical worldview at stake.

## The Baroque and the neo-baroque

When in the 1980s Bassan (1989) spoke of Carax along with Besson and Beineix in terms of a 'neo-baroque' he was not only identifying what were in his view certain shared characteristics, he was also hooking into an intellectual and aesthetic propensity of the era. In the 1970s and 1980s, in France, the Baroque – as the name for a set of intellectual and aesthetic principles – underwent a profound resurgence. The resurgence was not confined to a particular area of thought, and the concept was embraced by the Tel Quelists (Roland Barthes (1964) and Severo Sarduy (1975 and 1991)), by the psychoanalyst Jacques Lacan (1975), by the philosopher Christine Buci-Glucksmann in her study of Walter Benjamin and Baroque reason ([1984] 1994), by Guy Hocquenghem and René Schérer (1986) and by Gilles Deleuze in his study of Leibniz (from Italy, Omar Calabrese also made his contribution with *L'Età neobarocca* (1987)). However, 'baroquism' was even more widespread than this would suggest, and, via a predilection for Leibniz, it can also be felt in the work of the philosopher Michel Serres. Of the filmmakers who ranged on the side of the baroque, there are two names that are clearly apt: Raoul Ruiz and Werner Schroeter (to these we can also add Paul Leduc). Finally, the Latin American baroque (with which Ruiz and Leduc of course, along with Sarduy, have a close affinity) had its own influential voices in fiction (Lima, Carpentier) both outside and within the French context. With such a diverse range of individuals, coming as they do from distinct traditions and fields of endeavour, it would be absurd to assume that they present a united front on the question of what the Baroque, or, for that matter, the neo-baroque was. While there are many localised affinities and overlaps, there are equally as many divergences and points of disagreement between the thinkers and artists mentioned. For example, Ruiz feels an affinity with Deleuze, as do Hocquenghem and Schérer, while these two share certain of the convictions of Christine Buci-Glucksmann, especially in respect of the importance of Walter Benjamin's work on Baroque allegory. However, while he would share her sense of the importance of Leibniz for reflection on the cinema (and certainly Buci-Glucksmann for her part declares her support for Deleuze in her *Trafic* article (Buci-Glucksmann (1993)), Deleuze would want to stay aloof from many of the psycho-analysis-inflected theories to which Buci-Glucksmann subscribes. The difficulty of presenting an account of these revisitings of Baroque problematics notwithstanding, it is possible to make some rudimentary assertions about what characteristics or qualities might be considered neo-baroque when viewed from within the context provided by the resurgence of statements – however diverse – about the Baroque and the baroque. Once achieved, it will then be possible to select from these characteristics those which account for the specificity of Carax's neo-baroque on the one hand and which distinguish his work from other filmmakers who can also, from another point of view, be categorised as baroque.


## Four fundamental principles of the Baroque

### The Baroque is reason's other

For most thinkers – and certainly for those named above – the historical Baroque is antithetical in disposition vis-à-vis the central tenets of the age of reason. The key thinker as far as a French and European context is concerned is René Descartes (1596–1650). For the latter, the human mind (*res cogitans*), via the machinations of a divine being, imperiously surveyed what he termed *res extensa* (matter, or the material world). This consciousness perceived clearly and distinctly – that which it observed only in obscured or partly obscured form was due to its imperfections as perception's locus or host. The most important aspect, however, as far as we are concerned, is that obscurity was only contingent, and was, in effect, an illusion created by the failings of *res cogitans*. Such a model of human reason has been compared to a 'projective geometry'. Baroque reason shares this projective nature. However, in the Baroque, the situation becomes radically more complex. The distinction between clear and obscure becomes less watertight, and the unconscious is granted a signi-ficance that is wished away in the Cartesian formulation. In thinkers such as Leibniz, the human mind is immersed in a world of light and shade; it functions as a filtering mechanism sifting the possible from the 'incompossible' (that which is logically contradictory in relation to the possible). Although Leibniz installs a divine architect to oversee and underwrite terrestrial exchanges, there are, as Deleuze and Serres show, sufficient residual traces of 'noise' to undermine the imposed and imposing harmony of Leibniz's system, to render the Baroque, in this sense, 'reason's other'. As Buci-Glucksmann puts it, 'with its theatricisation of existence and its logic of ambivalence, [the Baroque] is not merely another reason within modernity. Above all it is the Reason of the Other, or of its overbrimming excess' (Buci-Glucksmann 1994: 39).

## Perspectivism

With the encroachment of unconscious perceptions on the once unchallenged tyrannical rule of consciousness, the Baroque sees the emergence of a perspectivist approach to the question of perception and knowledge. The idea of a central locus of perception, whether that be divine or human (*res cogitans*), undergoes, in the Baroque, a profound displacement. Centres proliferate, surfaces become inundated with focal points, giving rise to a failure of anchored encompassing perception. As Wölfflin, speaking in particular of architectural forms, put it, 'a (purely visual) movement is set going over the sum of the forms, independently of their particular viewpoint. The wall vibrates, the space quivers in every corner' (1950: 65). If as most commentators agree, the eye is the primary locus of inscription in the Baroque, then it is an agitated, 'ambulant' eye. Ruiz would make clear the utility of Leibniz's famous proposition nine in the *Monadology* when in his adapted version he declares the town equivalent to the infinity of points of view which can be brought to bear on it by the camera (Ruiz 1987: 102).

## Boundaries dissolve

In the historical Baroque the plastic and visual arts did much to call into question the status of the frame considered either as a physical territorial boundary, say as the physical frame around a canvas, or as a material and spatial limit on the material form (but also as a 'metaphysical' limit, say in the case of the imaginary 'boundaries' one might place on a sculptural form in order to interpret it). In Bernini's *The Ecstasy of St Teresa* (1645–52) the robes of the central subject appear to flee the figure at the centre of the complex sculptural form, resulting in what Alejo Carpentier identifies as a 'loss of central axis'. In his *Constantine the Great* (1654–70) a vast, self-supporting and entirely unnecessary (when viewed from the point of view of the demands of verisimilitude) swathe of garment rises to a dizzy height from behind the 'central' form. In *Bust of Gabriel Fonseca* (1668–75) the head and upper body of the sculptural figure emerge in three dimensions from a frame more accustomed to circumscribing a two-dimensional support. What is questioned simultaneously in these works is the idea of a central locus (for or in perception) and the ontological foundations of the frame itself.

## Fluidity

Or we might say, principle of turbulence. The Baroque uncouples the subject from its moorings, and permits it to float in a decentred and mobile realm. In the historical Baroque, such mobility (for Bernini the essence of the human being was only glimpsed in motion) tended to be reined in by theological and political pragmatism (and not least in Bernini). There remained, nonetheless, a turbulence that could not be entirely overridden by such pragmatism. Jean Rousset has a wonderful metaphor to describe this fourth Baroque principle: 'Qu'est-ce qu'une façade baroque? C'est une façade Renaissance plongée dans l'eau; plus exactement: son reflet dans l'eau agitée ... tout l'édifice ondule au rythme des vagues' (Rousset 1953: 157).[11] The solidity is compromised by a constitutive fluidity. For the historical Baroque, say, in the thought of Leibniz, fluidity is shored up by architectonics (by system), and hence does not compromise the belief that there is no void. In a more neo-baroque conception, however, a forgotten philosophical tradition is reinstated. Lucretius 'described, with precision, nature – the things themselves at their birth, at the moment of their birth, in and through turbulence. Turbulence is an intermittence of void and plenitude, of lawful determinism and undeterminism' (Serres 1982: 109). This fourth principle of the Baroque marks the point of convergence between the 'neo-baroque' and 'naturalism', two of the central concepts in this overview of the work of Carax.

Therefore, three centuries on, 'mannerist' and 'baroque' cinemas will not only compose shots according to these principles but narrative structure too will be affected, since the temporal order that resulted from Renaissance perspective and which was taken up unquestioningly by narrative-driven cinema will give way to new ways of connecting shots. This explains why the use of *tableaux vivants* became a favoured device among filmmakers exploring mannerist principles in the cinema, since, as Pascal Bonitzer has shown, the primary way to stop the narrative flow is through the use of this particular type of arrested but mobile image (*tableau vivant*). All of the mannerist and baroque masters of the cinema, from Welles to Cocteau, Robbe-Grillet to Ruiz, Pasolini to Carmelo Bene, have

11 'What is a baroque façade? It's a Renaissance façade plunged in water; or more precisely, its reflection in agitated water ... the entire edifice undulating to the rhythm of waves.'

invented exciting alternatives in response to the pressure to create predominantly narrative links between shots. The 'baroque' cinema of the twentieth century, just like its fine-art exemplar of the past, is recognisable through fantastical and convoluted narrative form, compositions that foreground the figural aspect of bodies and decors; characters that assume the most studied poses; a taste for anti-realist artifice; exaggerations of scale and size, distortions of perspective; films that savour illusionism of all kinds; anamorphosis and *trompe l'œil* effects; doubling procedures of many types including the immoderate use of mirrors, shadows and silhouette; startling disjunctions between a frontality in which fore- and background are barely distinguishable. To this can be added a dizzying exploitation of the possibilities of depth of field, the non-functional use of colour and light – often stretching to elaborate light displays – and excessive movement that the picture space can barely contain – in short the violation of every rule that derives from the Renaissance system of geometric perspective.

If there is one thing that differentiates the often difficult to distinguish mannerist and baroque tendencies of filmmakers it is to be found in attitude. Mannerism tends to carry with it an anxiety about its masters and therefore about the act of creativity itself. These films so often display a troubling concern with duplication of all types. However, if there is a doubling of perspectives, it is not the standard modernist device whereby what is facilitated is a retrieval of unity at another level. By contrast, truly baroque films tend to cast such reserve aside and are exclusively concerned with proliferating forms, formal devices and narrative strategies which destabilise any putative unity whether considered as prior or derived. If we take two films by Raoul Ruiz, *Hypothèse du tableau volé/Hypothesis of the Stolen Painting* from 1978 and *Les Trois Couronnes du matelot/Three Crowns of the Sailor* from 1983 it is possible to view the former as a paradigm of mannerist filmmaking focusing as it does on *tableaux vivants*, while the latter is primarily baroque, in its emphasis on narrative complexity and *mise en abyme* effects, deep-focus composition, humorous playing with logical paradoxes, and where the drive to duplication remains on the narrative level of doubling and exchange. Each mannerist or baroque film will tend to dwell on certain traits lent by these artistic developments. Sometimes the dominant emphasis will be on decor, or on taking an accepted form or genre to breaking point, or on

Russian doll style narrative complexity or lighting and colour. As should be clear by the end of this chapter, mannerist conceits predominate in *Boy Meets Girl*, baroque traits in *Mauvais Sang*.

Like its sixteenth-century model, the mannerist problematic began to appear in *Cahiers* in 1983 during a period of crisis, wherein it was aligned with Alain Bergala's diagnosis of the end of modernism as *the* problematic of the age (Bergala 1983, 1985). (On a wider scale, this was related to Jean-François Lyotard's account of the passing of the last remaining grand narratives – the equivalent for us of the High Renaissance 'loss of centre'.) Between 1955 and 1980 what drove leading filmmakers, Bergala argues, was a concern for truth. But now, Bergala could argue from the evidence around him, the false, the fake, the forgery and the lie were the dominant concerns of innovative filmmaking. This exploration of what Gilles Deleuze calls 'les puissances du faux' ('the powers of the false', Deleuze 1985: 165–202; Deleuze 1989: 126–55) often leads the cinematic image in the direction of mannerism – manifest in a concern with decor, theatre, costume, pretence, the fake, imitation, print and poster-style imagery. In the context of discussing *La Lune dans le caniveau/The Moon in the Gutter*, Bergala considers the value of Beineix's mannerist experiment: if the image is false and sound true as Bresson had said, and if Beineix responds 'I don't give a shit about truth', then Bergala concludes that if the cinema image is ontologically false (but no less ontologically real), there is no point in resisting this fact; there is nothing to do but investigate its theatrical powers. Hence in Bergala's eyes, the at least partial success of *La Lune dans le caniveau*, where Beineix manages to confer a theatricality even on the heaviest of milieus (the port). But the venture ends in failure, as Bergala makes clear, since the result is ultimately devoid of interest unless 'elle fait vaciller, dans un léger vertige de la représentation, la ligne de partage du vrai et du faux'; that is, this theatricality must be filmed so as to render truth and falsity indeterminate as opposed to a cinema which is already wholly 'avant filmage, du côté de l'illusion et de l'artefact' (Bergala 1983: 7).[12]

---

12 'it causes the dividing line between the true and the false to vacillate in a light vertigo of representation'; 'even before filming, on the side of illusion and artefact.'

## Gesture and decor

Perhaps the first things that strike the average viewer of a mannerist film are the artificiality of the acting and the excessive stylisation of the equally artificial decor. These aspects, however, must be understood in their larger context: they form part of a series of strategies designed to challenge standard representationalist cinematic conventions. In this context, it should be noted that the issue of the cinematic gesture concerns an area which Anglo-American film analysis has left relatively underexplored. Cinematic gesture is unique in that, according to Jean Douchet, it replaces the fixed attitudes and bearing that the theatre actor must find to lend a truth to her/his character with a new plasticity 'plus proche des poses que prennent les personnages en peinture' ('closer to the poses taken by figures in painting', Douchet 1995: 118), more created and invented than found. This imperative to create new postures and attitudes, ones more adequate to the concerns of the film one is making, is something that does not seem a conscious issue for most Anglo-American directors, whereas in France it has been essential. As Douchet makes clear, the future directors of the *nouvelle vague* when critics were still preoccupied with 'essayer de comprendre quelles propriétés le geste pouvait travailler, ce qu'il apportait au cinéma, étant entendu que la grande différence entre théâtre et cinéma était la façon dont un geste se situait dans l'espace et y traçait son graphisme' (Douchet 1995: 118).[13] In the cinema, the figure can easily obtain its autonomy from bodies and situations, and the potential is great for the fragmentation of bodies via framing and montage, whereby every pose or movement takes on a more abstract graphic quality and the distribution through the course of a film of these body parts becomes an essential element of the composition of the work.

Now mannerist filmmakers, in line with experimental filmmakers of every kind, tend to think of bodies and the decor they are placed in as such graphic or figurative compositions, albeit in three dimensions. Furthermore, there is the aforementioned consciousness of figural history and of the struggle between a wholehearted adoption of a pre-existent style and the desire to express through one's unique

---

13 'grasping the characteristics that a gesture could fashion, what it could bring to the cinema given that the great difference between theatre and cinema is the way in which a gesture locates itself in space and traces its figure there.'

personal stylistic traits. On both counts the limits of style are forced into the realms of artificiality.

Mannerist and baroque directors like Sternberg and Welles (to name but two) give the lie to the idea that Hollywood has never supported radical formal experimentation (as long as the public are willing to pay for it) while in Europe, and most notably in Italy – possibly because Italian audiences had acquired a taste for a measure of self-reflexivity in the medium through contact with the films of Fellini and others – mannerist and baroque cinemas flourished throughout the 1960s and 1970s in the work of Pasolini, Visconti and Bene.

But for Carax it is really the neo-baroque and mannerist films coming out of France in the 1970s that prove decisive. Bassan's influential account of the neo-baroque aspects of the films of Carax, Beineix and Besson is a bold attempt to discredit the many critics who had dismissed these films under the overly general rubric of '*cinéma du look*', a categorisation by way of which they were all considered to have based the surface texture and appearance of their films on that which was then in vogue in advertising and glossy magazines. The article 'Trois néobaroques français' was published in the journal *Revue du Cinéma* in 1989. Bassan cites three French films from the 1970s (all from 1976 as it happens) as direct influences on the three auteurs in question: Téchiné's *Barocco*, Rivette's *Duelle* and Garrel's *Le Berceau de cristal*. On the face of it this is an astonishing claim for those familiar with the films, especially when it is clear that Bassan believes that what he terms the first neo-baroque film, Beineix's *Diva*, owes something to Garrel and Rivette.

Let us examine each of the three 'source' films in question, in an attempt to probe more deeply into the matter of influences and precedence (in particular as it concerns Carax) than does Bassan in what is, despite its merits, still far too sweeping and unexplored a generalisation. Crucial, for example, is Bassan's 'forgetting' of the arrival of Chilean baroque master Raoul Ruiz in France in 1973. The latter injected an unprecedented dose of baroque effects, from excessive decoration and Pandora's box-type narratives structuring to near-pagan melancholy and superstition into a culture which would have preferred to carry on without it. As Ruiz himself has remarked (Ruiz 1993: 51): the average French citizen is a natural enemy of the baroque but, lodged in his office at the Ministry of Culture, Ruiz's thought and imagery soon had an immediate and direct influence on many French films, including *Barocco* by Téchiné and *Duelle* by Rivette. Bassan also curiously forgets to mention the work of Alain Robbe-Grillet, whose serialist experiments in narrative form often produced exciting baroque effects.

*Le Berceau de cristal* is certainly the joker in Bassan's pack, one of a series of partly mannerist, partly neo-decadent works by Philippe Garrel which exerted a somewhat subterranean influence on many young French filmmakers of the late 1970s (Noguez 1977: 312), and early 1980s. It is indeed a pity that Bassan did not follow up on his astute observation regarding Garrel's film: while it was an unpredictable link, it was nonetheless an inspired one in terms of tracking Carax's cinephilic development.

It is clear that a cluster of neo-decadent concerns had a great influence on the mood, thematic concerns and dialogue of Carax's first two films. Some of the defining features of Carax's neo-decadent philosophy can be traced back to the work of Baudelaire, while it is perhaps Huysmans (in *A Rebours*) who perhaps most thoroughly elucidates the decadent mindset proper. For Baudelaire, the world had witnessed in the middle of the nineteenth century a sundering of representation and meaning. In a condition of mourning for this lost link, allegory took the place once occupied by symbol (a phenomenon to which Walter Benjamin devotes much attention). Increasingly, the world became defined by the commodity; a symptom of this decline was, in Baudelaire's view, the commodification of women through prostitution. Carax's concerns differ, entailing as they do a generalised melancholy focused on the 'too late', combined with an interest in the theme of the impossible androgyne that echoes a more *fin de siècle* fascination. With Baudelaire also came a critical response to urban modernity in the shape of a theorisation of the role of the poet in the altered fabric of the metropolis. The response of Huysmans to the same issue a little later in the century can be measured in his critical attention to aspects of the work of Zola. Reproaching Huysmans for having, in *A Rebours*, undermined naturalism, Zola elicits Huysman's own criticism that 'le roman, tel qu'il [Zola] le concevait, me semblait moribund, usé par les redites, sans intérêt, qu'il voulût ou non, pour moi' (Huysmans [1884] 1981: 62).[14] In both cases

14 'the novel as he [Zola] conceived it seemed to me moribund, worn to a shadow by the wearisome repetitions that, whether he liked it or no, possessed no interest for me' (Huysmans 1969: xlv).

(Baudelaire and Huysmans), the response to the material world is to reinforce, rather than to diminish, artifice. The engagement in literature with the material world becomes a question of style, form, mode and manner.

## *Taedium vitae*

> Mais déjà, au début des années 70, le rock était quasiment fini, c'est comme le cinéma, comme à la guerre: il y a les éclaireurs, ceux qui vont en première ligne et se font descendre tout de suite, les mecs morts dans les années 60, Hendrix … Après arrivent ceux de l'arrière-garde, qui ne savent même plus pourquoi ils combattent, très protégés et beaucoup moins intéressants. Ce n'est même pas une nostalgie, c'est l'idée qu'on arrive après les choses. Par contre, le jus, l'électricité qu'il y a eu dans ce mouvement-là, je l'ai toujours recherché dans la vie, le cinéma, le montage. (Carax 1991)[15]

This quote from Carax is as good a definition as any of the contemporary relevance of the decadent mindset. It combines the feeling that one is arriving too late in an already worn-out world, and a mortal fatigue of living. There is, moreover, a belief that there is no more uncorrupted innocence, no more savage nature; in order to compensate for these gnawing absences refuge is taken in artificiality, in style for its own sake, as for example in dandyism as a mode (or *manner*) of living, which entails a seeking out of the excesses of refined living, and ever newer sensations. Decadence, then, as it is associated with late nineteenth-century aestheticism, is effectively one historically definable incarnation of the mannerist principle. All of this is close to Carax's heart in those first films. As Deleuze has demonstrated, Visconti is the filmmaker for whom the 'too late' has become a mode of being. Alex, however, is the Caraxian neo-decadent, with his Hamlet-like hesitancy and pallid demeanour, in isolation from society and the world and veering between bouts of ennui and mania, near-

15 'Already, at the start of the 1970s, rock music was almost dead, just like in the cinema, like in war. There were scouts, those who fought on the frontline and fell straight away, the guys who died in the 1960s like Hendrix. After that came the rearguard who no longer know why they're fighting, they're very protected and much less interesting. It isn't even nostalgia. It's the idea that one arrives after it's happened. On the other hand, the juice, the electricity that movement had, I've always sought it out in life, in cinema, in montage.'

catatonic langour and the ecstatic grasp of pure sensation or what Carax prefers to call emotion. 'L'emotion, c'est ce qui se passe ... c'est ce qui voyage à toute vitesse entre deux personnes' (Carax 1984);[16] 'emotion' is the blinding light, the flash or fulguration of an event provoking 'the smile of speed' (as one of the main themes of *Mauvais Sang* would have it – the expression comes from Léo Ferré (Philippon 1986: 17)). On the aesthetic level, such a philosophy of the event is translated into a cinematic system which might be thought of in terms of turbulence or perturbation: camera placement and lighting provoking both a troubled perception in a smooth space that lacks points of orientation, and a mood that veers from intense ennui to vertigo.

An interesting aesthetic consequence of this aspect of decadent thought is the elimination of the novelistic notion of the milieu or setting. For example, the classic-realist novel, or the realist film, always takes place in a well-defined, socially determined environment and describes the actions and reactions of characters in this recognisable space. Decadent art, however, removes the character from the social, and places her or him in a highly artificial realm of interiors in which the character is removed from the possibility of reaction and tends to dissolve in the luxuriant decor. Des Esseintes, Huysmans' quintessentially decadent protagonist for whom 'Il n'y avait, selon lui, que deux manières d'organiser une chamber à coucher' (134) is a case in point.[17] One of these ways is designed to contribute to 'une depravation de vieux passionné', while the other, which he opts for at this juncture, will 'obtenir l'effet absolument opposé, en se servant d'étoffes magnifiques pour donner l'impression d'une guenille; disposer, en un mot, une loge de chartreux qui eût l'air d'être vraie et qui ne le fût, bien entendu, pas' (Huysmans [1884] 1981: 134).[18] Hence, in the case of Carax, there is often the sensation that Alex, like Proust's narrator, is swimming slowly in the fluid and ambiguous

16 'Emotion is what happens between two people, what travels at full speed between them.'

17 'There existed two and only two ways of arranging a bedroom' (Huysmans 1969: 61).

18 'The depraved senses of an old voluptuary'; 'The opposite effect, using costly and magnificent materials so as to give the impression of common rags; in a word, to fit up a Trappist's cell that should have the look of the genuine article, and yet of course be nothing of the sort' (Huysmans 1969: 62).

element of time. In its permanently hallucinatory or dream world, decadent art lacks any impulse to tell stories – all that is sought is a decor that will provide the raw materials for conjuring up new sensations.

## Carax's cradle

*Le Berceau de cristal*, being the great neo-decadent film of the 1970s, produces all its tension, not from any dramatic events or psychological conflict but – and this is something that seems to have profoundly affected Carax – from stagings that in themselves make events dramatic; from *mise en scène* that is a series of dramatic tensions due to the positioning of the actors in the frame, their relation to the decor and above all to the light. But just as important in the context of the question of the film's influence on Carax's sensibility, is the overall mood of the film. The mood mirrors the film's tomb-like setting, presenting the actor (Nico) and her face as 'too late' for the light that seeks her.

Here is a decor which refuses to be doubled, incessantly disappearing as it does into the dark void whence it came: 'une obscurité sans fond, sans pouvoir d'émerger nettement ...'; whenever Nico's face 'capte la lumière, c'est pour mieux la redonner aux ténèbres' (Delorme 2000: 313).[19] Another notable influence on the nascent Caraxian aesthetic must be mentioned here: Godard's *Passion*. The following lines spoken by Jerzy the director in that film are like Godard's personal interpretation of *Le Berceau de cristal* and speak to Carax: 'what bursts into light is the echo of what the night submerges. What night submerges prolongs in the invisible what bursts into light'. Attitudes and postures here are neither theatrical – since they have no real target – nor real since they are more like the gestures of cadavers: 'les figures semblent habiter une chambre mortuaire, un tombeau', notes Stéphane Delorme (Delorme 2000: 313).[20] They are akin in this to Beckett's novel *Malone Dies*, where

19 'a darkness without end, unable to come to light in any distinct manner'; 'if it does catch the light it's only to give it back to the darkness.'
20 'the characters seem to inhabit a mortuary or tomb.' Pascal Bonitzer has coined the portmanteau word *cadaverité* to express the 'deathly truth' such a cinema can unveil (Bonitzer 1985: 84).

Malone is said to inhabit a kind of vault which no light penetrates.[21]
Alex's world is a world of dreams, of duplicated dreams, of dreams he
does not want to realise but, as he says, to repeat and repeat – this is
where the decadent and baroque sides of the Beckettian world come
together to mark Carax/Alex and where the only light comes, not from
the outside world, but from 'the two tiny yellow moons in his dream-
lover's eyes' (*Mauvais Sang*). It is tempting to note another affinity
with Beckett, since in *Malone Dies* the character exists only in so far as
he tells himself stories. As Serge Daney said of Garrel's later *L'Enfant
Secret* (1983), either one tells stories in order not to die or one tells
them to recover or because one is already dead (Daney [1983] 1996: 7).
Alex's frantic storytelling in the first two features can be attributed to
the same set of questions; this is the Scheherezade side of modern
cinema – she tells stories: (a) to avoid death; and (b) to keep her
interlocutor at a distance, in short to buy time (according to Daney's
formulation in the documentary *Jacques Rivette, le veilleur*). In *Le
Berceau*, in her vault, Nico courts artifice in the form of clothing and
cosmetics to ward off the exhaustion of the world in a space governed
by the seeming arbitrariness of unlocatable sources of illumination.
Here orientation is impossible, which leads her to seek a heaviness or
centre of gravity she can only find in the gun's metal and the bullet as
it tosses her down dead on her reading table. This film is a formidable
picture of the most primary search for sensation, for a fix of contact
with the material of life itself. 'Garrel cherche à créer une *stase*, l'état
prolongé d'un sentiment (un seul, la déperdition)' (Delorme 2000:
313),[22] without subjects, without social givens of any kind, without
reason, without cause and effect and with characters who can neither
act or react. All of this describes the key characteristics of the world of
Alex as we see him in Carax's first two films. Furthermore, *Les Amants
du Pont-Neuf* and *Pola X* will provide new variations of it.

Critics have long noted Garrel's obsession with originary experiences. Compare Alex in *Mauvais Sang*: 'can't I be reborn ... only first
times matter.' Despising the habits of the body and of a world become
the fodder of cliché-producing powers, decadence seeks metamorphosis, and this is why death takes on a new status in these films. As
Alex says to Mireille in *Boy meets Girl*: 'after 20 years of ... silence,

21  For more on Leibniz and Beckett, see Dowd 1998.

22  'Garrel is seeking to create a stasis, a single prolonged sensation, wastage.'

together we'll change our habits'. And in another variation from the same film: 'it's too late for everything ... we're too old to break our habits'. Of course the open and doubled ending of the first feature will leave us asking: is Alex too early or too late? One is left, therefore, in the space of ambiguity.

## The virtuality of artifice

Like Rivette's *Duelle*, André Téchiné's *Barocco* fills the screen with artificial decor and performances. Whereas the emphasis in *Duelle* is on an interplay of light and shade, Téchiné tends to emphasise the frame within the frame to the point of vertigo. Almost every frame is doubled or multiplied internally by means of further frames such as windows and doors. The film involves a convoluted plot involving politicians, thugs, sport and prostitution. An array of characters pursue the loot. Viewing the film, one cannot help but be struck by the extent to which it prefigures much of what was greeted as freshness and novelty in *Diva*. There is even a similar lift system at the sauna where the gangsters hide out. It is interesting to compare it to early Carax in order to define further the Carax–Beineix axis, and especially to enable further differentiation. What the film shares with Carax is a preoccupation with social exhibitionism whereby characters, most notably couples, seem to find their *raison d'être* when taking part in public displays. Perhaps this is a particularly French way of bringing mannerism on to the streets where post-new wave French cinema is at home. These people are images for others, for each other and for themselves. This ironic nocturnal thriller, Téchiné's take on *Vertigo,* complete with Hermannesque music, is full of lighting effects, high-contrast diagonal shots of cobbled streets at night, artificially excessive allegorical tropes (the near-apocalyptic scenes of rubbish-strewn streets, bodies filling the metro steps), exclusively neon-lit interiors, the figurative doubling of silhouettes, police mock-ups, water reflections and multi-framed mirrors – all of which is in the service of its delineation of an unsettling character duplication. Explicitly Caraxian moments include the pantomimic postures of the dying Samson and an intriguing moment when Samson's clone speaks for the first time in a slow, croaky, flat delivery somewhere between Alpha–60 in Godard's *Alphaville* and Alex's ventriloquist voice. There is even a Demy-esque burlesque musical number which summarises the 'look' of this film, wherein, as the heroine shoots the twice-removed mirror image of her lover, the chanteuse croons 'I see you see me, you see me see you, we see each other and knowing how to see is knowing we're in love'. The neo-baroque films of the 1980s then owed this film an enormous debt. Every kind of 'performance' and duplicated image is laid bare there, but it also shows us the essential difference between Beineix and Carax. Although techniques and stylistic traits may be shared by the filmmakers, this sharing needs to be seen in the light of the specific philosophical and intellectual principles underlying their use. *Barocco's* world is in the last analysis defined by class division, its line of dialogue 'in this world fortune smiles on one man or the other' merely a lack of revolutionary hope on Téchiné's behalf. The same is true of Beineix's universe. But Carax is much more concerned with metaphysical and cosmic issues which bring him closer to Rivette and Garrel, to limit ourselves to Bassan's holy trinity. If, as Deleuze says, Téchiné is able to 'considère comme acquis l'effondrement sensori-moteur sur lequel s'est constitué le cinéma moderne' (Deleuze 1985: 276),[23] as opposed to having to demonstrate or justify the collapse, and if in his 'intellectual' cinema 'le décor a une fonction cérébrale plus que physique' (Deleuze 1985: 276n.34),[24] then his particular mode of relating to the medium and to film history, in this case to Hitchcock's *Vertigo*, is analytical. To remake *Vertigo* is Téchiné's way of analysing it (as Van Sant so astutely said of his *Psycho* duplicate); filmmaking is his way of already doing criticism, whereas for Carax to dip into film history is simultaneously to probe the nature of the images all around us and inside us, and on an affective level to prepare the ground for an adequate engagement with his novel experiments.

There is a great deal of method behind Carax's notoriously *laissez-faire* attitude to film history. Rather than the retro image-thief or postmodern allusionist many see behind his work, Carax has more in common with certain kinds of sampling in popular music. His method is to *appropriate* and dismantle a scene or element taken from the work of another filmmaker (a Chaplin gag or Godardian flourish

---

23 'To take the sensory-motor collapse on which modern cinema is constituted as read' (Deleuze 1989: 212).
24 'The film set has a cerebral rather than physical function' (Deleuze 1989: 318n.34).

for example), extract one or two components, and then to insert them into his own image-series. The result is that the originals are thereby lent a new and contemporary affective charge.

As for Beineix, as the above suggests, most of what is interesting in Beineix's *Diva* comes from *Barocco*. As Deleuze shows, the windows and surfaces of Téchiné's film serve to dissolve the interior–exterior duality into a topographical question, giving us a 'topography of the mind', as Jill Forbes puts it (Forbes 1992: 253), but a mind or brain that is coextensive with the world, with the world's 'outside' as Deleuze would say, and which is no longer an interiority in any conventional sense. What Téchiné gives us (and Carax after him) are images now communicating vertically with their doubles rather than horizontally in an associative chain. But Beineix gives us back the associative chain, except that now, instead of the interstice that allows in the forces from outside, the forces that produce thought since they are precisely the forces of the new, what are being asked to become and link up images are recycled advertising clichés, dead images that can only form circuits of the most fake beauty. In an article published soon after the release of Beineix's *La Lune dans le caniveau*, Jean Narboni outlined the miserable miracles which in his view came to replace the goal of beauty in the new 'cinéma de l'image': magic, charm, seduction and spectacle. Commending Beineix's forthrightness in his famous 'fuck truth' declaration, Narboni adds:

> si l'Image est la nouvelle divinité du cinéma qui vient, alors il faut prendre acte que nous sommes entrés dans un moment de nouvelle piété iconique. Mais ce qui caractérise le plus souvent ces nouvelles images pieuses, c'est l'autosuffisance, l'écrasement des sensations sur un seul niveau, l'absence de modulation. D'où ... le manque total de tension interne, de rythme, et un sentiment général d'atonie. (Narboni 1983: 55)[25]

When Bergala announced the arrival of a cinema that has discovered the powers of the false, he stressed the difference between those filmmakers, like Beineix, seeking the false for its own sake, thereby

---

25 'if the image is the new divinity for cinema's future, then we must take stock of the fact that we are entering an age of iconic piety. But what characterises the new pious images is their self-sufficiency, the flattening of sensation onto a single plane, the absence of modulation. There ensues ... a total lack of internal tension, of rhythm and a general feeling of lethargy.'

giving us an impoverished fakery of style, empty decor and bad acting, and those who experimented with falsity on the vertiginous edge of reality, where the false is not celebrated for itself, but all distinction between truth and falsity is rendered indiscernible. The truth becomes a perennial question that one can only circle around forever, 'de décor en décor, de masque en masque, sans espoir de jamais la toucher, mais fascinés et exaltés par sa trop vive lumière, bien loin du cynisme triste des manipulateurs d'illusions désabusés' (Bergala 1983: 8).[26] Whereas for Beineix the working man will always return to the woman his class position has chosen for him, for Téchiné it is enough for her lover's döppelganger/killer to ask her to lie and tell him she loves him for both to leave together and risk their lives for one another. Why? Because here falsity has the power of meta-morphosis, each can become another in a demonic pact.

Now Carax too treads dangerously at the limit of the real, on the knife edge of truth. But contrary to Beineix, it is from here that the force of his cinema is derived. It is no coincidence that bridges play such a major role in all his films. As Ruiz says 'the bridge – il ponte – was a very important word in baroque thought' (Martin and Tuckfield 1993: 93). As he has one of his characters say, 'Je suis le passeur de frontières ... Je conduis les personnages d'un monde à l'autre' (Buci-Glucksmann in Buci-Glucksmann and Revault d'Allonnes 1987: 34).[27] In Beineix there is only one world, divided in two, whereas in Carax and truly neo-baroque auteurs there is a multiplicity of co-existing worlds.

## Sun goddess, moon goddess

What notions the stars do bring you, Mother. (Raoul Ruiz, City of Pirates)

Performance of a different kind defines the work of Rivette. There are many fascinating elements in Duelle, such as: the highly artificial setting, its baroque narrative strands, its lighting and decor, and

26 'from decor to decor, mask to mask, without hope of ever touching it, but fascinated and exalted by its too vivid light, far from the sad cynicism of the manipulators of disappointed illusions'

27 'I am a crosser of frontiers ... I lead characters from one world to the other.'

Rivette's ongoing aesthetic of contingency – whereby each completed film remains a work in progress. This is a paradox mirrored in the thematic and performative preoccupation with repetition (usually of a theatrical rehearsal) on the one hand, and a fidelity to the capturing of the irreducible singularity of each filmed moment on the other. Rivette's work is the model for every filmmaker who wants to preserve the rawness of the shoot in the final film (at its most extreme in Garrel's one-shot, one-take method). What is produced by this strange hybrid is a kind of staged cosmological documentary; if Téchiné brings mannerism onto the streets, then Rivette takes it into the world of direct cinema. However, unlike *Berceau de cristal*, this mannerism wants to bestow a minimum of narrative on an event captured in its unique occurrence (even the score by Jean Wiener is played *en direct* during shooting). In fact *Duelle* is one of Rivette's most structured films; Cocteau's influence is evident in the use of mythology and in the prominence of a refined decor. One critic has been led to the extreme claim that this is a 'film of pure mise-en-scène' (de Gregorio in Frappat 2001: 152), 'où la lumière devient l'unique matière, presque l'unique sujet du film' (Frappat 2001: 162): phantoms doing battle for the favour of light that has no interest in them, 'dans le dancing dont les murs sont des miroirs' (Frappat 2001: 199).[28]

Each great filmmaker explores different powers of the false. Rivette treats lies as a game, which is passed between characters but is never expressed. In Rivette, the lie is never expressed in a mono-logue:

> elle se construit dans un dialogue ou personne n'est dupé, puisque chacun préfère, à l'information la surprise ... à la 'vérité' son contourne-ment ludique ... pas une retention avare d'informations ... elle est un foisonnement généreux de fables, que la mythomane dispense, tout comme elle sème des billets de banque aux quatre vents ... les billets de banque sont des récits; ils crissent et passent de main en main ... une conversation est efficace lorsqu'elle rend réel le monde que ses complices inventent ... [ou] un complot qui sert à faire advenir des complices ... [L]a modernité consiste à inventer des complots d'ou toute intention a disparu: le manipulateur moderne en a fini avec l'intention de nuire, de maîtriser; il met en scène un 'complôt sans

28 'where light becomes the sole material, almost the sole subject of the film'; 'dancehall of which the walls are mirrors'

maître' ... machinations sans psychologie, vengeances non pas person-
nelles mais cosmiques. (Frappat 2001: 192–3)[29]

This superb distillation of Rivette's poetics has been quoted in full
because it so accurately accounts for that aspect of Carax's cinema that
none of the other influences we have discussed can explain: the sense
of cosmic forces and the part they play in the lives of Alex and those he
encounters. What Carax will do is to allow all of these influences to
pass through him and to forge a new hybrid, taking the lessons of
Godard, Ruiz, Téchiné, Garrel and Rivette into account. In the
briefest possible definition, we might say that he will give mannerist/
baroque form to a set of very contemporary yet neo-decadent concerns.
The remainder of this chapter will demonstrate these ideas at work in
*Boy meets Girl* and *Mauvais Sang*.

### Image mon beau souci

Thèse: l'image (le langage, le signe) ment sur le réel, et Ruiz désigne ce
mensonge. Antithèse: le mensonge est partout, il n'y a pas plus de
vérité dans le réel que dans l'image. Synthèse: ce 'mensonge' même
est l'ultime vérité; de par leurs béances et articulations l'image et le
langage, le rêve et la mémoire nous renseignent sur la structure du
réel. (Revault d'Allonnes in Buci-Glucksmann and Revault d'Allonnes
1987: 75)[30]

29 'it's constructed in a dialogue where no one is duped because each prefers
surprise to information, playful distortion of the truth to truth itself, less a
miserly retention of information than a generous proliferation of fables
dispensed by the pathological liar, just as she scatters bank notes to the four
winds ... bank notes are stories, they are crisp and pass from hand to hand ... a
conversation is effective when it renders real the world that her accomplices
invent ... or a plot serving to reveal accomplices ... modernity consists in
inventing plots from which all intention has disappeared: the modern
manipulator is done with intending to harm or control; he stages a "masterless
plot" ... machinations without psychology, acts of vengeance that aren't personal
but cosmic.'
30 'Thesis: the image (language, sign) tells lies about the real, and Ruiz points out
the lie. Antithesis: the lie is everywhere, there is no more truth in the real than in
the image. Synthesis: this same "lie" is the ultimate truth; by way of their gaps
and connections, images and language, dream and memory teach us about the
structure of the real.'

If Carax plays a key role in a 'cinema of the image' in the 1980s, then the nature of his involvement must be specified. Those who criticise him, on the basis of this classification, tend to think he overvalues the image to the detriment of a purported reality. However, if Carax foregrounds the image *as image*, it is in marked contrast to the manner of modernists like Antonioni or new wave films about filmmaking. Modernist reflexivity vis-à-vis the cinematic medium becomes for Carax a broader image–reflexivity, which no longer needs to be thematic in the manner of, say, *Blow Up* (Antonioni 1966), because it is taken as given that everything that exists is already an image. Moreover, that which is image necessarily falsifies, or at least casts doubt on everything presenting itself as true. 'The powers of the false' was a concept given some prominence in *Cahiers du Cinéma* throughout the 1980s. It was directly linked by *Cahiers* to what it identified as a generalised crisis of representation in 'postmodern' culture. A product of this culture, Carax knows from the outset that the only form of resistance to the regulation of images is to tap the powers of the false that are the image's potential. Resistance to the image is of necessity *by* the image. It is by way of a thoroughgoing exploration of the powers of the false that one can pit aberrant powers – what Deleuze will call 'time-images' – against the standardised images of advertising, television and the Hollywood action cinema, grounded as these images are on an ontological disjunction between the image and the real. This is the immediate *conjunctural* reason behind Carax's style: his taste for artificiality comes from recognising that it is no longer possible to think solely in terms of an image–reality duality and that cinematic innovation must pass the way of a monistic yet multi-dimensional view of the universe. By the 1980s, the false matches that violate continuity editing were no longer sufficient to provoke the thrill that goes with the subversion of norms or the dismantling of the comforting continuous space of classical cinema so dear to formalist critics: in short, everything that thrilled us in expressing what was unique to the medium, a medium desperately seeking to assert its singularity. Carax knew that what was needed was a new kind of *mise en scène* with the capacity to transform cinema lest it be superseded by other media, to reconfigure celluloid space and time lest they be replaced by electronic lines, by the table of information which replaces the conventional function of the screen in the new media. In many respects, Carax conforms to Deleuze's definition of epochal aesthetic mutation:

> Il arrive qu'un artiste, prenant conscience de la mort de la volonté d'art dans tel ou tel moyen, affronte le 'défi' par un usage apparemment destructeur de ce moyen même: on peut croire alors à des fins négatives de l'art, mais il s'agit plutôt de combler un retard, de convertir à l'art un domaine hostile, non sans violence, et de retourner le moyen contre lui-même. (Deleuze 1985: 348n.9)[31]

Carax belongs to the category identified by Deleuze, while his specific task is the 'reinvention' of the cinema with affects that will enable the side-stepping of the atrophied nature of the dominant image forms. His great coup is the creation of Alex the psychological automaton whose acrobatic body is capable of balancing the weighty and the weightless, of receiving into it all the force of the a-centred image.

Carax's work on decor, performance, colour and *mise en scène* in general has as its primary aim to multiply dimensions in the image–real of which the cinema is *one* actualisation. Starting from the most basic formal conceit of the frame within the frame (for example the butcher's shop window in *Mauvais Sang*), it is possible to follow Carax as he builds up layer upon layer of conjunctive and disjunctive plane, tension, rhythm – each layer contributing to the play of micro-*récit* that replaces narrative proper in early Carax (to pass from one layer or *récit* to another is to change duration, rhythm and speed). Yet one is not simply back in the 'baroque' deep spaces of Welles or Ruiz; rather, the proximity in question is to the shallow but spiritual dimensionality of Dreyer. It is doubtless an intellectual cinema, wherein the emotion stems from thought (an idea best expressed in Foucault's notion *la pensée-emotion*) and not the inverse.

Correlatively, Carax must dis-organise and disrupt the visual, while simultaneously installing poetry and poetic dialogue at the heart of the image. Such are the basic prerequisites to facilitate something to which Carax is clearly committed: the salvaging of thought

---

31 'Sometimes an artist, becoming aware of the death of the will to art in a particular medium confronts the "challenge" by a use which is apparently destructive of that medium: one might thus believe in negative goals in art, but it is rather a question of making up lost time, of converting a hostile area to art, with a certain violence, and of turning means against themselves' (Deleuze 1989: 331n.9).

and creation. Taking a cue from Godard's Lemmy Caution who says 'what transforms a night into light – poetry', Carax nonetheless departs from the Godardian move of accompanying the poetic drive with the lie of the image. For Carax, however, there is another Godardian axiom which comes closer to his position: 'It's not a lie, it's something imaginative, never exactly the truth, but not the opposite either. It's something separated from the real world by calculated approximations of probabilities'. These words from *Passion* go some way to explaining how that film crystallised in Carax's mind many of the elements discussed so far as he prepared his first features.

It is not so much that the image lies as that it renders all judgements of truthfulness inappropriate, and in so doing it presents characters who have become tricksters, forgers or, like Alex, who live in the element of falsity and lack a point of view on truth, judgement and action. We do not know who they truly are or what their past is. Their world comprises disconnected spaces and dechronologised moments, not subjective variations (Carax is no Tarantino) which modify the narrative. To be a forger or an impostor or stand-in (as Alex is in a variety of ways) signifies being multiple and being prone to metamorphosis. Indeed, it could be argued that, in the neo-baroque cinema as we have defined it 'le faussaire devient le personnage même du cinéma: non plus le criminel, le cow-boy, l'homme psycho-social, le héros historique … au détriment de toute action' (Deleuze 1985: 173).[32]

## Blocks

In terms of Carax's relations to the *nouvelle vague*, and to Godard in particular, it is now possible to situate Téchiné's diagnosis of the blockage caused by the encounter 'between the new wave and gauchisme' (Forbes 1992: 258). In his 1980s work Godard explores the work–cinema–couple conjunction, the ground of his reflections on the medium still clinging to an image–reality hiatus. The statements of this position proliferate in films such as *Passion*, where we learn 'you have to live stories before inventing them' (*Passion*), and

32 'The forger becomes *the* character of the cinema, to the detriment of all active agents, whether these come in the form of the criminal, the cowboy, the psycho-social man or historical hero' (Deleuze 1989: 132).

'work has the same gesture as love, not the same speed but the same gestures'. In Godard's 1980s films, the lighting creates relations and tensions between the characters, such that what matters is what happens between. 'We've lost the centre, so we search'; 'without extreme care, this explosion of incidental light would have disorganised the whole painting' says Jerzy. Just as is the case with Rivette's human phantoms, these workers, these human phantoms desperately seek to confront a light within the reach of which they have no reality. But, in addition to its materialism, Godard's film too is a cosmic adventure wherein the shot and the tableau do battle for illumination.

Now it is precisely Carax's links to the mannerist lineage that enable him to differentiate himself from this insistent background while remaining within the broad problematic which it elaborates. Carax's mode of artifice serves a form of mannerist doubling of the image. It is a struggle between two views, between his position as simultaneously acolyte and maverick. His question becomes: how to double the image not in the manner of Téchiné or Rivette or even Godard, in all of whom there remains a forced immobility and a struggle of the characters *against* something. Even in the *Cahiers* group analysis of cinema–painting relations in the 1980s the need was felt to deconstruct the tensions between the static image of painting and the incessant movement of cinema, that is between modes of representation, as mirrored in the transmedial struggle between mobility and immobility. Whereas in Carax by contrast (true to the new problems thrown up by the 1980s), in whose work every individual body, regardless of the decor, has become an element of a *tableau vivant*, there is no longer a need to have recourse to the model of painting. Here the world itself has become immobilised and the characters no longer engage in struggle. The cosmic element remains but is now allied to a sense of destiny that contains within itself its own resistance.

Carax thus substitutes for the Baroque struggle of good and evil, light and dark, a neo-baroque aesthetic in which is played out a struggle between fate and chance, heaviness and lightness. As he explained in the *Sight and Sound* interview (Carax 1992: 11), life and love are for him concerned with the irredeemable and *inespéré* (what one dare not hope for). Fate creates irredeemable lives and heavy bodies, whereas a simple throw of the dice (in the first two features turning an arbitrary twist of a radio dial symbolises this cosmology) can always bring the unhoped for or the passage to a lighter, more ecstatic level of existence. The prime example of this is the 'Modern Love' sequence in *Mauvais Sang*. In this sense, the production of images resists the blockage of life, as life simultaneously creates and runs down. As Carax's idol Epstein said 'Le cinéma pense une image de l'univers' ('Cinema thinks an image of the universe'), but by the 1980s that universe has definitively lost its centre, become unhinged, and, in a very confused and anarchic period of thinking about images, Carax draws the following conclusion: since images no longer represent reality and there are only images of different natures and dimensions at once real and unreal – or more accurately, images of the same type have $n$ dimensions – the end result is that, in a scene, two characters no longer necessarily share the same space or temporal dimension; rather, they may behave as if invisible to one another. Hence the tendency in the first two features for monologue to supersede dialogue, while apparently contributing to the latter. Scenes in Carax's films often function as passages between the multiple worlds his images have created. To some even benevolent critics, Carax indulges in a typically mannerist duplicity, since on the one hand he takes this anti-representational drive into account – hence his artificiality – while on the other he clings to the reality of emotion even if it is a mannered if not mannerist emotion, self-conscious and contrived. This however is a misreading. Rather, what Carax inaugurates is a new approach to emotion whereby the subject (chiefly Alex) 'spies on himself', and experiences the mannerist relationship between reason and passion described by Arnold Hauser: 'They despaired of speculative thought, and at the same time clung to it; they had no high hopes of reason, but remained passionate reasoners' (Hauser cited in Viano 1993: 108). The return to the Baroque and to its taste for unanchored images has allowed Carax to reconfigure the truth–falsity and real–unreal problems by way of steering a line through each pair driven by emotion but setting down nowhere. In Robert Gordon's words:

> Mannerist Figuration rather than giving a voice to aspects of
> subjectivity, gives them a look, a way of seeing [the world] which is
> itself a secondary figuration of the subject. [The world] is looked at as a
> tension between perceived forms ... particularly Mannerist connota-
> tions when the patterns of description are derived from existing
> iconography ... ways of seeing through artists' models, setting the self

against another eye. Mannerist, formal patterns of this kind create a profound, ontological link with the real, without recourse to mimesis, representing reality always with the imprint of subjectivity. (Gordon 1996: 147)

Therefore it is never a simple case of abandoning the 'real' or of taking refuge in narcissism, plagiarism or novelty for its own sake; everything is ambiguous, ambivalent, indeterminate. The crisis of the image is not solved by Carax (no single artist could do so), but its conditions are laid bare in his first features and dealt with in an innovative and profound manner. For Alex, the split subject, the already seen– already said is both a concrete weight he carries in his belly and the site of his division from himself, the crack which lets light(ness) in.

Just as the *tableau vivant* had served to halt the narrative movement in modernist film, now what stops everything flowing (and which ensures that narrative becomes even less important) is something that happens between the character and the world (but a character who is not separate from or 'in' the world but *for* it). Thereby he has to counter-ignite it (and the *récit*) as in the 'Modern Love' sequence in *Mauvais Sang*.

'To be human is to reside within the interval' (*Passion*). In the same film, Jerzy continues 'what bursts into light is the echo of what the night submerges. What night submerges prolongs in the invisible what bursts into light'. These examples from *Passion* demonstrate how Godard's 'objective' poetry can be compared to Carax's 'subject-ivism'. What Carax does with poetry, when writing poetic dialogue, is similar to what he does with cited images. He has to say 'I' because it is his way of countering the order words around him. Alex's 'I' is akin to the I of William Holden's character Joe in *Sunset Boulevard* (an already-dead narrator), or of those ubiquitous dead storytellers in Ruiz. Since the 1980s a host of strategies from various quarters have emerged to deconstruct the idea of first-person cinema, with the result that the auteur is now best described as a being-for-the-cinema after the manner of Godard in his most recent video work – one who moves and lives in the folds of the image.

As Alex says to Anna in a line Carax has said is crucial, 'j'ai l'sentiment si j'passe à côté d'toi, j'passe à côté d'tout pour très longtemps'.[33] Alex's hypothesis suggests the aberrant, undulating

33 'I have the feeling if I miss you [as target], I'll miss everything and for a long time.'

groove of the world with time in its infinite modulations as its only conceivable subject. It is no coincidence that many have spoken of Carax as the new Rimbaud. Deeper than the citations of the poems in *Mauvais Sang* is the omnipresence of Rimbaud's formula 'I is another', which has been glossed by Deleuze as 'mon existence ne peut jamais être déterminée comme celle d'un être actif et spontané' (Deleuze 1993a: 43).[34] Alex cannot be conceived of as:

> un être actif et spontané, mais d'un moi passif qui se représente le Je ... comme un Autre qui l'affecte ... le temps est cette relation formelle suivant laquelle l'esprit s'affecte lui-même, ou la manière dont nous sommes intérieurement affectés par nous-mêmes ... Forme d'intériorité ne signifie pas simplement que le temps est intérieur à l'esprit ... Ce n'est pas le temps qui nous est intérieur ... c'est nous qui sommes intérieurs au temps, et à ce titre toujours séparés par lui de ce qui nous détermine en l'affectant. L'intériorité ne cesse pas de nous creuser nous-mêmes, de nous scinder nous-mêmes, de nous dédoubler. (Deleuze 1993a: 43–5)[35]

Carax pegs Rimbaud's formula to the ambient neo-baroque aesthetic which, via the vertiginous fulgurations and mannerist duplications (Deleuze often writes of a schizo-essence of mannerism) to which it gives rise, becomes in Carax a splitting of time in the subject. Alex is at one and the same time the weight of the past and the giddy lightness of the present. 'I spy on myself' could be his motto. He is simultaneously the child and the old man – 'already a veteran', as *Boy Meets Girl* puts it.

In order to dramatise this split into I and ego Carax employs every cinematic means at his disposal: *mise en abyme*, mirroring, doubling and reflection. What the two films present is not, as his critics claim, a narcissistic trail of indulgent imagery, but rather the world or image-universe as its own subjectivity:

34 'My existence can never be determined as that of an active and spontaneous being' (Deleuze 1984: viii).
35 'A unique and active subject, but a passive ego which represents to itself only the activity of its own thought ... the I as another which affects it ... time moves into the subject ... is the form under which the I affects the ego, i.e. the way in which the mind affects itself. Time ... the form of interiority means not only that time is internal to us, but that our interiority constantly divides us from ourselves, splits us in two' (Deleuze 1984: viii–ix).

La seule subjectivité, c'est le temps, le temps non-chronologique saisi dans sa fondation, et c'est nous qui sommes intérieurs au temps, non pas l'inverse [...] Le temps n'est pas intérieur en nous, c'est juste le contraire, l'intériorité dans laquelle nous sommes, nous nous mouvons, vivons et changeons [...] La subjectivité n'est jamais la nôtre, c'est le temps, c'est-à-dire l'âme ou l'esprit, le virtuel. (Deleuze 1985: 110–11)[36]

Phil Powrie draws attention to Deleuze's account of the Baroque folding together of image, movement and matter, in which the human brain is merely one image among others. Following Deleuze, Powrie specifies that the 'turbulence of matter gives rise to the spiritual' (Powrie 2001: 24), for in *Le Pli* Deleuze describes the process whereby 'l'âme ... trouve en celui-ci une animalité qui l'étourdit, qui l'empêtre dans les replis de la matière, mais aussi une humanité organique ou cérébrale ... qui lui permet de s'élever, et la fera monter sur de tout autres plis' (Deleuze 1988: 17).[37] To be an auteur in the 1980s, a 'Rimbaud of the cinema', is to surrender oneself to a medium which is temporal by nature. An auteurism can no longer mean self-expression or pedagogy, but involves a new relation between director and spectator. No longer the unequal and distant relation of genius and pupil, but instead a kind of 'Crack'd Auteur' (to adapt the name of one of David Bowie's 1970s personae) offering 'ventriloquist glimpses of a volatile self' (Gordon 1996: 146).

### 'Crack'd auteur'

These are the contexts in which it is *initially* useful to see the use of disembodied voices in Carax: ventriloquism, telepathy, indeterminable sources of the voice, in the world of the already said. In short, one cannot locate the source of one's ideas and discourse. Even when silent the subject is never really self-identical. Alex and Mireille, or

36 'The only subjectivity is time, non-chronological time grasped in its foundation, and it is we who are internal to time, not the other way round [...] Time is not the interior in us but just the opposite, the interiority in which we are, in which we move, live and change [...] Subjectivity is never ours, it is time, that is the soul or the spirit, the virtual' (Deleuze 1989: 82–3).
37 'The soul ... discovers a vertiginous animality that gets it tangled in the pleats of matter but also an organic or cerebral humanity ... that allows it to rise up and that will make it ascend over all the other folds' (Deleuze 1993: 11).

Lise, or Anna may sit or lie around and dream as time and silence invade their bodies, but 'We don't keep silent, silence keeps us', as Alex explains in *Mauvais Sang*. In Carax's view, humans are ventriloquist's dummies, automata, pinned under the weight of cliché and regulated movement. This remains true unless the individual can somehow surf on the fold of things, on lines of flight, attaining a salvific lightness: even if it means pushing poetic language to the threshold of sense and bodies into mannerist or burlesque postures and attitudes. Alex/Lavant, or novel ways of inflecting language and of folding the body. Carax therefore is very much in the Artaud tradition, whose dilemma Deleuze and Guattari sum up as: 'on m'a fait un organisme! On m'a plié indument! On m'a volé mon corps!' (Deleuze and Guattari 1980: 197).[38] The inexhaustible repertoire of burlesque and vaudeville talents that Lavant brings to Carax's world enable him to negotiate these 'body-snatchers': getting from point A to B will involve a series of limps, detours and staggers. Alternatively, his body will embrace a state of 'becoming child', will blend with his milieu rather than acting within it – as in the beautiful *Limelight* tribute in *Mauvais Sang* where Alex's stagger becomes confused with that of the toddler.

To explore the capacities of postures is to explore thought, since it is the body that forces us to think – Carax seeks *pensées-émotions* in line with Ruiz's very baroque body–thought conjunction. Why is this so important? Because, as Deleuze thought, when the body forces us to think, it forces us to think life, while 'les catégories de la vie, ce sont précisement les attitudes du corps, ses postures' (Deleuze 1985: 246).[39] Therefore Carax's first works find a point of contact with Ruiz's films such as *Hypothèse du tableau volé* which seek new thought through new postures and attitudes of the body. To conjoin bodies and thought is to think life from a neo-baroque point of view.

### Do images communicate?

The problem of communication is another inherited from modernist film. However, by the 1980s the theme of 'alienated individuals

---

38 'They've made me an organism! They've wrongfully folded me! They've stolen my body' (Deleuze and Guattari 1987: 159).
39 'The categories of life are precisely the attitudes of the body, its postures' (Deleuze 1989: 189).

unable to communicate in contemporary society' that critics had found in Antonioni (in particular) was no longer relevant, or rather the leftist reading of the problematic had proved to be passé. An ontological response was needed. As Jean Narboni said apropos of Bergala and Limosin's film *Faux-Fuyants* (1982), in terms which could as readily apply to a whole range of post-new wave films including those of Carax:

> Etre-avec n'est pas communiquer, se pencher sur ou tenter de comprendre autrui. Nul dans le film ne s'avise de le faire avec personne, et moins encore les auteurs à l'égard de leurs personnages: ils se contentent de provoquer des mises en présence et d'enregistrer des effets. Non pas forcer le secret de l'autre, mais progresser de proche en proche, établir des connexions, tisser des relations, avancer du même pas (acteurs, personnages, spectateurs, cinéastes) dans un désordre d'apparences. (Narboni 1983: 54)[40]

It is not without relevance that this passage in Narboni's review is followed by a swipe at Beineix's *La Lune dans le caniveau* and 'the new divinity of the Image'.

Carax replaces the conventional notion of communicational or conversational utterances with a novel form of purely cinematic speech-act. What he achieves is to inflect the neo-baroque with a speech act dimension, giving rise to a schizophrenic mannerism of statements. Whereas Welles, Robbe-Grillet and Ruiz emphasise perspectivism on the level of shots, Carax often places the emphasis on speech-acts, yielding a poetry of 'strange associations', full of schizophrenic leaps on to new subjects, and, above all, 'subjectless' speech-acts which create subjects in being spoken which then disappear and are replaced by the next 'larval' or emergent subject. Speaking aloud as if to oneself or voices that seem to have no source – these are the norm in Carax's first films. There is no need for an 'official' voice-over in Carax because all voices function as voices-off. Hence the importance of Alex's condition as 'langue-pendue': with his peculiar language–body relations he can surf on the crestline

---

40 'Being-with isn't communicating, examining or trying to understand others. No one in the film thinks of doing this, still less do the auteurs vis-à-vis their characters – they're content to bring them together and record the effects. Not to force a secret from the other but to progress one step at a time, establishing connections, weaving relations, advancing along the same path (actors, characters, spectators, filmmakers), in a disorder of appearances.'

between 'du corps et du langage, une turbulence sonore à la limite de la formation de mots, la tangence ... d'un bruit de fond ... à la parole articulée' (Narboni 1977: 7).[41]

When time or duration forms the medium inhabited, it follows that worthwhile communication between characters can only be formed virtually, as when they pass close by one another in time in a manner comparable to comets and planets in space. Hence the centrality of the theme of Halley's Comet in *Mauvais Sang.* Quantum mechanics believes that:

> deux particules issues de la désintigration d'une particule instable semblent 'garder le contact' et continuent de former un système unique, quelle que soit leur distance, en s'informant instantanément l'une l'autre des propriétés qui leur échoient au moment même de leur observation. (Trias 2001: 17)[42]

So too Carax's couples are bound together by some lost unity whose trace is a sign in the nocturnal sky rather than by any present-tense physical or psychological attraction.

## Cosmopolis

It is quite appropriate that philosophy and cosmology be invoked in relation to these films. Carax is often very close to the Garrel of *L'Enfant Secret,* released in 1983 as Carax began serious work on the script of *Boy Meets Girl.* Garrel immediately recognised the affinity and requested an interview with Carax which was published in *Cahiers* in November of the following year (suggestively entitled 'Dialogue en apesanteur'). *L'Enfant Secret* is centrally concerned with the incorporeal rather than with the physical. Behind the seemingly 'centred organisms' (the bodies of the actors/characters and their encounters and attempts to communicate in specific milieus) there are occult phantasms, an entire network of ghostly presences and

41 'body and language, a sonor turbulence at the limit of the formation of words, "tangentiality" ... of a noise from the depths ... to the spoken word'
42 'two particles issued from the disintegration of an unstable particle seem to maintain contact and continue to form a single system, whatever their distance, and mutually inform one another instantaneously of properties which fall to them at the very moment of their observation.'

incorporeal beings. That which institutes this universe of virtual–actual co-existence is simply *love*. It is 'amour fou' which isolates the character from the rest of the world and its everyday demands. Just as in Rivette's film of that title such intensity cannot survive social interaction: it is only when the couple have literally carved themselves a new private milieu that it can be recaptured.

In a fashion comparable to Garrel, Carax's films multiply dimensions of reality. In the work of both it is very difficult to locate a 'present tense'; this is their 'Dreyer side' (Martin 2001a). Life is endowed with infinite layers or dimensions of reality, some visible, others invisible, but all subject to a temporal heterogeneity. In *L'Enfant Secret* some of these have names – The Cæsarian Section, The Ophidian Circle, The Disenchanted Forests. Others might be called The Black Hole or Childhood. In *Boy Meets Girl* it is Telepathy, in *Mauvais Sang* Halley's Comet. It is these 'hitherto unfamiliar stratospheres' (Martin 2001a) that bind and separate lovers. As in Proust, these spectres, even when together in space, exist in different temporal dimensions. Seldom in the cinema has love been shown literally to be such a fleeting thing. Alex and Mireille, Alex and Anna are like desire lines which form temporary points on different spatial planes of existence but whose cracked selves call out for incorporeal communion across time. One of the questions asked by this film is: what *can* a body *not* do? And its answer? 'It doesn't know how to occupy space when alone'. This is perhaps why one feels no resistance to Anna's comforting words to Lise on Alex's death 'you'll be together again'. Of course the only eternity of which one can speak today is of a cinematic or some other virtual sort. 'One day it'll seem as if we've lived all this before': Alex's parting words highlight the cosmological tenor of Carax's work. If the cinema 'thinks an image of the universe' then it is comparable to a cosmology with the capacity 'non seulement lever l'image de l'univers, mais aussi en imaginer les lois' (Trias 2001: 18).[43] Fuller's words describing the cinema in *Pierrot le fou* – 'love ... hate ... action ... violence ... death ... in one word ... emotion' – still apply to Carax. However, they apply no longer on the interpersonal level but, as Hélène Frappat writes of Rivette, on a cosmic plane demanding a *mise en scène* which:

---

43 'not only to exhibit the image of the universe but to imagine its laws'

s'attache au passage entre deux espaces. Passage entre la ville et la banlieue, entre l'extérieur et l'intérieur, entre la nuit et le jour ... passage entre deux sentiments, deux genres ... [elle] engendre un style d'état mixte ... la mise-en-scène ne prend pas parti, elle témoigne: elle est le tribut (ontologique) payé à la mort dans l'image, la dette (politique) payée aux morts dans l'histoire, le poème cosmique adresse aux astres qui se sont éteints. (Frappat 2001: 196–7)[44]

In this respect, it is certainly to Rivette that Carax is closest.

As in cosmology, perhaps it is more useful when thinking about this cinema to speak of relations and the principles of interaction which govern encounters than communication as commonly understood. The sequence following the 'Modern Love' dance in *Mauvais Sang* offers a good illustration of this point. When Alex returns to the shop and successively perceives a hair, a tissue and a cigarette – all of which are signs of Anna's absence but also of her virtual presence – one is in a universe common to a whole range of contemporary filmmakers from Wong and Kieslowski to Ruiz and Resnais (and in bowdlerised form in films like *Sliding Doors* and *Serendipity*) and their films which 'explore from film to film the ruling of human affairs by some impersonal fate, [they] view all people as figures within a pre-structured game or book of life' (Martin 2001b). Carax's original contribution to the development of this cinema was to marry the problem of communication reformulated by French post-new wave cinema to a cosmological concern, while succeeding in holding it all together on the level of emotion, albeit not the standardised version of emotion pedalled by the Hollywood programme and its supporters worldwide.

Pascal Bonitzer, in a cry of despair published in 1983 in *Cahiers du cinéma* and entitled 'Standards d'émotion', lamented the public's loss of appetite for any cinema which avoids standardised emotions. 'Le public veut s'y reconnaître, le nouveau l'indiffère' (Bonitzer 1983: 9).[45] The implication is that there has been a mutually determining standardisation of images (through their governed proliferation) and

---

44 'stages the passage between two spaces. Between the city and suburbs, between exterior and interior, between night and day, between two sentiments, two genres ... engendering a hybrid style ... the *mise en scène* doesn't prejudice, it testifies ... it is the ontological tribute paid to death in the image, the political debt paid to history's dead, the cosmic poem addressed to extinct stars.'

45 'The public wants to recognise itself in films, it is indifferent to the new.'

of emotions. Bonitzer identifies the turning point as being *Saturday Night Fever* (1977), when the hitherto heterogeneous practices of filmmaking and video-promotional creation were coupled together, thus opening up a bright new future for the entertainment industry. Perhaps this is one reason why dancing features so heavily in Carax's first three features – it must be reclaimed as an experimental possibility since, as Daney said, it has 'the miraculous power to set everything moving' (Daney 1982). Bonitzer goes on to pinpoint Beineix as France's chief representative of the new tendency: 'on y reconnaît ceux d'un imaginaire adolescent, nourri de pub, de BD, de fast-food et de rock industriel' (Bonitzer 1983: 10) and looks to a new auteurism, one for whom *mise en scène* = thought, which alone might be capable of combating this tendency.[46] A definition of auteur cinema follows from this: that which is auteurist is whatever with-draws from 'standards d'émotion', and in the process invents new emotions and new bodies – a definition not out of place in the context of Carax's contemporaneous project.

Indeed Carax's response to this blocked situation can be form-ulated in Bonitzer's terms: 'L'image d'avenir doit répondre à la prolifération des clichés, à l'inflation des signes, à la rédondance des informations par "plus de pensée"' (Bonitzer 1983: 13).[47] Here is the site of a potential confrontation with the universe of Bresson, whose characters are 'figures with a movement in which weight plays no part', to borrow Bergala's citation of Simone Weil's definition of grace (Bergala 1992: 65). What Carax does is to shift the emphasis from a grace–fall duality on to a more materialist cosmological plane, but without resort to the Godardian weight of the law. As Bergala says of *Passion*: 'Jerzy no longer expects validation of his work from a human law but from an external, necessarily non-human source, a sign from the light that he hopes will deliver him' (Bergala 1992: 66). If Carax too sees the way of salvation in the cinematic medium, unlike Godard he does not need to look beyond the self-imposed confines of the amorous situation, because there are always cosmic elements slipping between the characters, luminosities ensuring he does not need a *mise en scène* in the manner of a master painter since he is

46 'one recognises in [his images] those of an adolescent imaginary nourished on ads, comics, fast food and industrial rock.'

47 'The image of the future must respond to the proliferation of cliché, the inflation of signs, the redundancy of information by "more thought".'

content with his cinematic masters. One is reminded of Godard's
sketch 'Anticipation' which concerns the struggle between spiritual
and physical love. Jean-Pierre Léaud finds a concoction of both types
in the arms of prostitute Natacha (Anna Karina). 'Together they
invent the kiss, using the one part of the body which can both speak
and make love' as James Monaco comments (Monaco 1976: 141).

## Habitation

It is now time to turn to another area in which Carax innovates: that of
body–set relations. It is possible that the fundamental problem
haunting post-new wave cinema is how to inhabit space. An ambition
perhaps most succinctly expressed throughout the 1970s by Rivette in
what amounts to a manifesto for a new cinema, and which would be a
significant formative influence on Carax's generation (Assayas
2000). Rivette sought 'to discover a new approach to acting in the
cinema, where speech would play a role of "poetic" punctuation [and]
where the movement of bodies, their counterpoint, their inscription
within the screen space, would be the basis of the mise-en-scène'
(Rivette in Rosenbaum 1977: 89). Here, it should be recalled that for
Bonitzer *mise en scène* is equivalent to thought. 'To create one's own
space through the movements of one's body, to occupy and traverse
the spaces imposed by the decors and the camera's field' (Rivette in
Rosenbaum [1973] 1977: 91). It is not without relevance that this was
written in relation to one of his more 'mannerist' works, *Duelle*,
wherein Rivette attempts:

> to treat the text as material which plays a role exactly similar to the
> other materials in the film: the actors' faces, their gestures, the
> photographic texture ... the words carried by the images are not filmed
> for their meaning but rather for their materiality, as events and not as
> meanings. (Rivette in Rosenbaum [1973] 1977: 52)

Thus is provoked 'speech which carries no fixed reference in the
fiction and being completely erratic as speech' (Rivette [1973] 1977:
51). This takes speech into the realm of the poetic, since, as Rivette
implies, poetry seeks the senses before it makes sense. Despite the
differences between Rivette and Godard, there is also a vital link
between the latter and a certain conception of the poetic:

Godard's language is such an important focus of his films that it is almost a requirement to have printed scripts in order to appreciate the poetry fully – not the visual 'poetry', not the aural 'poetry', not the poetic sentiments, but the real, old-style, printed-on-the-page poetry. Jean-Luc Godard is one of the most vital French poets working today. (Monaco 1976: 163)

Carax can be located within this context too, since, as Daney said, he has a 'chose rare, un don pour la poésie' ('that rare thing, a gift for poetry'), while more recently Olivier Assayas declares: 'He's a true poet ... he has visions' (Assayas 2000).

## A tale told by a fool

Le monde est constitué de forces qui agissent les unes sur les autres, mais ces forces ne sont pas réductibles à des corps car ceux-ci les empêcheraient de s'exercer au-delà d'eux-mêmes, au-delà de leur enveloppe, les forces outrepassent la représentation des corps; d'où la différence de traitement des corps dans *L'Image-mouvement* et dans *L'Image-temps*: corps verticaux, stables, centres contre corps désarticulés, décentrés. Puisque le corps monocentré disparaît on peut poser la multiplicité des points de vue, l'hétérogénéité, le dispars. 'Le dispars fait fuir la représentation, la différence des points de vue trace une ligne de fuite', le sujet est dissout, il s'ouvre à une multiplicité de singularités en devenant véritablement temporel, il se fait faussaire. (Lacotte 2001: 85)[48]

In the world of Carax's crystalline narration both hodological space – grounded on the play of tensions in a centred force field – and a temporality wherein characters confront and overcome obstacles on a linear trajectory, are replaced by a collapse of the sensory-motor

48 'The world is constituted by forces which act on each other, but which are not reducible to bodies which impede them from being exercised outside themselves, beyond their envelope, forces pass beyond the representation of bodies; whence the different treatment of the body in *The Movement-Image* and in *The Time-Image*: vertical, stable, centred bodies against disarticulated, decentred bodies. Once the monocentred body disappears, the multiplicity of points of view, heterogeneity, the disparate can be posed. "The disparate puts representation to flight, the difference of points of view traces a line of flight", the subject dissolves and in becoming truly temporal, opens up to a multiplicity of singularities, giving birth to a forger.'

system and the rise of pure optical/sound situations. Confronted with
these, Alex cannot react – so great is his need clearly to see the content
of a situation. What there is to see in the situation is that the earth is
on the verge of exhaustion (signified by his cement-filled belly). Even
when threatened with prison or death, however, Alex during the
robbery, by holding himself hostage, may yet achieve the 'smile of
speed' and therefore reinvigorate the world. It is this that remains his
most (literally) pressing problem. In such situations movement can
either cease or become exaggerated, but it remains at the mercy of a
world movement. Rivette's manifesto for cinema finds its necessity
here – because space no longer supports sensory–motor links, performance can no longer be based on tensions or classical dramatic
confrontations or situations. As Deleuze concludes his account of
crystalline narration, in large part extrapolated from Bresson's work,
'le raccordement des parties n'est pas prédéterminé, mais peut se
faire de multiples façons: c'est une espace déconnectée, purement
optique, sonore ou même tactile' (Deleuze 1985: 169).[49] Deleuze cites
Michel Chion:

> Le modèle bressonien parle comme on écoute: en recueillant au fur et
> à mesure ce qu'il vient de dire en lui-même, si bien qu'il semble clore
> son discours au fur et à mesure qu'il l'émet, sans lui laisser la
> possibilité de résonner chez le partenaire ou le publique ... Dans *Le
> diable probablement* aucune voix ne résonne plus. (Deleuze 1985: 315–
> 16n.34)[50]

One effect of this is that speech is no longer a contributing factor to
plot development, nor does it serve the tensions and create the resolu-
tions. Since the 1980s, a specifically cinematic poetry, in the sense in
which this term is explained above, and verbal violence have proved to
be the two poles between which has drifted any cinema that wishes to
go beyond these sensory–motor system tensions.

49 'The connecting of parts of space is not predetermined but can take place in
   many ways. It is a space which is disconnected, purely optical, sound or tactile'
   (Deleuze 1989: 129).
50 'The [Bressonian model] talks as one listens, picking up as he can in himself
   what he has just said, to the extent that he seems to conclude his speech as he
   goes along uttering it [that is, the characters report their own words], without
   giving it the chance to resonate with the interlocutor or the viewer ... in *Le Diable
   Probablement* no voice is resonant anymore' (Chion cited in Deleuze 1989: 324,
   translation modified).

In this neo-baroque universe, force can no longer be said to be centred but is inseparable from its relations to other forces; each shot will produce a cluster of vanishing centres, and weights will have lost the centres of equilibrium around which they were distributed (hence Halley's Comet, prime emblem of the cosmic aspect in Carax); forces have lost the dynamic centres around which they organise space. In short, the Baroque question returns: is there a centre at all?

## 'So when this loose behaviour I throw off'[51]

It is now possible to isolate the three fundamental relations which a character in Carax's first films will be most likely to maintain with the decor/milieu. The first – which acts like a constant around which the others vary – is the relation of habitual activity, most often a restless inactivity in a neutral decor. Examples include Alex's room in *Boy Meets Girl* as he potters about watering plants, or the butcher's shop in *Mauvais Sang* as the planning is carried out on a daily basis. There is often a hyperactive edge to these scenes, since they carry with them an apprehension of resting, a fear that if one sits still things will stop moving. Around this constant, the first variation concerns the body's immobile states; it must surrender to a now highly stylised decor. As Carax says of his actor/character Mireille: 'je voulais qu'elle parle peu mais quand elle parle – c'est quelqu'un qui ne doit pas bouger' (Carax 1984).[52] These are often the moments of split subjectivity expressed through ventriloquism: when other-worldly spirits are unleashed, oracles speak, moments of extrasensory communication (the emphasis on telepathy in *Boy Meets Girl*) or of extraworldly coincidence arise. The last of these is marked, and not for the first time in this film, by a nod to Franju's short film *La Première Nuit* (1958), when Alex and Mireille unknowingly cross Bernard's path in the dead of night. In such sequences, Alex too becomes otherworldly, a ghost in a universe of cadavers. Another variation of this comes in the form of the overhead shots of Alex and the gang in the shop following the robbery, where they are rendered abstract, frozen by the decor. The third tension/movement is identifiable through characters from whom there is a spasm or acrobatic or athletic fulguration, often achieving

51 Shakespeare cited in *Mauvais Sang*.
52 'I wanted her to speak little and when she does speak she mustn't move.'

an equivalent of the elongation of the human form frequently found in Mannerist painting, as for example when Alex hangs out onto the street with the aid of a telephone wire in an effort to (spiritually) reach Anna in *Mauvais Sang.* What gives rise to these situations is a tension between the characters and their decor such that they become overwhelmed by uncertain gestures and feel not at home with their bodies. There are two chief variations on this model. The first concerns couples, where sudden discomfort can only be assuaged through a resort to clowning or some other game-playing. Examples include the shaving scene in *Mauvais Sang,* Anna's highly theatrical yawning when she meets Alex again following her night at the hotel, and his frantic card-trick session immediately following his call from Lise. This moment of unease can sometimes involve the reluctant recognition of the other's alterity as when Alex opens a door, perceives Mireille in a suicidal posture and calmly closes the door again. This is a kind of telepathic or inhuman empathy peculiar to Carax.

The second variation concerns the character alone with her or his body allied to the panic to which this solitude gives rise. Ever in search of an evasive equilibrium in this decentred baroque universe, the character can suffer the angst of too much lightness – a specific dread which in a tangental fashion links Carax to the literature of Kundera (Revault d'Allonnes in Buci-Glucksmann and Revault d'Allonnes 1987: 125). Two of the clearest examples involve Alex needing to walk backwards to keep grounded amidst the gravity-less spectres on the Parisian quays, and Mireille in her room, unable to sit still, but feeling compelled to launch into an acrobatic series of excessive postures. Alternatively, there is the angst of too much heaviness. Alex, for example, seeks a sense of lightness through shadow boxing, while in extreme cases of *pesanteur* there will occur an apprehensive turning of a radio dial. This anxiety is perhaps the quintessential Carax emotion, while the manner of his negotiation of the problematic leads him to some of the finest moments in his cinema. Taking as an example once more Mireille's dance scene in *Boy Meets Girl,* it can be asserted, moreover, that, as she tap-dances, 'un infime désynchronisme donne la sensation qu'elle vole, libérée de son corps, comme en état d'apesanteur ... un moment de bonheur immédiat et miraculeux' (Chévrie 1984: 73).[53]

53 'a tiny desynchronisation gives the sensation that she flies, liberated from her body, as in a state of weightlessness ... it is a moment of immediate and miraculous happiness.'

### 'How it feels when the universe reels'

These words from 'The Trolley Song' sung by Judy Garland in Minnelli's *Meet me in St Louis* (1944) serve to introduce another problematic and set of conditions that help to throw light on the manner in which Alex functions as a construct, and as a solution to a set of problems. From one perspective, he is the means that Carax employs to answer the question asked by the 'Trolley Song' and which may well be Carax's own fundamental question: how does it feel when the universe reels? Here the Deleuzian concept of 'movement of world' – touched on above – is once more helpful. For Deleuze, it is a kind of earthly justice that compensates a character whose heightened perception of things has rendered them immobile (Deleuze 1985: 81; 1989: 59). Through having recourse to the notion, Carax shows us once more that fate contains within itself its own ethical system. If Alex the frightened orphan can no longer move because of his cement-filled belly, 'le monde se met à fuir pour lui et l'emporte avec soi, comme sur un tapis roulant' (Deleuze 1985: 81).[54] The appearance of Halley's comet in the plot of *Mauvais Sang* is linked to this idea. The comet acts like the *passeur* between autonomous space-times. Is Carax's novelty here the neo-decadent one of a dying movement of world which Alex must save?

The set is now the motor of the *mise en scène* and no longer simply one of its constitutive parts; hence the story 'pourrait se réduire à un voyage à travers un certain nombre de décors qui mesureraient très exactement l'évolution du personnage' (Renaud cited in Deleuze 1985n.23: 85–86).[55] This description of Minnelli's use of decor *as mise en scène* leads to the inevitable comparison of major aspects of Carax's early work to the musical comedy.

As Alex tries to induce first Mireille (*Boy Meets Girl*) then Anna (*Mauvais Sang*) into his passion (through a kind of bullying hypnosis), Carax pushes the musical comedy back into the world of the burlesque. Carax emphasises a strong emotive, affective element of the kind to be found in 'les Pierrots lunaires du burlesque' ('the moonstruck pierrots

54  'The world sets about running away for him and takes him with it, as if on a conveyor belt' (Deleuze 1989: 59).
55  'Could be reduced to a journey through a certain number of film sets which would give a very precise measurement of the character's evolution' (Renaud cited in Deleuze 1989: 291n.25).

of burlesque'), variations of which type are found in the 'visage impassible et réflexif de Buster Keaton ... le visage intensif et variable de Chaplin ... Laurel ... Langdon dans ses sommeils irrésistibles et ses rêves éveillés' (Deleuze 1985: 87), but in his case it is read through the modernist burlesque of Tati, Lewis, Demy, even Godard.[56] If the burlesque character is still trapped in a sensory–motor obstacle course, in the pure optical and sound situations of the modernist burlesque, the character/Alex 'se met (involontairement) sur un faisceau énergétique qui l'entraîne, et qui constitue précisément le mouvement du monde, une nouvelle manière de danser, de moduler' (Deleuze 1985: 89).[57] There is inevitably a cosmic dimension as wave, wind or storm (or comet) depersonalises the character's movement. The body of Denis Lavant serves Carax astonishingly well as a link to the burlesque tradition.

This puts one in a better position to take stock of Carax's original contribution to contemporary cinema (in line with Rivette's demand for a new type of acting). Some critics have been too quick to compartmentalise: Carax is not a Godardian clone; his relations to Beineix and Besson, his presumed *cinéma du look* cohorts, are very tenuous to say the least; if he is mannerist, then it is a complex relation to the history of cinematic mannerism that can be opposed point by point to Beineix's. Likewise, if Carax is neo-baroque, then it is an intricately woven mode that, by way of tying together elements from diverse filmmaking manners, brought important questions and creative solutions to the cinematic medium in the 1980s. In the process, his work makes connections and untangles previously taken-for-granted links between filmmakers and styles from the history of cinema. If, for the sake of convenience, one temporarily considers Carax, along with Beineix and Besson as purveyors of the 'look', it must immediately be recognised that, unlike Beineix and Besson, Carax neither plagiarises nor borrows shopworn images *à la mode*. Instead, he problematises a historical situation in which the element we live in is one of images of all types and shows us how to struggle

56 'Buster Keaton's impassive, reflective face, and also in the power of Chaplin's intense and variable face ... Laurel ... Langdon with his irresistible sleeps and waking dreams' (Deleuze 1989: 64).
57 'Places himself (involuntarily) on an energy band which carries him along and which is precisely movement of world, a new way of dancing, of modulating' (Deleuze 1989: 66).

against the weight of a clichéd and atrophied reservoir of image and affect. In Denis Lavant, Carax found the perfect mediator for this series of aspirations.

### Le casting[58]

During the shoot of *Mauvais Sang* Carax used the screen perform-ances of Dana Andrews – one of the great underrated Hollywood stars of the 1940s – as a point of reference to assist Lavant in his role. Andrews was 'always an apparent hero with something to hide, he could suggest unease, shiftiness and rancour barely concealed by good looks ... he did not trust or like himself as if a so faraway bitterness haunted him' (Thomson 1994). It is possible to glean what Carax wanted to draw on here and to install and activate in Lavant – a kind of virginal personal attraction tied to a tough exterior. Lavant emits a 'regard fixe, avide' ('fixed, avid gaze', Philippon 1986: 17) and is the fulcrum of 'le regard devenu geste' ('the gaze become gesture', Philippon 1986: 17). His are hands which always, so to speak, have another trick up their sleeve, and which can turn a situation inside out by means of an acrobatic reorientation. Later of course this fearless physical aspect will take over, and by *Les Amants du Pont-Neuf* Lavant already looks like someone to fear. While Alex in this film is still the locus of these transformations and metamorphoses, his character is ultimately consigned to *thanatos*. He is already a corpse, already a *corps morcelé* (fragmented body). In Claire Denis's *Beau Travail* (1999), the 'resurrected' Lavant has subjected his anarchic body to the constraints of military disciplinarity: a form of 'mummification' which preserves within it vestiges of 'Alex' (as the final explosive dance scene confirms).

It may be useful here to compare what Carax was looking for in Lavant with Beineix's use of Depardieu (in his most mannerist work *La Lune dans le caniveau*) and Besson with Lambert in *Subway* (1985), in Bassan's view Besson's only neo-baroque film. 'Depardieu has the air of a rugby player (after a game played in heavy mud)', writes David Thompson in his *Biographical Dictionary* (Thomson 1994). Lavant, by contrast, suggests through facial and bodily movements fleeting

58 This section owes a great deal to conversations between Fergus Daly and Tony McKibbin.

moments of simian furtivity. These movements are coupled with a face that bears the type of light scarring that might come courtesy of a minor sporting accident or of a leisure pursuit gone wrong. He can give the impression of someone nursing pain. By means of gesture and posture Alex/Lavant also suggests hermetic closure, a body and mind sealed off from the outside. Yet, at the same time, his face is also a screen where other actors – in the form of facial tics mimicked – can fleetingly appear. This is why Alex's words and actions seem to bear little connection to each other. He sees himself as 'a cartoon figure with a bubble over its head' (*Mauvais Sang*) or in his description of Marc in the same film, which is in fact more applicable to himself, 'an unopenable safe with the keys inside'. There is a pressure in his interior that only death can release. For this Rimbaud whose senses are disordered, each thing seen (for instance in the scene in which he returns to the shop following the 'Modern Love' performance and, in a very strange scene, uncharacteristically filmed by Carax in isolated short shots, he stares at in turn a single hair, a tissue and a cigarette) is perceived as autonomous yet finally sharing a space because subject to a virtual process of unification that only the visionary is privy to. Christophe Lambert is in some ways Lavant's opposite. It should be noted that one draws Lavant and Lambert together *not* just because they are both perceived as *cinéma du look* actors, but because Lavant and Lambert through their respective styles suggest very different modes of being within a tradition that can be traced back to Gabin – a tradition that undeniably also includes Depardieu. Lambert is a 'lobotomised' presence; the sweet, sickly smile in *Subway* is that of a man as existential cyborg – a product of genealogical angst that has less to do with any notion of character than the generalisations of iconography: Lambert combines stylistically the Belmondo of *A Bout de Souffle* and the late punk drifting into the New Romantic so fashionable in the early 1980s. But this is the street punk with both a dress sense and a too-contrived sense of purpose. His clothes are carefully cut and he wants to set up a band; his character is, in a manner of speaking, a cyborg *à la mode* – as if Besson wanted to absorb a long tradition of purposelessness and despair and turn it into a mythic cool of desperation and inertia, but without negating the need for narrative momentum. Thus the cyborg element: Lambert does not evoke despair (the deep-rooted rage of Gabin in *La Bête Humaine* (1938), the feelings of entrapment Gabin feels as a second-class citizen in *Le Jour se lève* (1939)), but he serves as a useful cipher for tension: the viewer might side with him against the uncool of authority, be that Michel Galabru's police officer on his tail, or Jean-Pierre Bacri as lover Adjani's husband. The *cinéma du look* collapses notions of morality and psychology so central to Gabin's persona not in ironic questioning (as Godard did in reinterpreting the French icon and attaching it to Bogart), but in stylistic assumption. It is not necessarily pejorative to refer to a film like *Subway* as shallow – such an assessment is as close as we are likely to get to critical objectivity in respect of this film.

The central issue concerning the *cinéma du look* is really about types of shallowness. Here the comparison between Depardieu (an essentially pre-*cinéma du look* actor hijacked by Beineix for the director's own ends), Lavant and Lambert proves instructive. Lambert's shallowness in *Subway* is external, an image of existential fatalism. Lavant's shallowness in *Boy Meets Girl* is internal, a product of attenuated alienation, a shallowness that has in fact a curious depth. Lavant's depth, or shallowness, is the need to nurse solitude; this is the Truffaut side of Carax, with Lavant here both an Antoine Doinel and *L'Enfant Sauvage*. Of course, as some critics have done, both film and character could be written off as immature; however, it is more fruitful to look at Lavant's Alex as a protector of a space that is as yet undefined. *Boy Meets Girl* is clearly a one man and his room movie, as Schrader would phrase it, but it is also a one man and his room movie as Kierkegaard might perceive it: 'most people never really in all their lives manage to become more than they were in childhood and youth: immediacy with a little dash of reflection added' (Kierkegaard 1989: 88). In Alex's case, it is the other way round – it is as if he wants to stay within immaturity so he can maximise the 'epoch' of reflection. This is another sense of Alex as *enfant-vieillard*. His preoccupation with himself is central and with Mireille secondary. Or rather the preoccupation with Mireille through himself is central and the physical being of Mireille secondary. Alex may be immature, but he understands love as an act of faith and a product of the imaginary.

If Lambert is the shallow distillation of cinema past (a continuation and conflation of Bogart and Belmondo), and Alex shallow because he refuses to grow up, Depardieu in *La Lune dans le caniveau* is clearly less ethereally utilised, but instead Beineix uses Depardieu's physicality paradoxically. On the one hand Depardieu suggests tangibility in his presence, but on the other Beineix removes the realist *mise en scène* that would give Depardieu the opportunity to be physical. Beineix says that Depardieu's Gérard is 'seeking to reconcile himself with his other half', and believes 'it is a film that talks about institutions, about the rich and poor, without being interested in either wealth or poverty. It shows the existential suffering of two human beings' (Beineix cited in Kael 1987: 47). What Beineix underlines here is the Gérard dichotomy through contrast. What we have is poverty as a way of occupying space. How does someone used to occupying heavy, physical spaces (Gérard is a docker) and treating objects (and subjects) roughly deal with the intangibility of wealth and beauty, personified by Nastassja Kinski? And vice versa in Kinski's case. Of course, on one level, Beineix's film is without depth: Gérard is iconographically hewn out of Gabin (in *Le Jour se lève* and *Quai des Brumes*) but the fatalism now has less to do with a man who does not fit into a realistic (if equally studio-shot) and cruel world, and whose time is about up, than with a physical presence at odds with an artificial atmosphere. The unavoidable and distinctive billboard outside Gérard's slum dwelling may say 'try another world' but is this simply an ironic nod towards Gérard's lowly status, or is it, rather, saying something about his inability to live in Beineix's mannerist setting? After its release, Depardieu humorously referred to it as a 'film in the gutter'.

Hence there are three possibilities within the *cinéma du look*'s use of the actor. In Besson's use of Lambert an actor at one with the director's modishness as the iconic loner is drawn upon for the purposes of cool. In Carax, the cool is in some way inverted. Where Lambert's Fred, whatever his underground status, has a clearly social kudos, it is as if Alex protects a notion of cool that can never go beyond the first person, and which perhaps would not want to go beyond the first person. Besson's film is full of cool posturing, of ways to retain coolness, or even to gain it. There is the huge bodybuilder, the rollerskating thief, and Adjani rejecting her husband's polite little world during a dinner party sequence. Carax's work, however, appears indifferent to this type of cool. Cool in Carax is, if anything, a cool designed not for the purposes of oneself in relation to others, but for the purposes of oneself *until* in the presence of others, allied to an understanding of tenuous subjectivity. Cool here is simply what one needs to survive, a kind of false consciousness, of course, but is closer to a survival technique than a sought after mode of being, as in *Subway*.

Beineix's *Diva* (1981) occupies a middle position between the 'iconographising' of *Subway* and the first-person cool of *Boy Meets Girl*. There is the young postman and music buff who shares certain characteristics with Alex, and then there is the cool shoplifting Asian woman and of course Bohringer's super-smooth enigma. But Beineix's work in *La Lune dans le caniveau* is more adventurous in the way that he dehumanises the *cinéma du look*. One of the key problems for critics faced with the *cinéma du look* is the way it turns subjects into objects, where people are no longer the sum of their parts, but the singularity of their presentation. In *La Lune*, it is as if this is central to Beineix's curious politics. Does wealth amount to the ability to become an object accumulating objects, while subjectivity amounts to a subject accumulating subjectivity? Here 'ideal' subjectivity would be an echo of Spinoza's ideas about the more ways a body could be affected by forces the more force it would have (Deleuze [1962] 1983: 62). By the same token, the more a body accumulates dead forces (objects), the less force it may possess. From this point of view, there is a way of looking at the brittleness of wealth and the resoluteness of poverty that coincides with clichés of wealth and poverty but does not necessarily reiterate them. *La Lune* creates a brittle world at odds with the physical impact of Depardieu and asks if he wants to try the other world that has little need of his physicality. To be the sum of one's own parts (the inverse of Ruiz), or the singularity of another world – this is what Beineix seems to be getting at when he asks Gérard if he wants to try another world. Hence, though Beineix may be said to be superficial, and *La Lune dans le caniveau* taken as the ultimate example of *cinéma du look*, in some ways Beineix scientises the movement just as it can be said that Carax in *Boy Meets Girl* philosophises it. He turns wealth and poverty not into a political issue but an issue of texture; as a mode of behaviour based on tangible and intangible matter. Might the point be stretched to say that Beineix's mannerism is not metaphysics but physics itself? Such a take on the film justifies the apparently absurd choice of Depardieu in a *cinéma du look* film.

Of the three films and their use of their actors, Besson's is easily the most superficial, unthinking and predictable: he well earns pejorative labelling. But Carax and Beineix are doing something fresh with Lavant and Depardieu. Lavant has since gone on to become an underused but important actor who in his roles has given a kind of formal rigour to despair in *Mauvais Sang*, *Les Amants du Pont-Neuf* and *Beau Travail*. His approach furnishes what might be called a 'subjective correlative', in so far as it falls between the objective correlative of T. S. Eliot's demand for distance, and the formless subjectivity of much that might be deemed insane behaviour. This aspect is something clearly developed under the influence of Carax and the *cinéma du look*.

What Beineix does with Depardieu is interesting in a different way. Depardieu is a great actor of physicality. Pauline Kael once said 'Depardieu redeems physical coarseness: he's both earth and spirit' (Kael 1975). What he cannot be, however, is shadow and light, gesture and mood; he carries too much weight. There are some great actors of weightlessness – Astaire of course, as Deleuze points out, but also Pfeiffer (especially in *Scarface*), Reeves, Lancaster, early Delon, Newman, Dafoe, Schneider and Kinski and, and especially, Lavant. Of course this weightlessness has a lot to do with weight itself, and also with age, albeit not necessarily always. For example, Mastroianni was an old man and far from light when he made *Ginger and Fred*, but he had retained enough lightness of physical presence to pull off a role that could have degenerated into complete farce. Lancaster's dance with Cardinale in *The Leopard* (Visconti 1963) gained its impact by presenting an ageing character as one still capable of agility. In *La Lune dans le caniveau* Beineix seems to take this notion of weight (once more one thinks of the film's physics) and turns the film into the most extreme example of the weight of performance and weight-lessness of milieu. Apart from *One from the Heart* (Coppola 1982), most other loosely mannerist films of the 1980s did not do this: *The Loveless* (Bigelow and Montgomery 1981) with Dafoe, *Cotton Club* (Coppola 1984) with Gere, *Rumble Fish* (Coppola 1983) with Dillon and Lane, *Streets of Fire* (Hill 1984) with Lane, Pare and Dafoe. Other notable examples include *Scarface* (De Palma 1983) and *Ginger and Fred* (Fellini 1986). Beineix's 'miscasting' raises interesting questions about casting in relation to space, just as Carax's raises interesting questions about the combination of 'the non-stereotypical face' and 'cool', and as Besson fails to raise them by casting so completely within expectation in *Subway*.

## Observations on key sequences

> To be delivered from gravity was the only way to stay awake in his dream (Serge Daney (1982))

In order fully to appreciate the strength and importance of much of Carax's imagery and dialogue, it is necessary to engage in a close reading of its poetic quality and sense. Four key sequences are selected, two each from the first two features.


### 1 *Boy Meets Girl*: the intercom sequence

Serge Cardinal, in one of the few academic studies to take *Boy Meets Girl* seriously, analyses this segment of the film from the point of view of its dissolution of conventional cinematic spatial structure, based on homological relations between the point of view and the point of listening, and the construction of an alternative space based on disjunction and division. In this it mirrors the disintegration of the relationship between Mireille and Bernard. Conventional space 'se construit d'abord selon une succession de fragments liés par un point de vue et un point d'écoute unifiés, et par le corps du personnage, qui permet une circulation entre ces fragments' (Cardinal 1997: 79).[59]

What inflects *Boy Meets Girl* in the direction of the baroque, but in a highly original manner, is the play between voice-in and voice-off, exemplified by this early sequence which creates the tone for his entire oeuvre. In *Hypothèse du tableau volé* Ruiz had set up a truly baroque interplay between the commentary of the collector and that of the voice-off, creating two communicating heterogeneous spaces and, on occasion, as Bonitzer points out, leaving the spectator's eye in a space incompatible with that of her or his ear (Bonitzer 1978). Carax similarly scrambles the spectator's senses. This (highly baroque) sequence acts like the door into all that is great in the Caraxian universe. Before it begins, we have witnessed not quite a conventional piece of cinema but at least one that did not contest our viewing expectations, but as Bernard stands at a 90 degree angle to Alex and the voice begins to float into indeterminacy, our perception soon becomes unhinged.

59 'is constructed primarily according to a succession of fragments linked by a unified point of view and point of listening, and by the character's body, permitting a circulation between these fragments.'

Cardinal shows how we progressively lose all sense of a conventional filmic space constructed according to a succession of fragments linked by a united point of view and point of listening, and by the body of the character which permits a circulation between these fragments. From a centred visual order establishing a unified scene, we pass to a disordered space in which ear and eye have been disordered as elements in a eurythmic system. The homogeneity of the scene is imperilled; there is a displacement of landmarks, a flux; perception and cognition confront each other; music and voice are detached from their source and travel independently of it:

> ils ne transportent pas le poids des choses ... ces occurrences sonores ne créent qu'un seul environnement sonore au sein duquel se retrouve le spectateur, un espace tordu est créé, un espace en suspension illogique des lieux séparés ... un spectateur déborde, déssaisi par l'errance du son sur l'image. (Cardinal 1997: 96)[60]

This also breaks the union of body and voice 'qui prévaut à l'unité du sujet, à l'unité du personnage' (Cardinal 1997: 96); that is, there is a desynchronisation (of body and voice).[61] The result is that the monologue is detached from Bernard's body: 'le rapport intime de la voix au sujet, leur communion, qui en Occident est celle du corps et de l'esprit, se trouve repoussée et, avec elle, l'unité fondamentale qui mesure toute chose' (Cardinal 1997: 96).[62] In addition a general desynchronisation takes place 'entre le mouvement du corps de Bernard et le déroulement de son discours' (which tempts one to attribute it at the same time to Bernard and Alex): 'ultime division du sujet, il n'est que l'écho d'un autre, que le porte-parole, le ventriloque ... la cohabitation des points d'écoute déjoue les limites de l'intérieur et de l'extérieur de l'immeuble' (Cardinal 1997: 97).[63] Here the neo-

60 'they don't bear the weight of things ... these sonorous occurrences create a single sonorous environment only at the heart of which the spectator finds himself, a distorted space is created, a space in illogical suspension between separate places ... a spectator that overflows, borne away by the floating of sound over image.'
61 'which prevails on the unity of the subject, on the unity of the character.'
62 'the intimate relation of voice to subject, their communion, which in the west is that of body and mind, is pushed aside and, with it, the fundamental unity which measures everything.'
63 'between the movement of Bernard's body and the unfolding of his discourse'; 'ultimate division of the subject, he is now only the echo of another, the mouthpiece, the ventriloquist ... the cohabitation of points of listening unmakes the limits of the interior and the exterior of the building.'

baroque idea of 'les deux étages' ('the two floors') is evoked. As
Deleuze describes this invention:

> C'est un grand montage baroque que Leibniz opère, entre l'étage d'en
> bas percé de fenêtres, et l'étage d'en haut, aveugle et clos, mais en
> revanche résonnant, comme un salon musical qui traduirait en sons
> les mouvements visibles d'en bas. (Deleuze 1988: 6)[64]

Powrie has made use of the distinction in order to analyse the
interplay of image and sound in the films of Beineix; in additon he
asserts that Beineix's characters' striving for a better world is
'analogous to what Deleuze means by the "spiritual"' (Powrie 2001:
25), and that 'the use of light and other conceits of the mise-en-scène
are related to the separation but indissociability of the inside and
outside in Leibniz's metaphysics' (2001: 66). Rather than the
absolute (in Leibniz) Carax would prefer to have Alex say 'infinity'
(*Mauvais Sang*) or 'eternity' (*Boy Meets Girl*): by whatever name, it is
the force which cuts through Alex dividing him from himself yet
propelling him through life *à toute vitesse*.

## 2  *Boy Meets Girl*: Alex/Mireille in the kitchen

This long sequence (itself occurring in the party sequence which as a
whole takes up close to half the film), where Alex and Mireille meet
and speak at length for the first (and only) time, works more like a
series of monologues than the standard flirtatious or mutually
provocative dialogue of conventional cinema.

Mireille joins Alex and Carol in the kitchen and begins to hum the
Bowie song ('When I Live my Dream') heard earlier as Alex walked
along the quays. In this way, she acts like the siren drawing Alex into
her world or into 'eternity' (as he suspects), for Mireille is in many
ways Cocteau's Princess of Death: 'it's like a dream being here with
you ... a deep sleep ... like eternity'. Mireille speaks of death and
suicide, Alex of love, loss and responsibility: 'To think that you will
age ... old, wrinkled ... it's all my fault', but she is 'wrinkled since

---

64 'Leibniz constructs a great Baroque montage that moves between the lower
floor, pierced with windows, and the upper floor, blind and closed, but on the
other hand resonating as if it were a musical salon, translating the visible
movements below into sounds up above' (Deleuze 1993: 4).

childhood' – a fellow *enfant-vieillard* propelling him into a sense of
cosmic responsibility: 'we'll be an unbeatable team whatever our
signs, Libra or Leo, I'll sign up ... we'll change our habits'. For Carax,
it seems one has a responsibility towards the cosmos to free oneself
from the weight of cliché: 'you'll stop destroying yourself, you'll
respect the warmth of your blood'. Cliché is precisely what blocks
movement, and the ethical imperative is to keep moving with the
world, with its warp and woof, to 'pass the way of all things', as Alex
says in *Mauvais Sang*. It is to be *for* the world, while suicide is
unethical if it does not respect the movement of life. Only flows (of
bodies, the earth, words) can prevent it: 'mental diarrhoea ... I must
not bury my lover with words. But if I shut up she'll kill herself'. Thus
when the body begins to weigh one down, becoming a blockage, one
must literally jump out of one's skin (as in the case of Mireille's dance
in *Boy Meets Girl*, and Alex's gymnastics to 'Modern Love' in *Mauvais
Sang*) or let the words flow free of the body in a form of cosmic
ventriloquism. The final shot of the sequence shows Alex and Mireille
on a bus crossing the path of Bernard riding on a tram, as Alex's voice
continues its disembodied monologue: 'kisses won't seal our lips,
help me to take wing. I weigh a ton. Don't look I'm a truck. I'll never
live again Mireille never'. The impression one has is that only Alex's
arrival at the party has breathed life into these cadavers; suddenly they
can reveal themselves, even embrace one another – everyone in
Carax's neo-baroque world is capable of living in parallel worlds
simultaneously, of dividing into 'incompossible' bodies and voices
(these party guests are grouped like the *tableaux vivants* in Ruiz's
*Hypothèse du tableau volé*) and of an eternal subsistence cohabiting
with their present form. For example, in the case of Carol and the late
Stan, the superimposed image of Stan's face appears with all the
ontological insistence of the party guests, while Alex hopes that, while
he is speaking, fate will work its magic on himself and Mireille,
against or in spite of his words: 'we must fall in love, unaware of it,
wordlessly' but, and this is where Carax's neo-decadence tends to
override every other emotion or belief, he adds 'it's too late'. The
lesson: even if one succeeds in evading the power of cliché, even if one
forms an ethical assemblage with a lover *for* the world with fate on
one's side – it is already too late. The ground of existence, its supreme
force is entropy, decomposition, something that 'eats away at [it] from
within'. Perhaps this is what *Pola X* will later call 'the lies underneath

everything', the weight that for Carax is what defines 'irredeemable' lives.

Irrevocability is central to Carax's vision. Time is an arrow, it accrues weight but can never be reversed. Therefore, when Lise phones to tell him she has slept with Thomas his ethical priority is a concern, not for any personal pain or sense of betrayal, but for the ontological wastage to which they will have contributed: 'Don't you see you couldn't be unfaithful to me? ... [it's] something irrevocable ... for what? ... we've ruined everything, for what?'. Only first times count; thereafter all of life is a process of breaking down. As Thomas says to Alex 'you'll grow old very fast, you'll implode, like a TV set ... more loathsome dead than alive' – a simile echoed in what Carax calls 'a love that burns quickly but lasts forever' (*Mauvais Sang*). The importance of the Halley's Comet theme here is that it ties irrevocability as the effect of human action to a cosmic destiny of inevitable wastage, while simultaneously bringing about the possibility of another cosmology, one based on unpredictability: now it snows, next it is swelteringly hot. Carax seems to ask: chance or destiny, which one will you choose? To accept the cement-filled belly or to struggle to attain the smile of speed; to tie the philosophy of 'only first times count' to the infinite repetition or reflections of possibility, with the latter choice being one always prone to the equally unpredictable onslaught of the 'too late'. 'My life is a rough sketch ... a wave never reaching the shore, it's too late now to learn to live': the sense of the provisional and the 'processual' evoked in this line of dialogue applies equally to Carax's treatment of character and narrative: '[T]he characters are not fixed, or defined at the beginning, so that they can't surprise us. They can change, and at the end of the story the characters are not at all the same as they were at the beginning' (Rivette in Ochiva and Rapfogel 2000). As the sequence progresses, Carax plays more and more with selective focus such that the planes between the faces of Alex and Mireille seem to be set in motion as if the dimensions of the image are multiplying as we watch.

Whereas in the 'baroque' cinema of the past, depth of field 'théâtralisait les corps et êtres, traversait tous les plans dans un mouvement en trouée, spirale ou diagonale' (Buci-Glucksmann in Buci-Glucksmann and Revault d'Allonnes 1987: 11), here the *same* effect is produced using a shallow *mise en scène*, resulting in pure baroque effects of *trompe l'œil* and *trompe-l'esprit*, the Princess of

Death 'liant l'œil visuel de toutes ces 'images optiques' à cet œil de la
pensée et du souvenir qui voit des fantômes, cher à Hamlet' (Buci-
Glucksmann in Buci-Glucksmann and Revault d'Allonnes 1987: 11).[65]
*Pola X*, with its variation on the Hamlet character, will return to this.

## 3 *Mauvais Sang*: modern love

> It is a curious fact that classical dance always fails to get across the
> screen footlights whereas modern ballet is as happy there as a fish in
> water because it is a stylisation of real, everyday movements. Classical
> dance, which seeks an immobility in movement, is by definition the
> opposite of cinema ... Rather than a goal, repose in the cinema is on
> the contrary the starting-point for movement. A balustrade is no
> longer something to lean on but an obstacle to clear, a chair no longer
> something to sit on but a site for a delicate balancing act: everything
> becomes simply a pretext for the 'lines which displace movement'.
> (Godard [1958] 1972: 87)

This is in many respects the quintessential Carax moment (each of
the first three features contains a related sequence). Inside and
outside the characters everything suddenly begins to weigh heavily.
Falling into a depressive exhaustion Anna mutters 'nothing's
moving'. In response, Alex arbitrarily turns the radio dial (as Mireille
had in *Boy Meets Girl*): 1 ... 2 ... 3 ... and soon Bowie's song starts up
and provides the spark that will electrify his body and provide him
with the force to kick-start the pulse of the world. It is a case of the
exhausted earth using Alex's body as the spark to reignite itself – 'a
starting-point for movement' in Godard's words.

From a different perspective, the 'Modern Love' sequence would
involve less a line of flight than a dance of death, an ecstatic form of
self-extinction. In line with the classical musical comedy, when a
situation proves too much for a character and they do not know how to
respond, there is a moment of hesitation before the character is
carried away by the world substituting its movement for their own.
On the crest of a wave, the character will pass into the life of the loved
one. Carax too associates love with a kind of telepathic union in the
other's mind or dreams. From this perspective, when Anna says

65 'theatralised bodies and beings, traversing all the planes in a perforating, spiral
or diagonal movement'; 'linking the visual eye of all these optical images to this
eye of thought and memory which sees phantoms, dear to Hamlet.'

'nothing's moving' it opens up Alex's passage inside her and he is carried along by the sidewalk at tremendous speed, speed being the rush, the vertigo of *amour fou*. Perhaps this is what will enable Anna at the film's end to attain the 'smile of speed', even though on a personal level it will be too late – he will have burned himself out.

Summoned back to the butcher's shop by Anna's humming, Alex finds the space empty, or rather physically empty but spiritually full – the imprint of her body remains on the bed. One after another Alex finds in and around the imprinted bed, a hair, a tissue, a dying cigarette, material signs of her spiritual presence. Then he lies on the bed, next to her imprint in a spiritual form of coupling.

### 4 *Mauvais Sang*: the death scene

Facing the double terminalities of a gunshot wound and STBO, Alex reaches the getaway airfield at the point of death. His search for an ethos of lightness seems less a personal one than a vocational one thrust upon him – the smile of speed is something he can only assist others in attaining, never himself. This is the Kafkaesque side of Carax. Alex is like a ferryman or foyer between worlds. Ruiz too has persistently explored the baroque notion of the bridge (*il ponto*) and its personnage the 'passeur'. As explained above, the baroque world is organised along two vectors, a diving toward the lower depths, and a thrusting toward the upper regions (hence the Caraxian duality of gravity versus weightlessness). Add to this the autonomy of inside and outside in the baroque house, at once separate and joined, and one can speak of the foyer, both inside and outside, a reception area provided by the host who maintains the interior for the guest who comes from the exterior. On a cosmic level, Alex is such a host.

If the only conceivable lightness is an experimental, mobile light- ness, achievable only by way of self-experimentation through which one can learn to float in a space and time which has nothing to do with 'the given instrumentalities of program' (Rajchman 1998: 42), it must never be a search for any transcendent delivery. We can see how in several respects Carax belongs in the line of French Nietzschean- ism which reached its peak of popularity in the 1980s. The following quotations from Nietzsche could be lines of dialogue from any one of Carax's first films: 'are not all words made for the heavy? Do not all words lie to the light?' (Nietzsche [1892] 1969: 246), 'Everything heavy shall become light, every body a dancer, all spirit a bird' (247) or, in John Rajchman's recent take on Nietzsche: 'To lighten the earth itself, as though one were to insert oneself into it like a surfer in a wave' (Rajchman 1998: 47).

There are two poles to thinking about the 'cosmic game'. Either nothing is fortuitous and destiny is written in the stars, or everything is contingent, nothing necessary. Once more Carax refuses the either/ or. Alex is one who both feels a burden of destiny on his shoulders (but it is not necessary) and who feels free (but it is not wholly contingent). Carax puts the freedom–necessity issue on to the plane of romance, where it becomes a vitalist issue in so far as there is no transcendent law or judgement; rather, there is nothing but the immanent judgement of life on itself. But for Alex/Carax it is a life yoked to its own wasting.

As Alex lies dying – 'I'll speak from the inside, it'll be easier' – the baroque inside–outside dissolution (and the concomitant insepar-ability of upper–lower and interior–façade) applies here on the monadic level. As in the intercom sequence in *Boy Meets Girl,* the voice floats free. There ensues a 'déconstruction de l'unité interne/ externe de l'espace classique dans la multiplication des points d'écoute, déconstruction de l'unité intime du sujet dans la démonstration de sa perméabilité et de sa déchirure d'avec la voix' (Cardinal 1997: 97).[66] The only possible communication/communion for Alex is by way of ex-stasis: 'Je me désapproprie de moi-même par l'autre, je m'approprie l'autre à moi' (Marin 1981 cited in Cardinal 1997: 47).[67] 'Excommunion de la voix qui n'arrive à trouver un lien que divise-double' (Cardinal 1997: 97).[68] Only the floating voice, free of the body's weight and of the concrete-like gravity of subjectivity, can provoke Anna to find 'the smile of speed' in the final shots of the film.

At the moment of his death, it is as if all of Alex's force passes into Anna. She turns and runs at full speed across the airfield, seeming to levitate as she attains the smile of speed, the event given visual form by Escoffier's shimmering camera effects. It is a concluding shot

66 'deconstruction of the internal–external unity of classical space in the multiplication of points of listening, deconstruction of the intimate unity of the subject in the demonstration of its permeability and its being torn from the voice.'

67 'I disappropriate myself by the other, I appropriate the other.'

68 'ex-communion of the voice which can only find a link when divided-doubled.'

which obliquely suggests an inversion of Maurice Blanchot's *récit* *Thomas l'Obscur* which ends as Thomas, having learned the protocols of death from Anne, leaps, in abject capitulation, into a flood of 'images grossières' ('vulgar images', Blanchot 1950: 137). In *Mauvais Sang* by contrast it is Alex who has offered a physical treatise on death, but the ending attains for Anna both the smile of speed and the lightness that allows ascent into a pure image.

## References

Assayas, Olivier (2000), 'Critical instinct: interview with Fergus Daly', *Film West* 37, 44–7.

Barthes, Roland (1964), 'Tacite et le baroque funèbre', *Essais Critiques*, Paris, Seuil.

Bassan, Raphaël (1989), 'Trois néobaroques français', *Revue du cinema*, no. 449, 44–50.

Beineix, Jean-Jacques (1983), 'Man in the moon', *Film Comment* 19.4, 16–19.

Bergala, Alain (1983), 'Le vrai, le faux, le factice', *Cahiers du Cinéma*, no. 351, September, 4–9.

—— (1984), 'Le cinéma de l'après', *Cahiers du Cinéma*, no. 360-1, June–July, 58–62.

—— (1985), 'D'une certaine manière', *Cahiers du Cinéma*, no. 370, April, 11–15.

—— (1992), 'The other side of the bouquet', in Raymond Bellour ed., *Jean-Luc Godard: Son + Image 1974–1991*, New York, The Museum of Modern Art, pp. 57–73.

Blanchot, Maurice (1950), *Thomas l'Obscur*, Paris, Gallimard.

Bonitzer, Pascal (1978), 'Sur *L'Hypothèse du tableau volé*', *Cahiers du Cinéma*, no. 288, May, 22–3.

—— (1983), 'Standards d'émotion', *Cahiers du Cinéma*, no. 353, November, 9–12.

—— (1985), *Décadrages*, Paris, Editions Cahiers du cinéma.

Buci-Glucksmann, Christine (1984), *La Raison Baroque*, Paris, Galilée.

—— (1993) 'Drôle de pensée touchant Leibniz et le cinéma', *Trafic* 8, 71–80.

—— (1994), *Baroque Reason: The Aesthetics of Modernity*, trans. Patrick Camiller, London, Sage.

Buci-Glucksmann, Christine and Fabrice Revault d'Allonnes (1987), *Raoul Ruiz*, Paris, Editions DIS VOIR.

Cache, Bernard (1995) *Earth Moves: The Furnishing of Territory*, Cambridge, MA, MIT.

Carax, Leos (1979), 'La taverne de l'enfer', *Cahiers du Cinéma*, no. 303, September, 98–9.

—— (1979a), 'Festivals: "Hyères"', *Cahiers du Cinéma*, no. 304, October, 40–2.

—— (1980), 'Semaine officielle et retrospective du cinéma polonais', *Cahiers du Cinéma*, no. 307, January, 55–6.

—— (1984), 'Entretien' on France-Culture, November.
   Available online at *www.patoche.org/carax/interviews*
—— (1984a), with Philippe Garrel, 'Dialogue en apesanteur', *Cahiers du Cinéma*, no. 365, November, 36–40.
—— (1986), 'La beauté en révolte', *Cahiers du Cinéma*, no. 390, December, 24–32.
—— (1991), Rédacteur en Chef, Numéro Spécial de *Cahiers du Cinéma, Les Amants du Pont-Neuf.*
—— (1991a), 'A l'impossible on est tenu', *Les Inrockuptibles*, no. 32, December.
   Available online at: *www.patoche.org/carax/interviews/inrocks.htm*
—— (1992), 'Leos Carax', interview with David Thompson, *Sight and Sound*, 5:2 September, 10–11.
—— (1999), 'Nous dépasser, ou sombrer', interview with Laurent Rigoulet and Olivier Séguret, *Libération*, 14 May.
—— (1999a), 'Interview FNAC' with Pierre-Andre Boutang, CanalWeb, 15 May.
   Available online at: *www.patoche.org/carax/interviews/fnac.htm*
Cardinal, Serge (1997), 'L'espace dissonant. A propos d'un segment du film *Boy Meets Girl*', *Cinemas* 5:3 (*Cinelekta 1*), 77–98.
Chévrie, Marc (1984), '*Boy Meets Girl* de Leos Carax', *Cahiers du Cinéma*, no. 360, June, 73.
—— (1986), 'Introduction' in 'La beauté en révolte', Carax (1986), 24.
Chion, Michel, (1982), *La Voix au Cinéma*, Paris, Editions *Cahiers du Cinéma*.
*Cinergon* (2001), *No. 11 Special Issue 'Cosmologie'.*
Daly, Fergus (1999), 'Alex in the City', *Film West* 34, 30–1.
   Available online at: *www.iol.ie/~galfilm/filmwest/34carax.htm*
Daney, Serge (1982), '*One from the Heart*', *Libération*, 29 September.
   Available online at *http://home.earthlink.net/~steevee/daney_one.htm*
—— (1983), '*L'Enfant Secret*', *Libération*, 19 February.
—— (1984), 'Libé meets Carax', *Libération*, 17 May.
   Available online at: *www.liberation.fr/cinema/cine25/carax.html*
Darke, Chris (1993), 'Rupture, continuity and diversifiation: *Cahiers du cinéma* in the 1980s', *Screen* 34:4, 362–79.
Deleuze, Gilles ([1962] 1983), *Nietzsche and Philosophy*, London, Athlone Press.
—— (1969) *Logique du sens*, Paris, Minuit.
—— (1983), *Cinéma 1. L'Image-mouvement*, Paris, Minuit.
—— (1984), Introduction to the English edition, *Kant's Critical Philosophy* (1963), London, Athlone Press.
—— (1985), *Cinéma 2. L'Image-temps*, Paris, Minuit.
—— (1986), *Cinema 1: The Movement-Image*, trans. Hugh Tomlinson and Barbara Haberjam, London, Athlone.
—— (1988), *Le Pli: Leibniz et le baroque*, Paris, Minuit.
—— (1989), *Cinema 2: The Time-Image*, trans. Hugh Tomlinson and Robert Galeta, London, Athlone Press.
—— (1990), *The Logic of Sense*, trans. Mark Lester with Charles Stivale, New York, Columbia University Press.

—— (1993), *The Fold: Leibniz and the Baroque*, trans. Tom Conley, London, Athlone.

—— (1993a), 'Sur quatre formules poétiques qui pourraient résumer la philosophie kantienne', in *Critique et clinique*, Paris, Minuit.

Deleuze, Gilles and Félix Guattari (1980), *Mille Plateaux. Capitalisme et schizophrénie*, Paris, Minuit.

—— (1987), *A Thousand Plateaus*, trans. Brian Massumi, London, Athlone.

—— (1991), *Qu'est-ce que la philosophie?*, Paris, Minuit.

—— (1994), *What is Philosophy?*, trans. Graham Burchell and Hugh Tomlinson, London, Verso.

Delorme, Stéphane (2000), 'Désaccord majeur (quatre films de Philippe Garrel)', in Nicole Brenez and Christian Lebat eds, *Jeune, dure et pure! Une histoire du cinéma expérimental en France*, Paris–Milan, Cinemathèque Francaise/Mazzotta.

Douchet, Jean (1989), 'La rue et le studio', *Cahiers du Cinéma*, no. 419/420, May–June.

—— (1995), 'Le visage comme révélation' in Jacques Aumont ed., *L'invention de la figure humaine. Le cinéma: l'humain et l'inhumain*. Paris, Cinémathèque française/Yellow Now.

Dowd, Garin (1998), 'Nomadology: reading the Beckettian baroque', *Journal of Beckett Studies* 8:1, 15–50.

Forbes, Jill (1992), *The Cinema in France: After the New Wave*, London, Macmillan.

Foucault, Michel (1982), 'La pensée, l'émotion', in *Duane Michals: Photographies de 1958 à 1982*, Paris, Musée d'Art Moderne de la Ville de Paris.

Frappat, Hélène (2001), *Jacques Rivette, secret compris*, Paris, Editions Cahiers du Cinéma.

French, Philip (2002) *Observer*, 6 January.

Frodon, Jean-Michel (1995), *L'Age moderne du cinéma français: De la Nouvelle Vague à nos jours*, Paris, Flammarion.

Godard, Jean-Luc [1958] (1972), *Godard on Godard* (ed. Tom Milne), London, Secker & Warburg.

Gordon, Robert S. (1996), *Pasolini: Forms of Subjectivity*, Oxford, Clarendon Press.

Hocquenghem, Guy and René Schérer (1986), *L'Ame atomique: pour une esthétique d'ère nucléaire*, Paris, Albin Michel.

Huysmans, J.-K., *A Rebours* [1884] (1981), Paris, Imprimerie nationale.

— (1969), *Against the Grain*, trans. Havelock Ellis, New York, Dover.

Kael, Pauline (1975), *When the Lights go Down*, Rinehart and Winston.

—— (1987), *State of the Art*, Marion Boyers/Rogers.

Kierkegaard, Søren (1989), *Sickness unto Death*, Harmondsworth, Penguin.

Lacan, Jacques (1975), *Séminaire XX. Encore*, Paris, Seuil.

Lacotte, Suzanne Heme de (2001), *Deleuze: Philosophie et Cinéma*, Paris, L'Harmattan.

Martin, Adrian (2001), 'Perhaps', *Senses of Cinema* 13 (*www.sensesofcinema.com*).

—— (2001a), 'Gardens of stone: Philippe Garrel's *L'Enfant Secret*', *Senses of Cinema* 15 (*www.sensesofcinema.com*).

—— (2001b), 'The ever-tested limit', in Stuart Koop ed., *Value Added Goods*, Melbourne, Centre for Contemporary Photography.

Martin, Adrian and Christopher Tuckfield (1993), 'Never one space: the cinema of Raoul Ruiz', *Cinema Papers* (Australia) 93.

Mazabrard, Collette (1989), 'Leos Carax', in '80 Cinéastes des Années 80', *Cahiers du Cinéma*, no. 419–20, May–June, 43–9.

Monaco, James (1976), *The New Wave*, Oxford, Oxford University Press.

Narboni, Jean (1983), 'Manèges', *Cahiers du Cinéma*, no. 353, November, 53–5.

—— (1977), 'La quatrième personne singulière', *Cahiers du Cinéma*, no. 276, April, 5–13.

Nietzsche, Friedrich ([1892] 1969), *Thus Spoke Zarathustra*, Harmondsworth, Penguin.

Noguez, Dominique (1977), *Le Cinéma autrement*, Paris, 10/18.

Ochiva, Dan and Jared Rapfogel, 'Lost in the funhouse: interview with Jacques Rivette', *Cinema Scope* 8 2001.
    Available at: *http://insound.com/zinestand/cscope/feature.cfm?aid=9008*; accessed 31 December 2001.

Philippon, Alain (1986), 'Sur la terre comme au ciel', *Cahiers du Cinéma*, no. 389, November, 20–3.

Powrie, Phil (2001), *Jean-Jacques Beineix*, Manchester, Manchester University Press.

Rajchman, John (1998), *Constructions*, MA, MIT.

Revault d'Allonnes, Fabrice (1986), 'Le grand-méchant look' and 'Céline, Cocteau, Carax', *Cinema 86*, 4.

—— (1991), *La Lumière au cinéma*, Paris, Editions Cahiers du Cinéma.

Rivette, Jacques ([1973] 1977), 'Interview on *Out One*' and 'For the shooting of *Les Filles du Feu*' in Jonathan Rosenbaum ed., *Rivette: Texts and Interviews*, London, BFI.

Rohdie, Sam (1990), *Antonioni*, London, BFI.

Rosenbaum, Jonathan (1994), 'Leos Carax: the problem with poetry', *Film Comment* May–June, 12–18, 22–3.

—— (1977) ed., *Jacques Rivette: Texts and Interviews*, London, BFI.

Rousset, Jean (1953), *La Littérature de l'âge baroque en France: Circé et le paon*, Paris, Editions José Corti.

Ruiz, Raoul (1993), 'Interview with Laleen Jayamanne', *Agenda* 30/31, 51–3.

—— (1987), ' Entretien avec Raoul Ruiz', Interview with Fabrice Revault d'Allonnes and Christine Buci-Glucksmann, in Buci Glucksmann and Revault d'Allonnes (1987).

Russell, David (1989–90), 'Two or three things we know about Beineix', *Sight and Sound* 59:1, 42–7.

Sarduy, Severo (1975 and 1991), *Barroco*, Paris, Seuil.

Serres, Michel (1982), 'Lucretius: science and religion', *Hermes: Literature, Science, Philosophy*, in Josué V. Harari and David F. Bell eds, pp. 98–124.

Thomson, David (1994), 3rd edition, *A Biographical Dictionary of Film*, New York, Knopf.

Trias, Jean-Philippe (2001), 'Cosmologie du cinéma: introduction', *Cinergon* 11, 11–19.

Viano, Maurizio (1993), *A Certain Realism: Making use of Pasolini's Film Theory and Practice*, London, University of California Press.

Waugh, Katherine and Fergus Daly (1995), 'Samuel Beckett's *Film*', *Film West* 20, 22–4.

Wölfflin, Heinrich (1950), *Principles of Art History*, trans. M. D. Hottinger, New York, Dover.

# 2

# Feux d'artifice: Les Amants du Pont-Neuf and the spectacle of vagrancy

[D]o not allegory and the uncanny bring into play the same procedures: ambivalence, the double, the organic and non-organic, living/artificial body, fixation on sight and the anxiety of losing it, and above all dread of the fragmented body? (Buci-Glucksmann [1984] 1994: 166)[1]

Et n'oublions pas que si Carax donne parfois l'impression de faire un peu trop de cinéma dans ces films, c'est sans doute qu'il doit en faire à la place de tous les réalisateurs de sa génération qui n'en font pas assez. (Sabouraud 1991: 14)[2]

Between the completion of *Mauvais Sang* and the start of his next project Carax appeared in his second screen role, this time taking the part of Edgar in Godard's *King Lear* (1987). The circumstances whereby Godard came to sign a contract with the film's Hollywood producers, Golan and Globus of Cannon, have since become the stuff of legend, as has the story of how Norman Mailer stormed off the shoot and the much-heralded involvement of Woody Allen as the Fool came to be limited to a few minutes delivered to camera in the final cut. Of the roles taken by well-known non-actors (Mailer) or of actors also associated with other directorial projects (Allen) in the film – the fame attached to whose names was deemed crucial by the producers – the role of the lesser-known Carax as Edgar is, paradoxically, the most integral. *King Lear* sees Carax playing Edgar to Godard's Professor

---

1 In *Les Amants*, there is a concern for vision and an anxiety about losing it, as well as a focus on the theme of self-mutilation.
2 'And let us not forget that if Carax sometimes gives the impression of overdoing cinema in his films, it is doubtless that he must do so in place of all the directors who don't do enough of it.'

Pluggy, the Lear role being shared between the latter character and Burgess Meredith in the guise of one Don Learo as scripted – the film suggests – by Norman Mailer. Carax here also takes a role that evokes in certain respects a younger variant or double of Godard. For, the latter, here as Pluggy–Lear, and elsewhere in his roles in his other films of the 1980s, often goes the way of fools (the burlesque elements of *Soigne ta droite* and *Prénom Carmen* in particular spring to mind). Indeed Godard and Carax share a fondness for burlesque, for Chaplin and Keaton. Where Godard's character in *Soigne ta droite* carries the reels of film around, exchanging them in the end for a bauble as he lies face down at the airport, Carax, as Edgar, having fished one half of a film can out of the river, hits himself on the head with it by way of attempting to understand it. This, then, is Carax as 'fool' of cinema, but in the same sense as Lear–Godard, 'poor fool' being a typically Shakespearean fond address from parent to child. In more concrete terms, the film features a scene in which Carax 'stands in' for Godard by occupying a position on screen which for anyone familiar with Godard's *Histoire(s) du cinéma* project, must immediately call to mind the stance often adopted by Godard himself, in front of, or beside or partly obscuring a projected image or sequence of images.

But Carax–Edgar is also here a son of fire – presaging the Heraclitean aspects of Alex in *Les Amants du Pont-Neuf*. He collects kindling, and is charged with the task of carrying the rifle and – crucially – with passing the sparkler advocated by Pluggy to Cordelia (Molly Ringwald). Carax holds vigil at the entrance to a cinema in a post-Chernobyl era in which, according to the film, cinema must be 'excavated' and reconstructed, while in the absence both of film to be screened and the entire support structure of the film industry, no films are projected. None aside that is from Professor Pluggy's demonstration model comprising a shoebox with two holes and a sparkler (he rejects the lightbulb with which it is initially furnished). In this *mise en abyme*, Carax takes the role of usher, while Julie Delpy – from Carax's own *Mauvais Sang* – as Virginie (both as in Virginia Woolf and as in Virginia tobacco) sells the cigarettes.

The role is rich in metaphorical suggestion of the sort that the analysis in Chapter 1 was keen to take its distance. If *King Lear* shows us Carax as guardian of Godard's heritage, but also as slave to that weighty bequeath, it has been argued that Carax already goes a long way towards destabilising such a reading. However, the *King Lear* role does represent a distinct metaphorical *mise en abyme* of Carax's career. In the vestiges of cinema sequence, something of the impossibility of what Carax himself would attempt in *Les Amants* is poignantly indicated. In the miniature fireworks with which Godard as Pluggy is here content, sparklers are apparently all that remains of the projection that was once cinema. Carax himself, as director, would of course attempt to 'resurrect' cinema with a somewhat more expensive arsenal of pyrotechnical weaponry, and within a purged and highly symbolic space – Paris's Pont-Neuf.

Carax's spectacular and notoriously overbudget film of 1990 has tended in many accounts to be read as an allegory of social exclusion, and as part of the 'return to the real' (understood in a loose sense which includes both a higher degree of realism and a focus on reality as opposed to simulacra) which characterises many new French films of the 1990s including films by Zonca and Guédiguian, and latterly Dumont and Noé. In such analyses, the 'real' functions as a referent which enables, for instance, the simultaneously enclosed and excluded characters on the bridge to become a site of critique and contestation, and thereby to embody a rejection of the spectacular communal celebrations of the bicentennial of the revolution; that is they are both there to confront the spectacle with a debilitating and sapping counterflow.[3] When the celebrations are over, the city remains abundantly lit, and it is within this 'set' that the central characters perform their own joyous, but nonetheless parodic, celebrations. To a certain extent such a reading is entirely unproblematic; however, it would be overhasty to leap from this to the quite distinct assertion that in this film Carax announces by means of the alleged return to the real, his rejection of the *cinéma du look*, and of all of the qualities conveniently placed under the latter umbrella term. It must be remembered, after all, that the *cinéma du look* was an invention of the press, and, moreover, as Chapter 1 has argued, Carax already had marked his distance from the other directors allegedly identified by the term.

Indeed, as this chapter will propose, the haste with which the film has been categorised and in certain quarters thereby dismissed,

3 In an analysis which in many respects we endorse, Martine Beugnet (2000) uses the term allegory in this context. However, in her attention to the nuances of the film's interrogation of the frontiers of documentary and fiction, her study is exempt from the criticism which follows.

combined with the spectacular budget catastrophe and the myths developed around the on-set events, contributed to a widespread misunderstanding of the film, as well as to a certain blindness among critics as to the merits. The tendency to categorise this exorbitant film in part obscures its force and importance. Critical reappraisal, however, is well underway, for example in the 2000 assessment by Beugnet which extols the film as a crucial moment in French cinema of the 1990s. Beugnet signals Carax's markedly alternative vision to that of Beineix (and in particular *37,2° le Matin/Betty Blue*) and Patrice Leconte, mentioning in particular the tendency of these two directors towards the reification and objectification of (especially) the female body (Beugnet 2000: 175, 180).

However, the question of the status of the 'real' remains in some sense the enduring critical focal point for reflection on the film. What, one has to ask, however, is 'the real' as it has peppered debate about the film?[4] In one of the commonplace categorisations, the desire to situate the film can be traced to two principal causes: its *cinéma vérité*-style opening sequence suggests a commitment to verisimilitude and a refusal of artifice on the one hand (i.e. a 'realism' deriving mainly from the fact that genuine down-and-outs are captured on film), while the theme of homelessness gestures towards the traditions of naturalism (see Chapter 3), social and poetic realism on the other. The combination, then, paves the way for an entirely symbolic reading of the film to emerge, within which it is battened on to the supposed real; becoming its revealer (or, in the view of some, its betrayer, Carax being berated in some quarters for the crime of aestheticising poverty and homelessness). Part of the concern of this chapter is to offer an alternative to straightforwardly symbolic readings of the film by means of situating it within the context of those philosophical and aesthetic debates with which it maintains continuity. However, before broaching these issues in more detail, it is appropriate to turn to another narrative – that which recounts the troubled production that lies behind the film.

4 Beugnet displays the distance she would take from the hasty correlation of the film's 'realism' and the so-called return to the real, by insisting that the exclusion of Alex and Michèle is not only to be understood in terms of the separation of the couple from social normativity, but also from the normativity one might associate with cinema conventions (Beugnet 2000: 173).

## The troubled production

The view of Jean-Michel Frodon is that in order to up the stakes and to keep ahead of the other filmmakers of his generation, Carax needed to call into his service increasingly complex and costly arrangements, symbolised most comprehensively – if falteringly – in his view in the grandeur and folly of *Les Amants du Pont-Neuf*. The themes of expenditure and failure have invited much metaphorical reflection among critics. Stuart Klawans describes the film as 'an absurd imposture, a priceless gift' (Klawans 1999), whereas Jousse asserts that in being centrally concerned with the logic of *dépense* the film should be championed for managing – unlike many other films – to spend a lot of money without nullifying the film itself (Jousse 1991: 22). 'Il y a quelque chose de somptuaire dans *Les Amants du Pont-Neuf*, comme un excès impossible à combler, qui serait le sujet paradoxal du film' (Jousse 1991: 22, a point expanded upon below).[5] For Guy Austin, it is the inadvertent relocation of the film from Paris to an artificial set that is one of the contributing factors to its achievement, enhancing as it does the 'interplay between realism and artifice which runs throughout *Les Amants du Pont-Neuf*' (Austin 1996: 133).

In starting with a budget of 32 million francs, *Les Amants* was expensive (at around double the average for a film in that year – 1988) although hardly excessive. Key to Carax's plan was to be able to film on the Pont-Neuf while the latter was closed for repairs. However having obtained the permission of the municipal authorities to film on the bridge from 18 July (Prédal gives 15 July) to 15 August, Lavant seriously injured his hand and could no longer perform the many acrobatic feats required of him by the script. As Carax filled the time shooting scenes not set on the bridge, nor requiring a fully operational Lavant, work on a replica of the Pont-Neuf continued in a reservoir outside Montpellier. After a period, however, due to the increasing risk of the terminal collapse, not only of the set, but of the entire project, the insurance company refused to continue to prop up the imperilled project. At the time of their withdrawal of support just twenty-five minutes of salvageable footage existed.

The resurrection of the project – which came in June 1989 – was short-lived. The construction work on the replica had deteriorated and

---

5 'There is something sumptuary in *Les Amants du Pont-Neuf*, like an excess that is impossible to measure, and which would be the paradoxical subject of the film.'

had to be started from scratch. The duo who had bailed out the project, the Swiss financier Francis Van Buren along with the producer Philippe Vignet, under the name Pari-à-deux, injected 18 million francs into the film (now running at a cost of 80 million francs), and their investment succeeded in taking the total of usable footage to 40 minutes. The latter, however, it was some compensation, at least included the key scenes shot during the bicentennial parade – scenes which it would have been prohibitively expensive to replicate had they not been deemed successful.

In Frodon's account, the film polarised those with a vested interest in film in France; it especially divided those who saw Carax as symbol of a maligned *cinéma d'auteur* with its often enlarged sense of importance regarding personal vision, from those who championed the excess with which the project had become inadvertently associated. However, in defiant mode, upon its release, Strauss, writing in *Cahiers*, drew attention to the risible accountancy whereby one might judge the quality against the price, via, emblematically for him the question 'Alors, est-ce qu'on voit que c'est un faux Pont-Neuf?' (Strauss 1991: 24). As Chapter 1 has shown, the status of the false in Carax is such that it renders the question irrelevant:

> pour moi, que je filme un vrai clochard perdu dans ses pensées ou un couple de faux clochards qui dansent sur un faux pont sous les feux d'artifice, le regard est le même. C'est le sentiment qui change, sentiment de l'irrémédiable ou sentiment de l'inespéré. (Carax 1991a)[6]

The figure who would later emerge with the further 80 million francs required to salvage the project and complete the film, Christian Fechner, would, it transpired, ultimately alienate Carax by trying to impose an uplifting ending, eliding the suicide for Michèle envisaged by Carax. The reason for this elision is muddied by the many conflicting accounts of the events that led to its final version being included. For Frodon, it is a clear case of Carax being held to ransom by his producer (Frodon 1995: 792). However, in interviews, both Carax and Juliette Binoche attribute the powers of persuasion to Binoche rather than to the producer.

6 'for me it's the same whether I film a tramp lost in his thoughts or a couple of fake tramps dancing on a false bridge beneath fireworks – the gaze is the same. It is the feeling which changes, a feeling of the irredeemable or a feeling of what you dare not hope for.'

As Frodon reads it, in his diagnostic manner, the film self-reflexively withdraws from the realism of the Nanterre sequence into the realm of cinema proper. Cinema is thereby curled up on itself, folded in an implacable and abyssal torture of self-reflection. It interrogates itself at one level via characterisation. The three types who populate the bridge: a female artist who is going blind (destined to be cut off in the *future* from sight), a burlesque fire-eater (emblem of a cinematic *past*) and a theatre director (the profession of Klaus-Michael Grüber gestures towards an alternative to cinema) are for Frodon three symbols of cinema, but of a moribund cinema (Frodon 1995: 792). What takes place on the bridge is complete withdrawal, in Frodon's view, into an autistic universe. All lines of communication are broken aside from those leading to Vigo – even this one is rendered uncertain given the fact that the *Atalante* reference does not accurately reflect its appropriate register in Carax's planned ending. For Frodon, then, the film is symbolic not so much of the real, as it is a symbol of a necessary disaffection; it is a work of mourning and melancholia.

## Synopsis

The film opens with two startling sequences: in the first of these, Michèle (Binoche) and Alex (Lavant) encounter each other on the street. He staggers drunkenly in the middle of the boulevard de Sébastopol; she walks in a dazed state. When Alex eventually falls, he begins to rub his forehead on the tarmac. A car with two amorous occupants (seen only from behind) approaches at speed. Alex's ankle bears the full force of the car as it speeds over his protruding leg. The moment is registered by Michèle who happens to be passing at the same time in the opposite direction to the trajectory of the car. She approaches the inert Alex and thinks him dead. At this point the bus arrives to round up the homeless – of which Alex is one – and transport them to a shelter in Nanterre. Alex, whose first visit to the shelter it clearly is not – the *bleus* immediately recognise him – is carried on board and thrown in the corner of the packed vehicle.

At the shelter, Lavant is dragged naked to the shower where he is seen to languish abjectly sprawled on the tiles. Next morning at the hospital where his broken ankle is attended to, another homeless patient urges Alex to consider his options, to come with him to the south of France, but, above all, to reflect well before he acts. All that Alex can utter in response to his interlocutor is that he needs to return to the bridge. The film cuts to the bridge. The word 'Danger' appears on screen in a close-up of the fence and barrier closing off the bridge. In a mid-distance aerial shot, Alex negotiates his approach; another close-up displays the sign announcing the purpose and duration of the repairs which having begun in 1989 are due to terminate in 1991. Despite his injury, Alex swings around the fence and hobbles towards another dishevelled figure. This is Hans – another *clochard* who has in his keep a store of downers which he dispenses in order to enable Alex to sleep. Alex is informed by Hans that another man has taken his patch. Alex investigates only to discover that the stranger is not a man, but a woman wearing an eyepatch. The viewer recognises this as the woman who the night before had attempted to aid Alex after the accident on the boulevard de Sébastopol. Alex, however, being unconscious at the time, does not recognise her. While she sleeps, he looks through her portfolio of sketches. He runs off in order to wash himself and returns intent to make an impression on the visitor, only to witness Hans expelling the stranger from the bridge. Clearly in fear of the authority represented by Hans, Alex tentatively pursues her. Unobserved by Michèle, he unfastens the portfolio so that the drawings it contains drop to the ground. Alex thus finds a way to motivate his question, based on his research of the night before: is one of these drawings not a portrait of him? He asks to keep the portrait. After initially refusing, she offers him the deal: in return for sitting for a new portrait, she will give him the drawing. When Michèle faints and the work in progress falls into the Seine, Alex can find out a little more about the interloper. In her box of paints and artist's materials he finds an envelope addressed to Michèle Stalens. The envelope gives her an address in Saint Cloud, near the Bois de Boulogne

Alex visits the address and breaks in to startle Michèle's sister. Following an acrobatic exit, he returns to the bridge. He steals a fish from the market and he and Michèle eat it raw back on the bridge. He follows Michèle in the metro. She hears a cello in the station and rushes desperately to locate its source, whom she takes to be Julien, a former lover – who at any rate refuses to see Michèle when she attempts to visit him. Alex, who at this point has adopted the guardian/censor role played on the bridge by Hans, threatens the cellist who departs the scene just in time for Michèle to miss him. Michèle and Hans visit the Louvre by night to view a Rembrandt self-portrait by candlelight. They embrace and (it is implied) have sex off-screen. Alex and Michèle drug cafe habituées with the Alcyon capsules stolen from Hans's supply and steal their wallets. Troubled by the alteration which financial independence may cause in their relationship, Alex intentionally knocks the box containing their profits over the side of the bridge. Michèle suggests they go to one of the 14 July *bals*, but Alex insists they will see things better from the bridge. They get drunk together and, while the fireworks go on all around them, the two lovers dance across the bridge. Head-butting a dozing police officer Alex paves the way for a thrilling water-skiing escapade, with Michèle on the skis and Alex at the helm. She falls in, while he leaps from the moving boat to help her to shore. They return to the bridge to sleep. Alex uncouples an electrical connection to help her sleep, creating darkness on the bridge and turning off the lights of the Samaritaine building. On the radio that Alex has given to Michèle to give her news of the world beyond the bridge without having to leave it, she hears a missing person announcement concerning her. A poster campaign sees her face adorn every available wall. Alex attempts to destroy the posters; in the process he sets fire to a billposter. Michèle returns to her family and enters into a relationship with her doctor, while Alex goes to prison for three years. In prison, he has a hand amputated (he had earlier shot off a finger), while in the outside world Michèle is cured of her disease. On Christmas Eve the two lovers are reunited, in the middle of the traffic, on a snowy and now fully operational Pont-Neuf. Michèle informs Alex of the impossibility of their becoming involved again. Alex pushes her over the wall and follows her into the water. They resurface and get on board a barge helmed by an elderly couple. The barge with a cargo of sand is heading for Le Havre.

## The 'Nanterre sequence'

The popular success of the Dogme 95 manifesto rekindled debate in the second half of the 1990s concerning hand-held camera techniques and the use of natural light, live sound and the dismantling of a certain stratum of cinematic artifice to which such devices contribute. While such techniques are new to the Caraxian filmic world, there is a certain continuity at the outset marking the transition from *Mauvais Sang* to the synechdocal space of the bridge of *Les Amants du Pont-Neuf*. *Mauvais Sang* features several dazzling shots in a tunnel under La Défense; one in particular sees Alex turn around on the motorcycle to shoot a pursuing police officer. Of course Alex is heading towards his death at this point, sitting behind Lise as angel and messenger. In his third incarnation, Alex is announced by a camera this time descending into a tunnel. The camera follows the route out of the tunnel and then adds a tracking shot that takes us back to the opening sequence of *Boy Meets Girl*. We are decidedly in Carax's world.

Carax announces his two characters not by means of a direct shot, but by their being reflected in the rear-view and side mirrors of the car that swerves to avoid them in two separate manoeuvres, the same car – a taxi, appropriately – which has been both the viewer's and the camera's vehicle into the filmed space. This tentative relation between camera and characters establishes a world at a remove, which one cannot immediately and directly access.

The remarkable documentary-style sequence featuring Lavant amid the real homeless people on the bus and in the Nanterre shelter is unflinching in detailing the injured, malnourished, diseased bodies in close up. In the supplement which Carax edited for *Cahiers* in the form of a special number 'hors série' he includes photographs of gangrened limbs of several homeless people accumulated during the research for the film (Carax 1991). Genuine collapses of drunks and violent exchanges are filmed in ambient light and reproduced on screen. The murky light of this sequence is abruptly contrasted with the next sequence in the hospital in the first shot of which we see the plaster cast on Alex's ankle being finished off in pristine white. The *mise en scène* elaborates by showing, in the following shot, Alex being escorted by a white-clad fellow homeless patient (a non-actor whom Carax said showed remarkable professionalism, even doing his own overdubbing) along the corridor of the hospital. But, significantly in this film where one is dealing with a restricted range of choices, and where the characters mostly have to improvise within the confines placed around them by multiple hardships, there is little sense of what these options might be. That Dan is employing the rhetorical structures of reasoned argument, only serves to underline the unbridgeable distance between the world of Alex and that of the society within which choice and full agency do have a forum.

## Chance and non-derived images

In continuity with the cosmic forces animating the first two features, in this film chance is the force whereby the two lovers meet, literally by accident. However, Carax also retains that aspect of his early characters that keeps them under the threshold of full volitional subjectivity, in so far as the encounter is between two somnambulants who are only barely conscious of the encounter having taken place. This inability to register the meaning of what happens is indeed perhaps the central thematic concern of the film – it is complementary to and supplementary of the motif of *amour fou* as such – with Michèle going blind to begin with and Alex perpetually drugged or inebriated.[7] Carax, then, is interested in chance in two complementary ways: as the engine of the film's narrative, and as sustained by characters incapable of full conscious volition and perception. Of course the lack of a finished script, and the fact that Carax only gave the actors their lines on the day of shooting (in the manner of Godard) is further evidence of the importance of the contingent to his vision of cinema. More generally, however, it also signals a broad commitment to narrative and image forms not constrained by rationality or by a logic of strict causality. When Alex accidentally opens Michèle's paintbox it reveals not only her identity and address but also a loaded pistol. The pistol gives us on the one hand, *and in the same hand*, the girl and the gun, the ingredients of cinema according to Godard, but it is, in the view of Frédéric Strauss, more significant than that. In playing its strange anti-role in the film, it points up Carax's resistance toward too obvious scenarios (murder), and yet it does so by being at the centre, but not the *logically causal* generative centre of several scenes. When it does take a generative role in the narrative – in the scene where Michèle shoots Julien through the peep-hole of his apartment door – the incident is revealed to have taken place in a nightmare. It is by having Alex count the bullets in the magazine that Michèle proves to herself that it *was* only a nightmare – or, within the film as a whole, a spectre of another more predictable scenario. Taking up the other strand of Strauss's argument regarding the pistol, it is possible to see in the latter a metaphor for the film's weaknesses. The sights of the pistol are restricted, just as the confines of the bridge seal a reduced

7 Alex sees the moment at which she saw him on the street (she drew from memory, however).

space of engagement. If the pistol does not act other than in this circumscribed void, perhaps Carax's film occupies a similarly restricted space, and Carax remains enfolded in a 'Repli stratégique sur sa propre solitude dans un dialogue de sourds' ('Strategic folding up in his own solitude in a dialogue of the deaf', Strauss 1991a: 22). Strauss, however, would not deny that behind this criticism – and he has much to say that is affirmative too – lies a prescriptive assumption about what cinema should attempt to be. However, what Carax is interested in pursuing by means of these strategies is what Maurizio Grande has called '*images non-dérivées*' ('non-derived images', Grande 1997: 297). They are not so much embedded in a hermetic space as cast adrift of necessity in a *dérive*, wandering, fugue or flight. This for Deleuze is an essential characteristic of the new type of character required by the cinema of the 'time-image':

> C'est parce que ce qui leur arrive ne leur appartient pas, ne les concerne qu'à moitié, qu'ils savent dégager de l'événement la part irréductible à ce qui arrive: cette part d'inépuisable possibilité qui constitue l'insupportable, l'intolérable, la part du visionnaire. (Deleuze 1989: 31)[8]

The question of belonging also gives rise to that of attribution. To whom is the image to be attributed? Carax, then, in this film, continues to explore the possibility of a resistance specific to the image, as will now be suggested with reference to several key scenes.

## Observations on key scenes

### The fire-eating scene

*Cahiers du Cinéma* was generally full of praise for Carax's third feature. For Vincent Ostria, Carax in *Les Amant du Pont-Neuf* reveals himself to be 'le meilleur filmeur actuel du cinéma français' ('currently the best shot-maker in French cinema', 1991: 23). This is how another

---

8 'It is because what happens to them does not belong to theme and only half-concerns them, because they know how to extract from the event the part that cannot be reduced to what happens: that part of the inexhaustible possibility that constitutes the unbearable, the intolerable, the visionary's part' (Deleuze 1989: 19–20).

*Cahiers* critic describes the meeting of technique and expression in the fire-eating scene:

> Plans flashant des gerbes de feu, fluidité des mouvements de la caméra en miroir des acrobaties d'Alex, chaleurs du visage de Juliette Binoche, le montage d'une rare intensité émotive nous transporte ici au plus près d'un cinéma ou l'émotion c'est le mouvement même. (Niney 1991: 25)[9]

What the scene entails is more a question of intensity – an abstract manifestation of intensity – than of a close-up in which the actor *expresses* emotion. It is, then, a question of the bodies of the characters as given in speeds and vectors, rather than as necessarily expressive of emotion or sensation happening to them as subjects, or as representations of subjects. The rapidity of the flames, moreover, is echoed in the rapidity of the editing. In a remarkable piece of montage the flash of flame – from Alex's unofficial 'fireworks' – fills the screen with white light and is segued with a shot of open sky into which three jets – part of the *official* celebrations – fly dispensing the tricolour in the form of their vapour trails.

## The parade montage sequence

In a scene that acts as a variation on the fire-eating scene, this time it is Michèle who is in motion. Her movements are more direct than those which Alex must adopt owing to his damaged ankle and need for a crutch (for Beugnet, Alex is at times a latter-day Quasimodo (Beugnet 2000: 161)). Hence the camera follows her in a tracking shot. Binoche is seen running behind (but in the opposite direction to) an intermittent and mobile wall of bodies participating in the bicentennial parade. The appearance of the actor's body on screen is fragmented by the intervening masses of regimented bodies. But the sequence also features rapid montage which brings Alex into the frame. In the intercut shots, he is on the bridge drinking. As the montage gives us rapidly sequenced shots of the parade, Michèle and Alex, the camera gets progressively, in rapid zooms, closer to Alex. In

---

9 'Rapid rotational shots of sparks of fire, fluidity of camera movements mirroring Alex's acrobatics, the warmth on the face of Juliette Binoche, montage of a rare emotive intensity where emotion is movement itself.' See also our comments in Chapter 1 in this volume.

the last of these shots, Michèle also enters the frame and grabs his wine bottle from him, declaring breathlessly that she is thirsty too. The sequence then is notable for the stress placed on speed, a familiar Carax concern from *Mauvais Sang*. As Ostria puts it, it is a 'film admirablement rythmé. Et superbement mônté' ('an admirably paced and superbly edited film', Ostria 1991: 24).

## The passing *bateau mouche* scene

In his analysis of the embrace scene on the Square du Vert Gallant, Thierry Oudart notes how the lovers' bodies are illuminated by the lights of the passing *bateaux mouches*. The bodies are then filmed in an overexposed sequence, and are in fact almost elided by the flash of white. As the boat passes, the position of the bodies as projected in shadow also changes. For Oudart, Carax here shows an affinity with 'la pensée moderne selon laquelle toute translation produit une transformation, tout mouvement renvoyant à un changement dans la matière' (Oudart 1995).[10] The scene confirms, through its synechdocal role, that the eye as metaphor is omnipresent (if not always all seeing) in *Les Amants*, which fact prompts him (and he is not the only critic to do so) to quote Derrida: 'L'expérience du regard voue à l'aveuglement'.[11] The question of the centrality of vision in *Les Amants* will be taken up again below, but, of course, it is worth noting – as did Chapter 1 – the pre-eminent position of the eye in the Baroque. It is in this context that some historical contextualisation of the fireworks in the film is demanded.

## The Baroque economy of *les feux d'artifice*

In the historical context of their first flourishing, fireworks served to provide a spectacular and transient symbol of the eminence and splendour of the monarch who was responsible for their taking place. On the one hand they served to display the surplus wealth of those presiding – a surplus which is converted into a transient and literally

---

10  'modern thought according to which all translation produces a transformation, all movement harking back to an alteration in matter.'

11  'The experience of the gaze is dedicated to blindness.' See Derrida (1990).

wasteful display of artifice (*feux d'artifice*). As such, the brief but spectacular display becomes a signifier of the distance between the plebeian people and the monarch or court, while also being a short-lived and evanescent focal point for their attention during the *fête* or *fiesta* (see Maravall [1975] 1986: 246–7). For José Maravall, there was also a philosophical dimension to fireworks in this historical context: 'With their illumination, the arts of fire were the answer to the zeal to replace night with day, overcoming the night's obscurity by means of pure human artifice' (Maravall [1975] 1986: 247). Of course this philosophical element, allied to the spectacle of court power, was also in the end political: 'This capacity to transform the order of the universe, however fleeting it might have been, showed overwhelmingly the greatness of whoever had so much power over natural and human resources as to achieve such effects' (Maravall [1975] 1986: 247). This is the penultimate sentence of Maravall's book on the Baroque. It ends not with politics but with a description of the *performance* of a *simulacrum* of political power.

Carax's film is implicated in a series of questions attached to those above, albeit no longer within the period of the historical Baroque. For a start, the importance of the fireworks sequence cannot be under-estimated. Carax makes it the centrepiece of the film. However, it is already the showpiece of the bicentennial celebrations in Paris (even if Carax ends up having to reproduce the fireworks elsewhere). That is, it was originally Carax's intention to harness the fireworks that were scheduled to take place in Paris in July 1989 and to parasite them by means of his own filming. The fireworks as they function in the world of the film, then, do have a link to the display of state power, and they do form the focal point of a collective celebration.[12] The difference is that in 1989 fireworks do not produce wonderment (or reinforce subjection) to the same extent as they did in the Baroque era. However, as far as the restricted ambit of the film is concerned, the display has no intending viewers; indeed it has no viewers whatsoever. No one looks at the spectacle: the display is denied the power of

12 The display of state power is evoked also by the parade. Of course the scene where Michèle runs parallel and in a direction opposite to the mass of bodies, horses and tanks is clearly a reference to Godard's use of Eisenhower's visit in *A bout de souffle*. Austin also identifies the intertextual references to Bresson's *Pickpocket* (1959) in the prison sequence and to Truffaut's *Les 400 Coups* (1959) (Austin 1996: 134).

looking at Alex and Michèle and of forming them as citizens. Alex and Michèle celebrate but are cut off from the spectacle and do not actively look at it. Instead they contribute their own fireworks (as Alex has already done in several ways) by shooting the pistol. Theirs is a world from which the centripetal force of baroque public display has been removed. The grand narratives, one might say, adopting a phrase of Jean-François Lyotard, which we have already cited, have given way to micro-narratives: for the display as expression of centrality we get, instead, the display harnessed as accidental backdrop for the performance of mutating and transient subjectivities (in Carax's favoured form, namely dance).

Having placed the opening sequences squarely in the neo-realist tradition, Austin goes on to argue that 'Carax's film also features a nocturnal Parisian fantasy so exaggerated as to at once parody and celebrate the most spectacular offerings of the *cinéma du look*' (Austin 1996: 134). For Austin, the hyperactive oscillation between the poles of neo-realism and fantasy is indicative of the breadth of Carax's achievement here:

> In this context, the waterskiing sequence is both an ironic exaggera-
> tion of the bicentennial fireworks (and of the *cinéma du look*'s reliance
> on the spectacular) and a desperate escape fantasy on the part of the
> protagonists, who have already escaped Paris once for the lyrical
> interlude on the coast. (Austin 1996: 134)

While the first of these assertions is not open to dispute, it is necessary to take issue with the assumption underlying the second, namely that the action needs to be grounded in character motivation in the first place (see the comments on non-derived images above). The sequence begins in a burlesque manner with Binoche letting her weapon (a bottle) fly from her hand as she attempts to render unconscious a river police officer who appears to have revelled too much. The water-skiing itself can be seen as the apogee of the stunts with which Carax inundates his work. There is always an element of the irrational about these turns, which erupt onto the screen and often dissipate in fade-outs or superimpositions (as is the case here) in the manner of fireworks themselves.

## Corporeal resistors in the circuitry of desire

The body in *Les Amants du Pont-Neuf* is conceived of as a site of impedance on a trajectory, as is suggested by the fact that Alex is lame and Michèle is losing her sight. Fire on the other hand flows freely from Alex's mouth, as does wine into the mouths of both Alex and Michèle. The body here is the site of regulation and controlled release – as underlined by the fact that Michèle wants to wait before having sex with Alex. The body in *Les Amants* is the locus of the coagulation of flows (Chapter 3 will have more to say on the body in this respect). Occasionally, these bodies are released from the sumptuary arrangement – as in the coastal idyll where in silhouette Michèle 'pulls' Alex along the shore by his erect penis. But to be released – as far as the logic on the bridge is concerned – is to become quiescent, as does Hans when he falls, without displaying an effort to save himself, into the Seine to drown.

When Michèle is given a last chance to ameliorate her rare eye condition (and rare diseases and obscure unnamed ailments, as we know from *Boy Meets Girl* and *Mauvais Sang*, are something of a recurrent interest for the director) and to be released from the nightmare – as she puts it – of her current predicament, Alex does everything in his power to keep her 'plugged' into the restricted circuit on the bridge. The body for Alex with his heavy burden – discussed in Chapter 1 – must remain a restricted/maimed (and metaphorically fragmented) entity, divorced from its totality. The space beyond the bridge however – space of totality, encompassment – seeps in and contaminates. It transpires that this perhaps has been Hans's fear in respect of Michèle: it is an expression of a wish to keep the frontier with the outside in place. It is also possible that he wishes to keep the bridge pure of sexual desire – she reminds him of his wife, and she later allows him to have sexual contact with her in return for his having helped her see the painting (a Rembrandt self-portrait) by candlelight. To the end of maintaining a certain stability, a strict set of regulations characterises the sumptuary arrangements operative on the bridge. The vagabond-automaton as it takes shape in Hans, it seems, requires stability in order better to swing between the poles of void and plenitude. Too much to drink and there will be no *ampoule* for Alex; Michèle can stay for a few days on condition that Hans does not have to set eyes on her.

## Milieu, centre and totality

Three distinct zones form the setting for the film: bridge, river and métro.[13] As Marc Augé describes them such spaces as métro tunnels are a kind of locus without specificity (Augé 1992; 1995), and yet as he points out the Paris they occur in is at the centre of a thoroughly centralised country. As Augé explains, even the smallest town in France has its 'centre ville' ('town centre') 'où se côtoient les monuments qui symbolisent l'autorité religieuse (l'église), l'autre l'autorité civile (la mairie, la sous-préfecture ou la préfecture dans les villes importantes) (Augé 1992: 84).[14] The central squares come alive on certain dates such as market days or feast days, among which the most notable is, of course, Bastille day on 14 July. On especially prominent celebrations such as the latter, civil and military institutions combine to form a two-headed people–state phylum. It is fitting, then, that Carax chooses to film his third feature on *l'amour fou* in the centre, and surrounded by the elaborate complex of parades, performance and spectacle which greets the bicentennial celebrations. (Of course, the suburb also features as the space to which the *clochards* are rounded up and deposited, the better to enable the display of state pomp and festivity.) However, this particular part of central Paris is cordoned off and in abeyance *as centre*. Carax does not locate his *amour fou* in the clearly and literally liminal space of, say, the first half of Beineix's *37,2° le matin*, nor in an immediately identifiable periphery such as the Nord Pas de Calais which has, in the eyes of some, become the pre-eminent space of exclusion in contemporary French cinema (as filmed in Dumont's *L'Humanité* (2000) for example). If anything, the choice of this paradoxically decentred centre permits Carax's film to stage the dichotomy identified by Verena Andermatt

13 In their respective essays dealing with the films of Carax, Keith Reader and Jonathan Rosenbaum draw attention to the place occupied by them in a long tradition of French filmmakers who have treated Paris as a playground, among them Rivette (*Paris nous appartient* (1959), Godard (*A bout de souffle*), Varda (*Cléo de 5 à 7*), to which list can be added Rivette's *Pont du nord* (1980) and several films made after the publication of the essays in question, among them Rivette's *Haut bas fragile* (1995) and *Va Savoir* (2000), and Assayas's *Irma Vep* (1995). See Reader (1984) and Rosenbaum (1994). On the métro in French cinema, see Berry (2000).

14 'Containing monuments that symbolise religious authority (church or cathedral) and civil authority (town hall, *sous-préfecture* or, in big towns, the *préfecture*' (Augé 1995: 65).

Conley (adapting Michel de Certeau) when she speaks of the dynamic of space of exclusion (or 'ejection') versus space of 'election' (Conley 1996). Indeed the film mimics very closely this dynamic, with Alex first ejected to the shelter and then returning to reformulate the bridge as a site of 'election'.[15]

The loci wherein this reformulation (in instances of what de Certeau calls 'arts de faire') is to be found are, variously: fire-eating, begging, theft, breaking and entering, gun-shooting, dance, drunkenness and sex. These are among the small-scale counterflows against and within the urban fabric knitted together in the conformity uniting the population in acknowledgement of the bicentennial celebrations. These experiments and radical experiences amount to a creative re-mapping of atrophied urban space. Once remapped, however, not only do social norms need to be remodelled, but dimensions and spatio-temporal co-ordinates warp or do not hold. This, the utopian dimension of the film, is signalled most forcefully by the scene where the two drunk lovers lie in the gutter and pavement respectively of a bridge which has seemed – along with the wine bottles and cigarette ends strewn around them – to acquire gargantuan proportions. This, for Taboulay, is a scene which succeeds in combining elements of 'Lewis Carroll, Jack Arnold et Hergé réunis' (Taboulay 1991: 17). One of the notable aspects of this scene is that if the shift in proportions is associated with the drunkenness of the characters, then any disorientation in respect of the image and its internal proportions is as much the result of a 'drunken' camera as it is as a consequence of an inebriation attributable to them as characters. The scene is shot from above without any other point of view shot to anchor the aberrant imagery in the perceptual hub of either character. In this respect, the film accords with one of the neo-baroque principles identified by Christine Buci-Glucksmann in her *Trafic* article, in positing an *im*possible all-seeing eye to survey the possible world below (Buci-Glucksmann 1993). Keeping the camera at this angle, Carax refuses to make the scene subservient to a motivating ground or generative centre which would provide the rationale: they are drunk, hence their perceptions are faulty. Here, rather, the point of view furnished by the camera remains 'impossible'.

15  See Conley (1996) for more on this distinction.

## *Espace quelconque*[16]

Place and location, then, enjoy a special status in Carax's work. The Pont-Neuf itself appears in each of the four films he has made to date. But, aside from geographically identifiable sites, with co-ordinates, Deleuze's concept of *espace quelconque*, or the 'any-space-whatever' may be helpful in thinking about the nature of the film's figuration of space. Such a space is one which has left behind 'ses propres coordonées comme de ses rapports métriques. C'est un espace tactile' (Deleuze 1983: 154).[17] The 'drunk perception' scene is a good example of figuration according to the 'espace quelconque' model. Such a space is characterised by powers and forces, by intensities; it is not a Euclidean space, and is unmoored from co-ordinates proper; it belongs to the domain of what Deleuze and Guattari call intensive ordinates. 'Espaces quelconques' obey the logic of what they elsewhere call 'counteractualisation'; an abeyant constituent part or stratum holds them back from actualisation. *Espaces quelconques* are simultaneously given and withheld, and oscillate on a threshold of becoming (to remain within a threshold zone of becoming is what 'to become' means in Deleuze and Guattari's terms). Réda Bensmaïa in a commentary on Deleuze and Guattaria takes up a related point:

> Si l'espace quelconque et l'espace effectué sont toujours contemporains et se conjuguent, ils ne peuvent être confondus pour autant, car ils ne participent point du même 'ordre': la virtualité de l'un met toujours l'actualité de l'autre en sursis; mais, en même temps, l'actualité de tel 'espace effectué' – ce terrain vague, ce parking etc. – est toujours grosse de la virtualité qui viendra le transformer en 'espace quelconque'. (Bensmaïa 1997: 148)[18]

In this sense – of an ontological commitment to the potentiality of space – the purpose of cinema in Deleuze's view is not to reproduce the real, but to give us spaces which do not yet belong to this world

16 'Any-space-whatever.'
17 'Its own co-ordinates and its metric relations. It is a tactile space' (Deleuze 1986: 109).
18 'If the any-space-whatever and actualised space are always contemporaneous and conjugated, they cannot however be confused, because they do not participate in the same "order": the virtuality of one always holds the actuality of the other in abeyance, but at the same time, the actuality of an "actualised space" – this waste ground, this parking lot, etc. – is always pregnant with virtuality which will come to transform it into an "any-space-whatever".'

(Bensmaïa 1997: 149). The concept of the *espace quelconque* is part of Deleuze's strategic adherence to this capacity inherent to cinema for transfiguration and transformation. Thus the *espace quelconque* in Deleuze's hands becomes much more or less than an anthropological habitat, or a phenomenon caused by historical and political agencies; it is a 'conceptual persona' – and Bensmaïa is insistent that the concept demands to be read in this way – which engenders the 'spiritual automaton' capable of giving rise to the 'powers of the false'.

The powers of the false – this central Deleuzian concept, as Chapter 1 has observed – finds its hollow echo in the *cinéma du look*, that, albeit short-lived, category of filmmaking with which Carax was briefly associated. The work of Beneix and Besson of this period is defiantly under the sway of the simulacrum – but in the Baudrillardian sense of that term, rather than the Deleuzian sense. Carax's work, however, negotiates the powers of the false in a much more inventive and less abject fashion.

Thus, while one can see the logic behind the reading given by Graeme Hayes when he asserts that the *cinéma du look* is driven to its impasse in the fireworks spectacle presented by Carax in *Les Amants* (Hayes in Powrie 1999: 201), the film has much more to offer than a facile affront, or even pastiche. The film once more is partly about establishing the conditions for the sheltering of 'the event', the *inespéré*, and is operative at this abstract level. The spectacle is not just the spectacle of the *cinéma du look*. Carax's neo-baroquism is more profound and paradoxical than the concept of an attention to surface images implies. His work is about the engendering of possible worlds, ones not yet created. For Carax, it is decidedly not a question, as it appears to be in Beineix of the 'try another [ready-made] world' of *La Lune dans le caniveau* for example. Instead of a choice between contending possibilities, Carax's characters inhabit a laboratory for their own mutant subjectivities – as Michèle clearly embodies this in her 'becoming-homeless'. These characters occupy a space of disjunction, and of what Deleuze calls inclusive disjunction – a way of being host to alterity and heterogeneity – rather than exclusive disjunction – which serves to banish alterity and heterogeneity. It is this aspect that gives to the film its political force, which Beugnet sums up as follows:

> En outre, et crucialement, en alliant l'exploration du potentiel esthétique du médium avec une dimension politique et sociale, *Les*

*Amants du Pont-Neuf* devient une expression, à travers l'image et l'espace filmique même, des tensions complexes – attirance, résistance et rejet – que génère l'exclusion. (Beugnet 2000: 187)[19]

## France, commodity culture and the bridge as radio dial

Without its temporary barriers, the bridge would be a place of transit and exchange. Its part in the economy of the city is signalled very clearly by the looming presence at the top of the frame of the illuminated sign of the Samaritaine department store. In fact we have here the coexistence of several distinct Parisian temporalities, in the manner evoked by Baudelaire in *Tableaux parisens* – 1789, Baudelaire's own nineteenth century and the 1989 of the lovers. Where Godard in his commissioned film *Lettre à Freddy Buache*, gives us Lausanne as a spatial archaeology of intersecting and interleaved planes (Cache 1995: 6–15), Carax gives us Paris as a temporal conundrum, layered behind transient signifiers of other times.

Indeed there are other strands in the film that can be linked to Benjamin's conception of Paris as capital of the nineteenth century. The department store is, after all, a symbol of the commodity culture of that century. Under its shadow, Michèle sketches on the hoof, in a manner which indeed strives to capture 'the ephemeral, the transient, the contingent' (Baudelaire). More crucially, the film seems to inter-mingle the two things woven together in the thought of Benjamin: commodity culture and allegory. As Graham Gilloch explains:

> The experience of the commodity is that of ruination. The modern city, the site of the smug celebration of progress and the conquest of the natural world, is critically revealed through the allegorical gaze as the space of ruin. (Gilloch 1996: 136)

This is almost literally rendered concrete in and through Carax's film. The Samaritaine building becomes literally empty – just a façade of scaffolding and wood on the bank of a reservoir. Carax's narrative – a narrative partly scripted by the city of Paris itself, in the shape of its

19 'Furthermore, and crucially, in allying the exploration of the aesthetic potential of the medium to a political and social dimension, *Les Amants du Pont-Neuf* becomes, through the image and the filmic space itself, an expression of complex tensions – attraction, resistance and rejection – which exclusion generates.'

municipal authorities – places a site of ruin within the city in celebration (of progress, of France). But allegory overspills and threatens
to decimate the film's avowed core. Leaving aside, however, the
question of to what extent the allegorical impulse in the film swallows
it up, and focusing merely on the film itself, rather than its blighted
production history, Carax's set places the ruin and the commodity
together, and even sets up a continuum between them via the wiring
and connections, exposed by the building works, which Alex can use
to turn on and off the lights both on the bridge itself and in the
department store. This is how Benjamin describes the method of
Baudelaire:

> tearing things out of the context of their usual interrelations – which is
> quite normal where commodities are being exhibited – is a procedure
> very characteristic of Baudelaire. It is related to the destruction of the
> organic interrelations in the allegorical intention. (Benjamin 1985: 41)

For Benjamin, the allegorical gaze fragments but rebuilds at the same
time. If Carax had used the ending he wanted, the redemptive aspect
which is present in the film as it stands would have been less in
evidence. If *Pola X* is Carax's next *tableau parisien*, the emphasis will
now shift entirely to the side of catastrophe – what one reviewer called
'caraxysm' (Hoberman 2000).

## Margins, centre and locus/co-ordinates

In being set amid the build-up to and celebration of the bicentennial,
*Les Amants* has a special relationship with the question of France in
modernity, France as forged in the smithy of the Enlightenment, with
its enshrining of a sense of the enlightened individual along with a
collective (*le peuple*) in which individual freedoms were supported and
upheld. The red, white and blue of the celebrations abound but are
never spoken of by the protagonists. Parallel and outside – yet
curiously invaded in the form of falling fireworks by the celebrations
– the two lovers do enact their own celebration. The framing music
which will return once the lovers have danced and run back and forth
along the bridge is French accordion music. The first piece of music
to which the soundtrack switches is of north African origin, the
second is a rock track by Iggy Pop ('Strong Girl'), the third a rap track

by Public Enemy and the fourth a waltz (Strauss). In a characteristically inventive inscription of music on soundtrack, Carax has the
sideways movements of the lovers along the bridge operate as if along
a kind of dial. As they move, the soundtrack tunes in to the four
different 'bands' (or channels) and back again. The four tracks, allied
to the accordion music represent together a disjunctive melange of
music forms, none of which (aside from the 'framing' accordion) is
especially evocative of France or of Paris, but, rather, variously, of
Vienna, New York, the Berlin of the late 1970s – as inhabited by Iggy
Pop and Bowie – and, finally, perhaps most significantly in this film
about centres and margins, the former colonies. The bridge becomes
in these moments a kind of keyboard in an immense spatio-temporal
circuitry as sparks rain down from extinguished fireworks on the
dancing automatons on a Pont-Neuf music box.

The bridge, however, because of the repairs, is functionally removed
from the centre, and removed from modes of relation; vectors of
movement and transfer reach an impasse at the barriers which only
the protagonists are able to get through, or, in Alex's favoured acrobatic mode, round. If de Certeau's definition of space as 'frequented
place' (de Certeau 1990: 173) is to be held to, then the bridge reverts to
a *place* when it is cordoned off – since it is no longer frequented. But
occupied as it is by Hans (a latter-day Père Jules presiding over two
young lovers), Alex and Michèle a mode of occupancy is re-
established. '[D]es relations s'y reconstituent' (Augé 1992: 101).[20]

Just as Deleuze's distinction between *espace quelconque* and actualised space is in no way a mutually exclusive one, neither does
Certeau's distinction between place and space subscribe to a logic of
reciprocal exclusion. Augé takes up this point: place is never completely
erased, while non-place is never totally completed. They are to be
thought of, rather, as 'palimpsestes où se réinscrit sans cesse le jeu
brouillé de l'identité et de la relation' (Augé 1992: 101).[21] Thus it is
entirely appropriate that Hans in this film elects himself as authority
over relations and over the economy of the bridge. He is the dispenser
of downers needed by Alex to sleep – he has been and remains, then,
at many levels a 'caretaker'. In other words, relations are restored, and

20 'relations are restored and resumed in it' (Augé 1995: 78).
21 'Palimpsests on which the scrambled game of identity and relations is
ceaselessly re-written' (Augé 1995: 79).

with them power relations, including patriarchy and the phallocratic order. Within this space of resumed and restricted relations – but which for all that restriction opens on to the entire fabric of capitalism, the nation (*la patrie*) and patriarchy – however, Carax is careful to allow the unfolding and elaboration of the minuscule economy of relations between Alex and Michèle. Two sets of intensities rather than intentionality driven individuals, they are individuations ('haecceities') in Deleuze's terms, operating by means of an 'automatism' which can be traced back to Cocteau or perhaps to Murnau.[22]

If it is said of Alex that he has failed to enter the symbolic (Hayes in Powrie 1999) – although this study has tended to avoid psychoanalytic categories – then it is at this level. His rejection of identity and intentionality (through alcohol) is allied to his burning of the missing person (everyone in this film is a missing person) poster. All intentionality and identity must pass, from Alex's perspective, through fire, and through *feux d'artifice*. The Heraclitean side of Alex is significant. Fire (standing in for flux generally) is his medium. In addition to his feats of pyrophagia, he can ignite space and light up the bridge. His mouth is more eloquent with flame than it is with language (again the lure of the suggestion that Alex can be interpreted as not having yet entered the symbolic is apparent). It is for this reason that the poster man dies by being burned: it must be so within the economy of fire over which he presides and through which he moves. Against the mirror image of the poster, which Michèle for her part will not be able to see, Alex wages war. She cannot see, while he refuses to recognise. The well-off background from which Michèle comes and to which she will return is of course highly significant here. Moreover, the military father links her to a state apparatus against which Alex is also seen to struggle.

22 Glossing Artaud, Deleuze writes 'Thought has no other reason to function than its own birth, always the repetition of its own birth, secret and profound' (Deleuze 1989: 165). Artaud believed that surrealist approximations to dream imagery (Dulac, etc.) only went so far in solving what he called the problem of thought. 'Artaud believes more in an appropriateness between cinema and automatic writing, as long as we understand that automatic writing is not at all an absence of composition, but a higher control which brings together critical and conscious thought and the unconscious in thought: the spiritual automaton (which is very different from the dream, which brings together a censure or repression with an unconscious made up of impulses)' (Deleuze 1989: 165).

This composite of resistances may appear a romanticised vision of auto-creation, a nihilistic rebellion that lapses into the black hole of what Deleuze and Guattari call 'déterritorialisation' ('deterritorialisation') at too fast a rate. It matters little whether or not Carax has as his primary intention a critique of contemporary bourgeois French society; what does matter is that this film sets up internal localised circuits of becoming. The set pieces such as the counter-celebration on the bridge in the form of the dance sequence mentioned above, along with the water-skiing sequence, make the film rank high as one of the most innovative contributions to the iconography, temporality and corporeality of *l'amour fou* since the landmark foray of Rivette into that turbulent domain.

If indeed it is true that at a certain level in *Les Amants* we witness too swift a deterritorialisation at the level of the film as a whole, it is important to stress that the film is averse to the prescriptions of totality and teleology. If every narrative is, as Certeau insists, a narrative of journey (Certeau 1990: 171), *Les Amants* manages to insert itself into such a framework, while avoiding teleological finitude and closure, even if it has been bound to the parenthetical space of the closed bridge. What matters is not the signification of the final scenes – is the journey towards the terminus of death or not?[23] – but their effect of unfurling the characters from the space they have inhabited on the bridge. While the underwater scene recalls Vigo, and the barge takes us more directly to the space of *L'Atalante*, the important thing is that it is an 'unfold', deployed from the fold of the once sealed now open bridge. Little did Carax know at this juncture that his space of election would prepare him for a long tenure in the space of ejection, and that when he returned it would be without Binoche, without Lavant and without Escoffier. In summarising what for her are the splendours of the film ('Carax vient de nous donner un film lustral et férial': Taboulay 1991: 17), Taboulay declares 'Commençons à attendre le prochain' (17); little did anyone at that time know that the critic was announcing a full eight years of anticipation.[24]

23 Le Havre in Vigo's film is a decidedly purgatorial space.
24 'Carax is about to give us a lustrous and celebratory film'; 'We begin to await the next one.'

## Visions, the excessive, 'emergencies'

> Quel sainte image attaque-t-on? Quels cœurs briserai-je? Quel mensonge dois-je tenir? – Dans quel sang marcher? (Rimbaud [1872])[25]

There has always been something of the visionary in Carax's approach to cinema. Carax as a latter-day Rimbaud (*Mauvais Sang* – its title taken from one of the books of Rimbaud's *Une Saison en enfer* – is just one of the many references to the French poet) sees himself as part of a visionary tradition. Rimbaud advocated a 'derangement of the senses', a relocation of the borders by means of which these are differentiated. The task of the poet becomes a 'synaesthetic' one, requiring language to smell, thought to touch, touch to become 'visible'. Carax as seer then is a compelling notion, and Carax as 'synaesthetist' likewise. Like Michèle in *Les Amants*, the seer by definition always sees with eyes that have been 'damaged', and that require one of the other senses to supplement them – touch for example. Camille Taboulay, in her review of the film for *Cahiers*, reminds us of the exhibition curated by Jacques Derrida at the Louvre – the same museum as visited by Michèle to view the Rembrandt self-portrait – 'Mémoires d'aveugle', the presiding concept behind which is the idea that one is wounded by what one sees (Taboulay 1991: 16–17). This notion of a parasitic constituent inhabiting the sensory field embraced by a given sense finds an abundance of echoes in the film.

## Soundtrack, vision-track

In the metonymic form of the film's two lovers, Carax places the two 'tracks' of cinema together. The audio and the visual collide when Alex and Michèle encounter each other on the street in the opening sequence. Importantly, however, both the audio and the visual as represented by their respective 'bearers' are impaired: Alex will not speak and Michèle is losing her sight, as we see in the scene in the métro tunnel where to her patch Alex's crutch is now added. Clearly, in this film so concerned with, and so linked to, a question of excess, there will also be a pronounced interest in the themes of limits and of

---

25 'What sacred image are we attacking? Whose heart shall I break? What lie should I tell? – In whose blood shall I walk?' (from the Wallace Fowlie translation).

limitation. Vision confronts its limit in the figure of Michèle: she collapses when sketching Alex, and faints when watching him perform his fire-eating act. She cannot tolerate the pain of observing paintings in their usual lighting and can only bear to observe them by candlelight. Michèle's, then, is an impaired vision but also a transient and mutating vision. This sense of (undesired) attenuation, which she suffers as a consequence of her disease, finds its counterpart in Alex's need of downers to enable him to sleep. However, it is precisely the necessarily impaired nature of the perception that sets up the possibility for the arrival of the Caraxian *inespéré*. This notion, which has been invoked several times in these pages, is in *Les Amants du Pont-Neuf* given a very specific formulation by means of this self-reflexive inscription. The audio and the visual (the two tracks of cinema) are each embodied in characters and each is impaired. Carax's ongoing negotiation of limits takes on a new form – by placing them on/in/ around his characters in this film. This is tantamount to an experiment in what Deleuze refers to as the unthought within thought:

> d'une part la présence d'un impensable dans la pensée, et qui serait à la fois comme sa source et son barrage; d'autre part la présence à l'infini d'un autre penseur dans le penseur, qui brise tout monologue d'un moi pensant. (Deleuze 1985: 218–19)[26]

The ability to testify to emergence, to the 'event' as it might be called in the idiom of Deleuze's *Logique du sens* (or Carax's *inespéré*), is part of the lineage of filmmaking to which Carax lays claim in this film. Deleuze turns to the work of Jean-Louis Schefer to identify the essential question: 'en quoi et comment le cinéma concerne-t-il une pensée dont le propre est de pas être encore?' (Deleuze 1985: 219).[27] Clearly such endeavours will not characterise all cinema, and Deleuze is quick to remind us that the type of cinema which Schefer has in mind will be close to that envisaged by Artaud, and whose best exponent will be found in the figure of Philippe Garrel. The work of Carax is partly, not entirely, it has to be said, to be located within this

26 'on the one hand the presence of an unthinkable in thought, which would be both its source and its barrier; on the other hand the presence to infinity of another thinker in the thinker, who shatters every monologue of a thinking self' (Deleuze 1989: 168).

27 'In what respect and how is cinema concerned with a thought whose essential character is not yet to be?' (Deleuze 1989: 168).

lineage. Contrary to Eisenstein who wished, through the dialectics of montage, to reveal thought itself as visible, the cinematographic image, 'dès qu'elle assume son aberration de mouvement, opère une *suspension du monde*, ou affecte le visible d'un *trouble*' (Deleuze 1985: 219),[28] such that what emerges, within the 'emergency' of this disturbance, is neither strictly speaking visible, nor strictly speaking thinkable: the unseen, the unthought – monstrous visions and perceptions. In the words of Eric Alliez:

> Propelled by the cinematographic postulate of a world become image, this amounts to the affirmation of a plane of immanence in which consciousness is no longer consciousness of something; rather, consciousness is something, an eye in things grasped by a camera-consciousness, the eye in matter undergoing universal modulations such that all images vary in relation to one another, a machinic consciousness open unto duration as a whole. (Alliez 2000: 293–4)

This machinic consciousness is open to flux, fluidity and to the *informe* – all of which rumble beneath a putative threshold of identity and molarity. The 'emergency' brought about by this scopic disturbance gives birth to the 'spiritual automaton' in cinema:

> C'est la description de *l'homme ordinaire du cinéma*: l'automate spirituel, 'homme mécanique', 'mannequin expérimental', ludion en nous, corps inconnu que nous n'avons que derrière la tête, et dont l'âge n'est ni le nôtre ni celui de notre enfance, mais un peu de temps à l'état pur. (Deleuze 1985: 220)[29]

Carax does his apprenticeship at the school of the *nouvelle vague* and incorporates many of their innovations meticulously in the first two features – the *nouvelle vague* being largely synonymous in Deleuze's formulations, with the break with sensory-motor schemata. 'La rupture sensori-motrice fait de l'homme un voyant qui se trouve frappé par quelque chose d'intolérable dans le monde, et confronté à quelque chose d'impensable dans la pensée' (Deleuze 1985: 220–1) – the

---

28 'As soon as it takes on its aberration of movement, carries out a *suspension of the world* or affects the visible with a *disturbance*' (Deleuze 1989: 168).

29 'This is the description of the ordinary man in cinema: the spiritual automaton, "mechanical man", "experimental dummy", Cartesian diver in us, unknown body which we have only at the back of our heads whose age is neither ours nor that of our childhood, but a little time in the pure state' (Deleuze 1989: 169).

sentence could well describe the situation from which *Les Amants* departs.[30]

Perhaps the clearest sense in which Carax's films seek out a Deleuzean 'suspension of the world' is the extent to which his characters are separate from the world. Godard said of his own film about a trio of misfits in *Bande à part*:

> Ce sont des gens qui sont réels, et c'est le monde qui fait bande à part. C'est le monde qui se fait du cinéma. C'est le monde qui n'est pas synchrone, eux sont justes, sont vrais, ils représentent la vie. Ils vivent une histoire simple, c'est le monde autour d'eux qui vit un mauvais scénario. (Godard, cited in Deleuze 1985: 223)[31]

*Les Amants*, viewed retrospectively, now clearly signals a shift in Carax's project. Whereas the appellation 'neo-baroque' becomes increasingly apt as one moves from *Boy Meets Girl* to *Mauvais Sang*, *Les Amants* is to be located within a distinct set of aesthetic and philosophical questions – the connivance with simulacra has become more critical and rigorous. The dance sequence (as in *Boy Meets Girl*) or the rapid walk-dance (as in *Mauvais Sang*) however is still, here, to be thought of within the logic of a breakdown in sensory-motor schemata. In short, what Deleuze says of the dance routines in *Pierrot le fou*, *Bande à part* and *Une femme est une femme* remains true of Carax up to and including *Les Amants* (*Pola X*, while still echoing Alex's fugues, in the form of Pierre's limping lurches, bids farewell to the dance as limit):

> tandit que la danse, dans une comédie musicale classique, informe toutes les images, même préparatoires ou intercalaires, elle surgit ici, au contraire, comme un 'moment' dans le comportment des héros, comme la limite vers laquelle tendent une suite d'images, limite qui ne sera effectuée qu'en formant une autre suite tendant vers une autre limite. (Deleuze 1985: 240)[32]

30 'The sensory motor break makes man a seer who finds himself struck by something intolerable in the world, and confronted by something unthinkable in thought' (Deleuze 1989: 169).

31 'These are people who are real and it's the world that is a breakaway group. It is the world that is making cinema for itself. It is the world that is out of synch; they are right, they are true, they represent life. They live a simple story; it is the world around them which is living a bad script' (Godard, cited in Deleuze 1989: 171).

32 'Whilst dance, in a classical musical comedy, informs all the images, even

Thus in Carax the dance diffuses into a sequence leading to the fire-eating performance, which in turn will be linked via another sequence to the métro station acrobatics.

## The lives, death and afterlife of Alex

Alex the medium, Alex the ventriloquist and the ventriloquised, Alex the supple individual: Alex in the first three features is more than a character. He is a site of impedance (he impedes normativity) and thoroughfare (he releases flows), an orphan (severed from family) and *Orphée* (conduit of visionary perceptions) of chaos. This is a new type of character for cinema, and the innovation of Carax should not be underestimated. Claire Denis seems to have been attentive to this novelty by managing to transport (in the process transforming) aspects of Alex to her own project in *Beau Travail*. One of Alex's possible worlds (he is on the eve of his military service in *Boy Meets Girl*) is thereby given form. That 'Alex' has had this curious afterlife (even including a remarkable dance scene with a solitary Lavant/Galoup in a mirrored discothèque) is testament to the specificity of Lavant himself, as well as to the new type of acting and character he brings to the screen. One of Deleuze's best anglophone interpreters Brian Massumi has elaborated on a category of literary character that comes close to evoking something of the specificity of Carax's characterisation in respect of Alex – the 'supple individual'. This character is partly an inheritor of the protagonist of Melville's 'Bartleby the Scrivener', who says 'I would prefer not to' (Melville [1856] 1990). I bend and I evade, this character seems to say: I resist – I ply but am not compliant. The supple individual is especially appropriate to cinema, with its combination of accretive and dissipative qualities: its fades, superimpositions, zooms, accelerations and decelerations. 'A supple [pliant] individual lies between the molecular and the molar, in time and in mode of composition' (Massumi 1992: 55). Alex is such a persona, both physically supple and metamorphic

---

preparatory or intercalary ones, it arises here, in contrast, as a "moment" in the behaviour of the heroes, as the limit towards which a sequence of images is moving, a limit which will only be realised by forming another sequence moving towards another limit' (Deleuze 1989: 184).

as he passes from film to film in the trilogy. By investing as heavily as he did in the persona of Alex in his first three films, Carax made of Denis Lavant a screen within the screen, a screen both to be projected upon and a filter. Alex as sieve, as screen, as supple individual lying between a chaotic, turbulent matter and aesthetic assemblage, may have gone in *Pola X*, but as the next chapter will show, Carax's dealings with chaos are in that film, nonetheless, pushed further still.

## References

Alliez, Eric (2000), 'Midday, midnight: the emergence of cine-thinking', in Gregory Flaxman ed., *The Brain is the Screen: Deleuze and the Philosophy of Cinema*, Minneapolis, University of Minnesota Press, pp. 293–302.

Augé, Marc (1992), *Non-Lieux: Introduction à une Anthropologie de la Surmodernité*, Paris, Seuil.

—— (1995), *Non-Places: Introduction to an Anthropology of Supermodernity*, trans. John Howe, London, Verso.

Austin, Guy (1996), 'The *cinéma du look* and fantasy film', in *Contemporary French Cinema: An Introduction*, Manchester, Manchester University Press, pp. 132–5.

Baignères, Claude (1991), 'Zola congelé', *le Figaro*, 16 October.

Bassan, Raphäel (1989), 'Trois néo-baroques français', *La Revue du cinema*, no. 449, 45–53.

Benjamin, Walter (1977), *The Origin of German Tragic Drama*, trans. John Osborne London, Verso.

—— (1983), *Charles Baudelaire: A Lyric Poet in the Era of High Capitalism*, London, Verso.

—— (1985), 'Central Park', trans. Lloyd Spencer, *New German Critique* 34, winter 1985, 28–58.

Bensmaïa, Réda (1997), '"L'espace quelconque" comme "personnage conceptuel"', in Oliver Fahle and Lorenz Engell eds, *Der Film bei Deleuze/ Le Cinéma selon Deleuze*, Weimar, Verlag der Bauhaus-Universität Weimar/ Presses de la Sorbonne Nouvelle, pp. 140–52.

Berry, David (2000), 'Underground cinema: French visions of the Métro', in Konstantarakos ed., *Spaces in European Cinema*, London, Intellect Books, pp. 8–22.

Beugnet, Martine (2000), 'Filmer l'exclusion: *Les Amants du Pont-Neuf*, Marginalité, Sexualité, Contrôle: Questions de Représentation dans le Cinéma Français Contemporain*, Paris, L'Harmattan, pp. 157–87.

Binoche, Juliette (1991), 'La croix et la foi', interview with Juliette Binoche, *Cahiers du Cinéma*, no. 443/444, May–June, 37–40.

Buci-Glucksmann, Christine (1984), *La Raison Baroque*, Paris, Galilée.

—— (1993), 'Drôle de pensé touchant Leibniz et le cinéma', *Trafic* 8, 71–80.

—— (1994), *Baroque Reason: The Aesthetics of Modernity*, trans. Patrick Camiller, London, Sage.

Cache, Bernard (1995), *Earth Moves: The Furnishing of Territory*, Cambridge MA, MIT.

Carax, Leos (1991), *Cahiers du Cinéma numéro spécial Les Amants du Pont-Neuf*, rédacteur en chef: Leos Carax.

—— (1991a), 'A l'impossible on est tenu', *Les Inrockuptibles*, no. 32, December. Available online at: *www.patoche.org/Carax/ interviews/inrocks.htm*

—— (1992), 'Interview' with David Thompson, *Sight and Sound*, 2:5, 10–11.

Certeau, Michel de (1990), *L'Invention du Quotidien. 1. Arts de Faire*, Paris, Gallimard.

—— (1984), *The Practice of Everyday Life*, trans. Steven Rendell, Berkeley/Los Angeles, University of California Press.

Conley, Verena Andermatt (1996), 'Electronic Paris: from space of election to place of ejection', in Michael Sheringham ed., *Parisian Fields*, London, Reaktion Books, pp. 162–74.

Daly, Fergus (1998), 'Alex in the cities', *Film West* no. 34, 30–1.

Deleuze, Gilles (1983), *Cinéma 1. L'Image-mouvement*, Paris, Minuit.

—— (1985), *Cinéma 2. L'Image-temps*, Paris, Minuit.

—— (1986), *Cinema 1: The Movement-Image*, trans. Hugh Tomlinson and Barbara Habberjam, London, Athlone Press.

—— (1989), *Cinema 2: The Time-Image*, trans. Hugh Tomlinson and Robert Galeta, London, Athlone Press.

Derrida, Jacques (1990), *Mémoires d'Aveugle. L'autoportrait et autres Ruines*, Paris, Louvre, Réunion des Musées Nationaux.

Frodon, Jean-Michel (1995), 'Leos Carax, tous derrière et lui devant', *in L'Age Moderne du Cinéma Français: De la Nouvelle Vague à nos Jours*, Paris, Flammarion, pp. 787–93.

Gilloch, Graham (1996), *Myth and Metropolis: Walter Benjamin and the City*, Cambridge, Polity.

Grande, Maurizio (1997), 'Les images non-dérivées', in Oliver Fahle and Lorenz Engell eds, *Der Film bei Deleuze/Le Cinéma selon Deleuze*, Weimar, Verlag der Bauhaus-Universität Weimar/Presses de la Sorbonne Nouvelle, pp. 284–302.

Hayes, Graeme (1999), 'Representation, masculinity, nation: the crises of *Les Amants du Pont-Neuf* (1991)', in Phil Powrie ed., *Contemporary French Cinema: Continuity and Difference*, Oxford, Oxford University Press, pp. 199–210.

Hayward, Susan (2000), 'The city as narrative: corporeal Paris in contemporary French cinema', in Myrto Konstantarakos ed., *Spaces in European Cinema*, London, Intellect Books, pp. 23–34.

Hoberman, J. (2000), 'Desperate remedies', *Village Voice*, 6–12 September.

Jousse, Thierry (1991), 'Argent', short entry in 'L'alphabet des amants', *Cahiers du Cinéma*, no. 448, 22.

Klawans Stuart (1999), 'Bridge over troubled water', *Nation* 269:3, 19 July, 34–6.

Konstantarakos, Myrto ed. (2000), *Spaces in European Cinema*, London, Intellect Books.

Lavant, Denis (1991), interview with Vincent Ostria, *Cahiers du Cinéma*, no. 448, October, 18–20.

Léonardini, Jean-Pierre (1991), 'L'œil s'éclate', *l'Humanité*, 16 October.

Lyotard, Jean-François (1971), *Discours, Figure*, Paris, Klincksieck.

Maravall, José Antonio [1975] (1986), *Culture of the Baroque: Analysis of a Historical Structure* (1975), trans. Terry Cochran, University of Minnesota Press and Manchester University Press.

Massumi, Brian (1992), *A User's Guide to Capitalism and Schizophrenia: Deviations from Deleuze and Guattari*, Cambridge MA, MIT.

Melville, Herman [1856] (1990), *'Bartleby' and 'Benito Cereno'*, New York, Dover.

Niney, François (1991), 'Feu', brief note on Carax in 'L'alphabet des amants', *Cahiers du Cinéma*, no. 448, October, 24.

Ostria, Vincent (1991), 'Equilibrisme', brief note on Carax in 'L'alphabet des amants', *Cahiers du Cinéma*, no. 448, October, 23–4.

Oudart, Thierry (1995), 'Cinématographe et septième art', *Études de Langue et Littérature Françaises*, Université Seinan-Gakuin, no. 33, winter.

Prédal, René (1996), *50 ans de Cinéma Français (1945–1995)*, Paris, Editions Nathan, pp. 546–51, pp. 719–21.

Reader, Keith (1984), 'Cinematic representations of Paris: Vigo/Truffaut/Carax', *Modern and Contemporary France*, 1:4, 409–15.

Rosenbaum, Jonathan (1994), 'Carax: the problem with poetry', in *Film Comment* 30, May–June 1994, 12–18, 22–3.

Roussel, Christophe, 'Leos Carax', *http://chtiforce.com/carax/texte.htm* (accessed 31 January 2002).

Sabouraud, Frédéric (1991), 'Leos Carax', short entry in '20 Cinéastes pour l'an 2001', *Cahiers du Cinéma*, no. 443/444, May–June, 13–14.

Strauss, Frédéric (1991), 'In vino veritas', short entry on Carax in 'L'alphabet des amants', *Cahiers du Cinéma*, no. 448, October, 24–5.

— (1991a), 'Balles à blanc', in 'L'alphabet des amants', *Cahiers du Cinéma*, no. 448, October, 22.

Taboulay, Camille (1991), 'Explosante fixe', *Cahiers du Cinéma*, no. 448, October, 78–80.

Thompson, David (1992), 'Interview with Leos Carax', *Sight and Sound* 2:5, 10–11.

Thompson, David (1992a), 'Once upon a time in Paris', *Sight and Sound* 2:5, 46.

Toubiana, Serge (1990), 'Le pari du Pont-Neuf', *Cahiers du Cinéma*, no. 434, July–August.

Udris, Raynalle (2000), 'Countryscape/cityscape and homelessness in Varda's *Sans toit ni loi* and Carax's *Les Amants du Pont-Neuf*', in Myro Konstantarakos ed., pp. 42–51.

Vincendeau, Ginette (1993), 'Juliette Binoche: from gamine to femme fatale', *Sight and Sound* 3, 22–4.

# 3

# *Pola X*, or Carax's ambiguities

## *Pola X*: 'le siècle est détraqué'[1]

In the year of the fiftieth anniversary of the Cannes Film Festival, the organisers asked Carax to send them 'un film court, comme une lettre adressée au Festival' ('a short film, like a letter addressed to the festival'), which would give some news from the wilderness he was consigned to after the financial catastrophe of his 1991 film *Les Amants du Pont-Neuf*. The film he sent them is *Sans titre*. The distinctly Godardian elements of his discordant essay would, for the most part, not make it into *Pola X*, the film of which it is in some ways a draft outline – this despite the fact that Godard's influence is clearly registered throughout *Sans titre*, from its grave voice-over to the burlesque presence of the director on screen. Carax's self-reflexivity here has its counterpart in Godard's roles in *Soigne ta droite* (1987), *Prénom Carmen* (1982, with Anne-Marie Miéville) and *King Lear* (1987) – a film in which Carax himself played Edgar. Nonetheless, the film of 1999 into which *Sans titre* would develop *does* retain a sense of the procedure of naming by way of not naming. The title *Pola X* was decidedly cryptic for most when they first heard it, except perhaps for mathematicians who may have thought that the unpredictable *enfant gâté* of French cinema had made an unlikely foray into the world of partially ordered linear algebra, or POLA. They were of course wrong: 'Pola' was in fact an acronym of the title in French of Herman Melville's novel of 1852, *Pierre, or The Ambiguities*, that is, *Pierre, ou les ambiguïtés*. As for the X, it could be the marker to represent the family

1 'The time is out of joint.' Shakespeare's phrase is more usually rendered in French as 'le temps est hors de ses gonds'.

name which the character Isabel/Isabelle is denied, she being the possible secret progeny of an extra-marital relationship; in this way it could stand for the family secret, therefore, an element so central to the naturalist tradition in late nineteenth-century fiction. Carax in interview himself reminds us that it is suggestive of that which is taboo, and that it could therefore mark the space and time of the incestuous sex between Pierre and his half-sister. Indeed, speaking of this latter aspect, and of the explicit nature of the sex scene between Pierre and Isabelle, the X also suggests X-rated. While Carax is aware of each of these possible readings of the X – a marker rather than a signifier proper – he is adamant that its provenance derives from the fact that the script went through ten drafts on his computer before being regarded as ready to become a film. But of course that gives rise to the question: if the title given to the finished product contains a coded statement of it being generated by a tenth *draft*, then there is lodged in the title a sense of the incomplete, the provisional, the unfinished. In this respect, Carax can be seen to have performed for his own film something akin to Robert Musil – the other key literary source for *Pola X* – who, by withdrawing the galley proofs of the final book of *The Man Without Qualities*, left us with an incomplete novel which is yet one that is spoken of as a whole, as a unit, as a work.[2]

This sense that *Pola X* is provisional is corroborated by the fact that Arte in 2001 screened another version of the film as a three-part television series. This time the material was screened not with the title *Pola X* but *Pierre, ou Les ambiguïtés*, which fact would seem to suggest that it is the definitive version. Final version or not, however, there is an aspect of the project in its three manifestations, or partial manifestations, as well as in its literary sources and models – Melville, Musil and Shakespeare – that invites reflection on the question of 'remains' and waste. There is a trace left within the project of a type of wastage, one which holds it in abeyance from completion and wholeness. For, 'X' could be said to name the structure of ambiguity itself, which always, in the view of Andrew Benjamin, entails an irreducible remainder (Benjamin 2001: 89). It is possible, then, to think of the ambiguities in *Pierre*, the absence of qualities in the case of Musil's *Man without Qualities*, and the indecision of Hamlet, as various literary precedents which find themselves abbreviated in the X of Carax's title.

2 Musil died in 1942.

When Carax first read Melville's novel in his youth at the prompting of his long-term friend and collaborator Elie Poicard (who is credited with the role of 'discontinuité' in the film's credits), he was, in finding it an immensely difficult book, echoing many generations of readers. Having struggled through it, however, he came to realise that it was, in some sense, 'his' book, one which asked 'toutes les bonnes questions pour moi' ('all the right questions for me', Carax 1999a). One reason the novel spoke so directly to him was that in *Pierre* he finds a great Melvillean figure – the impostor or a version of the 'confidence man'. Carax has – as Chapter 1 shows – aligned himself with this formidable if marginal lineage in literature, and regards himself as a kind of impostor (it is easier to be one in cinema than it is in literature he has commented), one who can 'get away with it'. In his interview for the Arte programme *Métropolis* Carax explains to Pierre-André Boutang:

L'imposture, ça commence dès la sortie ... L'imposture, c'est qu'on n'est pas à sa place et qu'on a volé la place ... Déjà, l'imposture, c'est qu'on ne sait rien faire et qu'on essaie quand même ... C'est qu'on fait semblant d'écrire sa vie alors que c'est les autres qui l'écrivent pour soi ... C'est mille choses. Mais *Pierre* est un beau roman sur l'imposture. Et le titre de Cocteau, *Thomas l'imposteur*, est un des plus beaux titres de roman. Moi j'aime bien les personnages d'imposteurs. (Carax 1999a)[3]

The film is loosely adapted from Melville and the setting moved to contemporary France. It is quite appropriate that *Pierre* be relocated, and not just because of the protagonist's name, but because Melville is already deeply indebted to Balzac (specifically for his short story 'Luck and Leather: A Parisian Romance'). Indeed the 'evil French influence' on Melville's novel of 1852 was noted by an anonymous reviewer writing in 1919 (Haydock 2000: 70 n.14), while one of the film's reviewers notes that Pierre's motorcycle forays take place in a landscape that belongs to the world of Balzac (Léonardini 1999).

This adaptation of an amorphous, sprawling literary curiosity was

3 'Imposture is there right from the outset ... Imposture is when you're not in your place and when you have stolen your place ... Imposture is when you don't how to do anything but you try anyway ... It's when you pretend to write your life story whereas others write it for you ... It's a thousand different things. But *Pierre* is a great novel on imposture. And Cocteau's title, *Thomas the Imposter* is one of the most beautiful novel titles. I am very fond of characters who are imposters.'

the end product of Carax's years in the wilderness. It is worth dwelling on the extent to which the film to come was announced in abbreviated and cryptic form in the film essay *Sans titre*. The short begins with sound – applause over a black screen. Then a barrage of images follows: Cannes festival delegates, stars arriving in highly treated and remixed images, a dance sequence from a film by the Lumière brothers. The globe spins on its axis while a voice-over intones words from Shakespeare's *Hamlet* as rendered in the French, 'le siècle est détraqué'.[4] Alluding to a scene which the film itself excerpts from Vidor, Carax struggles up urban steps. An interior scene features a baby swaddled on a desk next to Carax and his computer screen; the sound of Leonard Cohen plays over a hand in silhouette recalling the vampire's hand in Murnau's *Nosferatu*, and then a silhouette profile in which Carax's own eyelashes feature prominently. An intertitle announces the next section: 'Hamlet's Sisters'. A series of images of children playing and bathing is intercut with images (which obliquely gesture towards a scene in *Mauvais Sang*) of Carax lying on a bed with painted images of vaguely foetal bodies on the bed-linen, but which have suggestions of genitalia marking them as male (Carax taking and leaving the place of the 'male' image) and female (the image of the 'female' remains unoccupied throughout). The image of a photograph of Carax as a child flashes twice on screen (the same photo features in the *hors série* edition of *Cahiers* which he edited). An extract from *The Night of the Hunter* shows the fleeing children on the river (Pierre and Isabelle will be swept along in a river of blood in *Pola X*) and then in bed wishing each other goodnight (and warding off the bites of bedbugs). Planes bomb a graveyard. Golubeva and Depardieu walk along a street. Deneuve, wearing a tiara drives a sportscar muttering to herself. A camera sits on a snowy esplanade in front of a (Godardian?) lake. Carax jogs towards it but slips in the snow. A reproduction of Courbet's *L'Origine du monde* burns and brings the series of images to an end.

The film into which these fragments grew would lose practically all of the elements which cause one to think of Godard, aside from the opening sequence which in many respects – some of them coincidental

4 The lines from *Hamlet* are: 'The time is out of joint; O, cursèd spite,/That ever I was born to set it right!' (*Hamlet* (1601) act I, sc. 5. l. 188; Shakespeare 1980: 96).

(found footage subject to new montage) – echoes the Godard of *Histoire(s) du cinéma* (1988–98). It loses the burlesque elements, the intertitles, the touch of Godardian self-reflexivity (could this scene even be filmed on the banks of Lac Leman?).

Despite the many ways in which the film bids farewell to the world created in the first three films (it features horseback riding for example), with *Pola X* it can be argued that paradoxically it reconfigures the central concerns albeit it in a context that few, based on their knowledge of the first three features, would have predicted. In this chapter, in addition to assessing what is new in the fourth feature, the ways in which Carax's most recent work at the time of writing sheds new light on what came before will be considered. The film, it will be shown, underlines the shift from neo-baroque to what will here be identified as 'naturalist' concerns. This claim requires immediate qualification on at least two fronts, however: if the neo-baroque and naturalism are present as *puissances* (one of the many invaluable suggestions in the French journal *Vertigo*'s recent reappraisal of the baroque in film (*Vertigo* 2001)), then it may be that it is a question of a *foregrounding* of naturalism in *Pola X*, while the neo-baroque 'powers' withdraw but do not disappear. Second, and equally importantly, it must be stressed that the shift in emphasis, and the modification of forces, were nascent from the outset.

## Synopsis

The credits sequence features found images of the Luftwaffe bombers of the Second World War unleashing their cargo on a cemetery. A discordant rock track by Scott Walker plays over the sequence of images. (A blasted empty plain with plumes of smoke visible on the horizon is the setting for the first shot of the Arte version. A bulbous rock protrudes from this parched landscape. Pierre walks towards it, leans against it, and is joined by his mother). Then comes the first shot of the film proper: a pastoral setting, a magnificent château in the heart of the French Normandy countryside. An array of arcs of water from sprinklers frames the foreground, while the landscape as a whole is bathed in late morning light. Pierre Valombreuse (played by Depardieu *fils*) is on a motorcycle on the way to see his fiancée, Lucie de Boiseux, while his mother Marie (Deneuve) lies asleep upstairs.

We learn in a subsequent scene, with Deneuve looking through the contents of a trunk, that Pierre's father, Georges, a diplomat based in Eastern Europe, has passed away some time ago. Marie occupies some of her time as director of an unspecified business. Pierre, for his part, is the author of a best-selling novel entitled *A la lumière* under the pseudonym 'Aladdin'.

Pierre, however, is not entirely content in this at once fixed and restrained (by tradition) and liberated (from routine and regular employment) milieu. He takes to the roads on his father's motorcycle, 'traversent vite des paysages qu'on dirait balzaciens' (Léonardini 1999),[5] much to the displeasure of his mother. Subsequent to a premonition that there is someone or something haunting the château grounds, on one of his rambles, Pierre, having joined his cousin at a café, notices a woman observing him from across the street. His observer is Isabelle, who to judge from her accent may be a refugee from Eastern Europe, and possibly the Balkans. Once transfixed by this mysterious apparition, Pierre joins Isabelle on a crepuscular march through the forest. This is the occasion for Isabelle to recount her past in a seamless monologue – a past characterised by 'cadavres partout' ('corpses everywhere'). The uncanny bond between them intensifies to the extent that Pierre ultimately forsakes Lucie, his impending marriage, and his family, and sets off for Paris with Isabelle, along with her female companion Razerka and child. Thus Pierre replaces one expanding family circle with another ready-made one. Believing little to have changed aside from the identities of the members of the latter, Pierre soon finds that his own identity and privilege are neutralised by the members of his entourage. Hotel owners immediately identify his companions as *sans papiers* – as illegal immigrants – and refuse them entry. After several rejections, and an increasingly unhinged Pierre in evidence, they manage to find accommodation in a less than salubrious *pension*. The transition from impending marriage within the *haute bourgeoisie* to urban squalor and alienation has been rapid. The death of the child after she is struck by a man on the street outside the hotel precipitates their expulsion from their accommodation. Soon the group finds shelter in a vast warehouse squat where it shares meagre facilities with, among others, a noise-based, experimental music collective led by an enigmatic central

5 'quickly crosses landscape which could be described as Balzacian'

figure (Sharunas Bartas) who may also be the leader of a paramilitary group. Pierre is set up with an improvised writing desk where he works on his novel. Razerka and Isabelle endeavour to assist Pierre who during this period becomes increasingly obsessive and changes in appearance, wandering the streets, barely recognisable from the golden boy of the opening sequences. He is spurned when he does attempt to interact with society – as in his earlier ejection from his cousin's party – and is disowned by his mother. Pierre and Isabelle consummate their prolonged inadvertent courtship in one of the film's central scenes – to judge by the prominence it is given by Carax. Then in a startling reversal, Lucie follows Pierre to Paris, where she announces that she will happily endure Pierre's relationship with Isabelle. Pierre's own departure then has set in motion a series of events, unravelling all that was once secure. Pierre's mother, in order to underline this aspect, dies soon after in a motorcycle accident. The world of the squat – 'dans une ambiance technomisérable baignée de perçus électroniques' (Séguret 1999) – and of the surrounding Parisian space becomes increasingly violent and unaccommodating.[6] Pierre himself is now also in one sense *sans papiers*, since he has been disowned by his own family and deprived of income. The novel therefore becomes his only potential source of earnings. However, his new novel is lambasted by the publisher who sends him a rejection letter describing the manuscript as not only a mess, but as reeking of plagiarism. A dejected Pierre finds some hope of redemption when a chat show appearance is organised to bring into the light the person behind the mysterious pseudonym Aladdin. However, Pierre falters in his responses – enduring shouts of 'imposteur!' from the audience – and projects the image of a catatonic, dazed and possibly unhinged individual. Unable to capitalise on the possibilities that the television appearance might have occasioned, Pierre is soon catapulted back into the frenzied and violent world of the *sans papiers*. Having shot his cousin Thibault, Pierre is driven away in a police van as Lucie looks on and Isabelle throws herself in front of a passing truck.

6 'in a technomiserable ambience bathed in electronic percussion'

## Naturalism x 3 in the thought of Deleuze

Some initial qualifying remarks are necessitated by the use made here of the term 'naturalism' itself. In order to achieve clarity at the outset it must be underlined that the term 'naturalism/t' is used here in a specific way. When it is employed in the pages which follow it is not in the sense equivalent to 'realism/t' as this term is normally used in film studies. An explanatory section therefore will form a symmetrical counterpart to the explanatory section (in Chapter 1) on the neo-baroque. For the moment, however, it is important to note the context in which Deleuze employs the term, since it is his theoretical explora-tion of the concept both in and beyond cinema that the current study draws upon. As defined by Deleuze, naturalism has a philosophical source on the one hand and a literary source on the other. The respective essays pertaining to each of these – on Zola (1967) and on the father of philosophical naturalism, Lucretius (1961) – are reprinted in his *Logique du sens* (1969), while the term 'naturalism' resurfaces in the first of his volumes on cinema (1983). These three texts of Deleuze combined yield a unique insight into naturalism in cinema and help to gain an understanding of Carax's concerns in *Pola X*.

Naturalism is the name for a philosophical model which refuses to 'devalue Nature by taking away from it any virtuality or potentiality, any immanent power, any inherent being' (Deleuze 1990: 268). In the thought of Lucretius (*c.* 94–*c.* 55 BC) there is a declared affiliation to a heretical belief system which allows the void and being to co-exist. For the naturalists, there was the void and there was being and the twain *did* meet; they were not, then, mutually exclusive categories. By contrast to the position held by Parmenides (early to mid-fifth century BC), then, Lucretian thought has no time for an absolute (etymo-logically, 'absolute' means divide) distinction between being and non-being (or nothingness): 'Le vide et le plein s'entrelacent et se distribuent de telle manière que la somme du vide et des atomes, à son tour, est elle-même infinie' (Deleuze 1969: 310).[7] Atoms are said by Lucretius in his *De Rerum Natura* to 'fall'; precipitation is their manner of coming into being. A world described only in these terms would be a wholly deterministic one. However, each atom is deter-mined by a clinamen, an angle of declination:

7 'The void and the plenum are interlaced and distributed in such a manner that the sum of the void and the atoms is itself infinite' (Deleuze 1990: 269).

Again, if all movement is always interconnected, the new thing arising from the old in a determinate order – if the atoms never swerve so far as to originate some new movement that will snap the bonds of fate, the everlasting sequence of cause and effect – what is the source of the free will possessed by living things throughout the earth? (Lucretius 1997: ll. 251–6)[8]

The naturalist philosopher is committed to a philosophy of expression, as Deleuze points out in his study of Spinoza – another naturalist in Deleuze's sense – to a univocal nature as plane of immanence, bereft of a transcendent Deity. As a philosophical system, 'naturalism' does not need to look to gods, while in denouncing myths it is also attacking the source of humanity's unhappiness: 'Les événements qui font le malheur de l'humanité ne sont pas séparables des myths qui les rendent possibles', as Deleuze comments (Deleuze 1969: 322).[9]

The *clinamen* was, in Lucretius, a force of differentiation, or an originary differentiator. Naturalist literature, in the form this takes in the work of Zola, has its equivalent to such a force in the inherited impulse said to issue from an 'originary world'. It is from this latter reservoir that what Deleuze calls a derived milieu emanates. The central problem which naturalist literature as conceived by Deleuze explores is the persistence of the originary world in the derived milieu. The centrality to naturalist novelistic discourse of heredity has been widely noted. Deleuze, for his part, makes a distinction between two forms of heredity: the small and the epic, or the heredity of instincts and the heredity of the 'fêlure' ('crack', Deleuze 1969: 377; 1990: 324). Where the first, 'small' heredity transmits instincts, and *reproduces* what it transmits along the way (thereby labouring in the name of same) the heredity of the crack transmits only itself. It traverses the body destined to act as its host in the form of a crack, and is apt to swerve in different directions as it follows silently the line of least resistance.

Though he adds philosophical nuance to the portrait, in his use of the term naturalism in the context of the work of Zola, Deleuze is – at

8  Jean-Louis Leutrat has written of a Lucretian vein in the work of Godard, and of an 'atomic discontinuity' counterbalanced by a 'continuity of flux and flow'. See Leutrat (2000: 183).

9  'The events which bring about the unhappiness of humanity are inseparable from the myths which render them possible' (Deleuze 1990: 278).

first glance – merely adding his own backing to a well-established orthodoxy, the roots of which are to be found in Zola's own account of his method, and to the manner in which his writing relates to its subject matter.

In the work of Zola, individual beings, *bêtes humaines*, are studied in relation to their environment and social and economic conditions, with characters 'conditioned and controlled by environment, heredity, instinct, or chance' (Pizer [1966] 1984: 10–11). Naturalism shares with realism the accumulation of details, as well as a commitment to 'la cohérence et la cohésion logico-sémantique interne du récit' (Hamon 1983: 28), associated with a mimetic agenda, but varies from realism by means of what has been described variously as its pessimistic materialistic determinism, 'violent death [as] utopia' (Sundquist 1982: 13), 'extraordinary and excessive in human nature' (Pizer 1984: 11), or what Hamon, speaking specifically of Zola, calls naturalism's 'volonté de décrire exhaustivement le réel ... un réel considéré de surcroît comme "milieu agissant sur l'individu"' (Hamon 1983: 129).[10]

There is, in addition, a naturalism specific to cinema, which shares something with its literary correlates, but is not, for all that, equivalent to them. For example, the positivist impulses and faiths of Zola are not a feature of cinema's naturalists, and certainly not of Buñuel, one of Deleuze's key examples. Naturalism in cinema, as defined by Deleuze, describes a range of filmic experiments that have in common an examination of the interaction of forces of formation and deformation. The films loosely classed as naturalist in some instances closely translate the conventions of, say, Zola from the domain of literature to that of cinema (notably Renoir's adaptation of *La Bête humaine*, 1938).[11] Other films may be naturalist because their formal characteristics foreground an entropic erosion of an ordered and formed milieu or status quo. In the cinema of Luis Buñuel, for example, one might note a propensity for deformations in the service of pure optical affects (as in *Un chien andalou* (Buñuel and Dalí 1929) for instance), or of a depiction of transgressions of logic and breaking

10 'internal logico-semantic coherence and cohesion of the récit'; 'the will to exhaustively describe the real ... a real which is moreover considered as "environment acting on the individual"'. See Seltzer (1992: 43) for a compelling and concise statement on the realism–naturalism relation.

11 See Lagny (1990) for an analysis of the Renoir film tracing its adherence to key elements of the Zola novel.

of taboos (as in *Belle de jour* (1967) or *Viridiana* (1961) for instance). Clearly, one is already quite some distance from Zola, in speaking of Buñuel.

There remains space, however, within the naturalist tradition as defined by Deleuze, for the powers of the false. That this is the case helps us to understand the fact that the neo-baroque and the naturalist are not opposed. For example, Buñuel's *Terre sans pain* (1933) is ostensibly a realist, positivist-in-intention, documentary essay on the inhabitants of Las Hurdes, in which the director's camera appears faithfully to record the inhabitants struggling with a cruel nature which acts as an uncooperative host to their abject humanity. In many ways this is Buñuel proffering figures every bit as stereotypical, and just as acted upon by environment, as those of Zola. But of course, as we now know, Buñuel had a large hand in *pre-fabricating* the conditions of abjection for the film subsequently 'faithfully' to reproduce. The film is naturalist, then, at one level, that is, in its adherence to what appears to be a positivist motivation underpinned by a putative transparency of the medium, but is also a fabulation, fabricated by an impostor, by a purveyor of the powers of the false. The contradictory aspirations of Naturalism in literature are well pointed up by Huysmans in his own response to Zola's calling into question of the mutation to which naturalism succumbs in the former's work. Writing twenty years after the publication of *A rebours*, the author places his novel of 1884 in the context of the predominant naturalist concerns of his contemporaries:

> le naturalisme s'essoufflait à tourner le meule dans le même cercle. La somme d'observations que chacun avait emmagasinée, en les prenant sur soi-même et sur les autres, commençait à s'épuiser. Zola, qui était un beau décorateur de théâtre, s'en tirait en brossant des toiles plus ou moins précises; il suggérait très bien l'illusion du mouvement et de la vie; ses héros étaient dénués d'âme, régis tout bonnement par des impulsions et des instincts. (Huysmans [1884] 1981: 53)[12]

12 'Naturalism was getting more and more out of breath by dint of turning the mill for ever in the same round. The stock of observations that each writer had stored up by self-scrutiny or study of his neighbours was getting exhausted. Zola, who was a first-rate scene painter, got out of the difficulty by designing big, bold canvases more or less true to life; he suggested fairly well the illusion of movement and action; his heroes were devoid of soul, governed simply and solely by impulses and instincts' (Huysmans 1969: xxxv).

The end result in Huysmans's view is that Zola's characters become mere 'utility men' bearing the heavy burden of the ideas that they are there to represent.

When naturalism as it has been defined above comes to the cinema, however, in many of its exemplars it succeeds in shaking off the enduring genetic link with realism (as identified by, among others, Seltzer 1992: 143), and thus also the requirement that we are in the presence of a 'real' considered as 'milieu agissant sur l'individu' ('environment acting upon the individual', Hamon 1983: 129). There will remain this exchange or communication between environment and 'individual'; however, the exchange need no longer be between a milieu conveyed according to mimetic aspirations and a character given solid – however stereotypical – dimensions. The extent of the mutation is made clear in Deleuze's delineation of the salient characteristics of naturalism in cinema. It usually entails, he points out, a geographically defined space such as a house, country or region ('des milieux réels d'actualisation, géographiques et sociaux' (Deleuze 1983: 174)) – as opposed to 'espaces quelconques' ('any-space-whatevers') – which is somehow in communication with what he calls 'un monde originaire' ('an originary world', Deleuze 1983: 174).[13] This originary world, Deleuze explains, is often marked by either a highly artificial studio set (one thinks immediately of *Les Amants du Pont-Neuf* which was mostly filmed on a reconstructed artificial Pont-Neuf near Montpellier) or a genuine, natural space such as a desert or forest. *Pola X* conforms to these requirements, first in the centrality to its topography of the château world (a real milieu of actualisation) and second in the shape of the oneiric spaces that encroach on that domain. As a final preliminary point about naturalism, it is not coincidental that Carax's own model for *Pola X, Pierre, or The Ambiguities*, is one of Deleuze's examples of 'naturalism' in literature.[14] As a way of describing certain aesthetic principles, naturalism, we will argue, then, offers a way of getting close to Carax's concerns in this film.

13 'real milieus of geographical or social realisation' (Deleuze 1986: 123). There is a discussion of the concept of 'espace quelconque' in Chapter 2 of this volume.

14 Deleuze would probably elicit only tacit support for this assertion from specialists in North American literature: 'In pre-Darwinian United States the boldest novelists, and especially Herman Melville, had sensed most of these ideas, but nobody could combine such loomings into an integrated vision and technique' (Budd 1995: 29).

It has been remarked that the Paris sequences of the film recall the opening documentary-style scenes of *Les Amants du Pont-Neuf*, not simply in terms of technique, but also in their raw evocation of the world of the *sans papiers*, of those who are forced to survive at the margins of French society. At a superficial level, then, the film can be said to share Zola's fascination with the exotica of the 'lower depths'. What is perhaps more notable, however, is the choice made by Carax to locate both sets of lovers in a space architecturally separated from normativity, but which is also a space of ruin. From the bridge of *Les Amants* to the squat of *Pola X*, however, there is quite some distance, notwithstanding what we might term this structural affinity. The squat (a remnant) is far from the centre of Paris, whereas the bridge (under repair) was at its heart. The utopian aspects, however, of *Les Amants* only arise due to an accident – the closure of the bridge for repairs. The utopia is made possible by a caesura in time, or by a fold in time which also creates a space, a niche (just as *Mauvais Sang* with the passing of the comet yields a fold in time). In *Pola X* no such possibilities obtain, and thus the margins have to exist in the geographical periphery of Paris itself.

One might be tempted to speak of the Paris sequences, as many have done in respect of the opening sequences of *Les Amants*, in terms of realism, or of naturalism in the Zolaesque sense. Given the claim made by several commentators regarding the atrophied Zolaism (a 'Zola congelé' according to Baignères's (1991) review) of *Les Amants du Pont-Neuf* it is already possible to see an affinity between naturalism and that film. With regard to Deleuze's suggestion that artificial sets are a key feature of one strand of naturalism in cinema, there is another aspect of the film to prompt the question of a specifically cinematic naturalism. However, the artificial set of *Les Amants*, along with the spectacular events and set pieces of that film, remain located within the predominantly neo-baroque aspirations of Carax in this period. Simply to point out that there is a lack of artifice, or a reduction of the intervention of artifice between camera and objects filmed, is not sufficient evidence to corroborate the claim that this amounts to a return to the real – not unless that return is taken in its proper context. Certainly, it is far from true of *Les Amants* that it follows Zola in 'replacing ... pure imagination by ... observation and experimentation' (cited in Jameson 1971: 173), when it comes to the film once the opening sequence is over. If anything, what the film is in part concerned to do – a concern evoked by the opening sequence in the context of the film as a whole – is to ask the question of whether allegory can be restored as anything other than 'a pathology with which in the modern world we are only too familiar' (Jameson 1971: 72).

There is in cinema, Deleuze asserts, an entropic and a cyclic naturalism. In cinema, its representatives are von Stroheim and Buñuel respectively. The originary world, in Deleuze's conception, is operative as a force of turbulence which undermines the derived milieu and subjects it to a process of degradation, decomposition or unravelling. The difference, Deleuze asserts, between the two primary examples of naturalist cinema, is that in von Stroheim there is an entropic pulsion, symbolised most forcefully by the rubbish dump which is the destination of the corpse in *Foolish Wives* (1921); by contrast, Buñuel's is a cyclical naturalism, the clearest idea of which can be gleaned from the repeated undoing of the respective derived milieus in *Le Charme discret de la bourgeoisie* (1972) – the event to which the characters repeatedly address themselves does not take place despite the repeated setting up of the conditions for the successful completion of the meal. Thomas Vinterberg's film of 1998, *Festen*, belongs to this strand of naturalism. The destabilising force represented by the protagonist's memory of child sexual abuse keeps returning, despite his repeated expulsion from the hotel where the celebration of the film's title repeatedly and defiantly attempts to proceed.

A forgotten violence upon which the derived milieu is founded, or an excluded force of destabilisation, often excluded by means of a similar act of violence: these would essentially be the two sides of the originary world. *Pola X* in different ways features both sides. Isabelle and her companions are the displaced survivors of a war, excluded from their homeland, but excluded also in their adopted home in France. They come, then, to haunt the derived milieu of another nation space, but also to trouble the very idea of the *heimlich*. Thus updating and transposing Melville, Carax succeeds in having the film register a very strong sense of what Julia Kristeva (1989) calls the phenomenon of 'étrangers à nous-mêmes'. As both the excluded part of the family, and its buried secret, Isabelle is also, however, an affirmative and metamorphic force once she bursts into the château grounds, hinterland and the family enclave. In its essential aspects, the figure of Isabelle as *unheimlich* corresponds to the structure of the originary in the thought of Walter Benjamin. In allegory, according to Benjamin, 'the observer is confronted with the *facies hippocratica* of history as a petrified, primordial landscape [*erstarrte Urlandschaft*]' (Benjamin 1977: 166). In *Pola X*, moreover, Isabelle evokes aspects of the angelic as this concept informs Benjamin's thought. She comes first via the telephone, where she remains mute on the other end of the line; she is nothing but, as Deneuve's character puts it, a *souffle* ('a breath'). She haunts the periphery of the château grounds. In *Pierre* the novel, the ghostly apparition – and the 'demoniacal' qualities – of Isabel are more emphatic still. For Benjamin, such interruptions, where the observer is forced forward but while gazing backwards, issue in a utopian possibility (hence their redemptive and messianic quality), are made available through and in ambiguity itself: 'Ambiguity is the figurative appearance of the dialectic, the law of the dialectic at a standstill [*Dialektik im Stillstand*]. This standstill is Utopia' (Benjamin 1983: 171). If there is standstill in *Pola X/Pierre, or The Ambiguities*, what it facilitates, in the idiom of Benjamin, is a 'blasting' out from the linear–chronological time of family and patrimony.

This is how Deleuze and his co-author Félix Guattari describe the forces channelled through Isabel in Carax's model, *Pierre, or the Ambiguities*:

> Pierre gagne la zone où il ne peut plus se distinguer de sa demi-sœur Isabelle, et devient femme. Seule la vie crée de telles zones où tourbillonnent les vivants, et seul l'art peut y atteindre et y pénétrer dans son enterprise de co-création. (Deleuze and Guattari 1991: 164)[15]

Carax's interest in the novel betrays a similar emphasis. He views Pierre's incestuous desire as a desire to 'become-woman',[16] an act of undoing (of molar identity) and liaison with a molecular force or set of forces):

---

15 'Pierre reaches the zone in which he can no longer distinguish himself from his half-sister, Isabel, and he becomes woman. Life alone creates such zones where living beings whirl, and only art can reach and penetrate them in its enterprise of co-creation' (Deleuze and Guattari 1994: 173).

16 In Deleuze and Guattari, 'woman' is on the side of the molecular, whereas 'man' is identified with the complex of molar forces that serve to preserve phallocentric social practices. The figure of becoming-woman – and it is a figure and not intended to designate either a literal transformation or even literal biological difference – has drawn both criticism and support in equal parts from feminist theorists and commentators on their work.

> L'inceste vu comme un rapport avec soi même, pas forcément le rapport sexuel [...] Je pense que Pierre ou Isabelle c'est la même chose, c'est la même personne [...] Isabelle, elle serait l'expérience. Pierre, il a vingt ans, il a pas d'expérience.[17] (Carax 1999b)

The zone of becoming referred to by Deleuze and clearly invested in by Carax also features in Deleuze's account of philosophical naturalism. Deleuze remarks of the originary world – as background – in terms which are immediately promising as far as *Pola X* is concerned: 'On le reconnaît à son caractère informe: c'est un pur fond, ou plutôt un sans-fond fait des fonctions non-formelles, actes ou dynamisms énergiques qui ne renvoient même pas à des sujets constitués' (Deleuze 1983: 174).[18] It is also, for these reasons, the world of affect as opposed to affection. The originary world is one prior to differentiation, a world where the line of demarcation between, say, human and animal is not yet operative (hence Zola's 'bêtes humaines'). The film conforms on a superficial level to this model, opening as it does with, as 'derived milieu', a château framed by highly manicured countryside which will provide the 'setting' for a denouement, while Carax has stated that Isabelle is an animal, mineral and vegetable force as much as a character (Carax 1999b). Pierre, following Melville's novel, has a relationship with his mother not without ambiguity and a hint of suppressed sexual desire. Here, as in other respects, the film at once invites and repels a psycho-analytic reading (the question of its resistance is returned to below).[19] However, it is not Pierre's ambivalent relationship with his mother – based on an impulse (a sexual one) 'prior' to the derived milieu of the family – that is indicative of the 'originary world' in these opening sequences. A sign that Pierre is hooked into the originary world is that

17 'Incest viewed less as a sexual relation than as a relation with the self [...] I think that Pierre and Isabelle are one and the same; they are the same person. Isabelle would be experience. Pierre is 20 years old and has no experience.'

18 'It is a pure background, or rather a without-background, composed of unformed matter, crossed by non-formal functions, acts, or energy dynamisms which do not even refer to the constituted subjects' (Deleuze 1986: 123).

19 Psychoanalysis, in Deleuze's view, is entirely inadequate when it comes to understanding affective states. It is content 'de donner des objets interdits aux affections répertoriées, ni de substituer aux zones d'indétermination de simples ambivalences' (Deleuze and Guattari 1991: 165); 'give forbidden objects to itemised affections or substitute simple ambivalences for zones of indeter-mination' (Deleuze and Guattari 1994: 174).

he is apt to flee from the house in spasmodic and spontaneous flights on foot, motorcycle and horseback, and to range widely and chaotically in the surrounding countryside. Via the house, and in particular via the strange past of its occupants, and the emergence of Pierre's half-sister Isabelle, there is, however, also another channel of communication with an originary world governed by impulse and the irrational.

In beginning to unearth a buried family secret – one which is not fully revealed to Pierre until a highly pregnant viewing situation later in the book in the case of the Melville model – Pierre hooks into a series which will send him on a vertiginous exit from the house and from the family. There are both emancipatory and constricting consequences to be engendered through this line of communication. On the one hand, Isabelle precipitates Pierre into a potentially creative relationship, one wherein he can further his ambitions as a writer and artist (he has a lot, but as Carax points out, what he lacks is experience: Isabelle is 'experience' (Carax 1999b)); on the other, the originary world is also that of Cain (as, following the novel closely, the film attests in the 'fraternal' rivalry between Pierre and his cousin Thibault).[20] The link which Carax forges – via the opening credits' 'dream sequence' – with the conflict in the former Yugoslavia is important in this context:

> C'était quelque chose que j'avais … qui se passait en Bosnie … et on pourrait penser qu'Isabelle elle sort d'une de ces tombes bombardées et elle marche vers nous comme dans le film d'Abel Gance *J'accuse* où les morts de la Première Guerre marchaient vers le caméra, marchent vers nous … C'est un peu ce fantôme là, elle est … Elle est la part maudite (Carax 1999b);[21]

The images are from the Second World War with Luftwaffe planes bombing a graveyard, but it is used to render the dream that Carax says was at the origin of the film, namely of bombs falling on a Balkan graveyard (Carax made several visits to Bosnia during the conflict). If one is aware of this, then the opening sequence is specific enough to allow the association of the images with (Carax's oblique experience

20 The point about Cain is made by Deleuze (1983: 175).
21 'It was something that … that happened in Bosnia … and one could think of Isabelle that she comes out of one of those bombed tombs and she walks towards us like in Abel Gance's film *J'accuse* wherein the dead of the First World War walk toward the camera, walk toward us … She is somewhat like that phantom. She is the accursed portion.'

of) the Balkan conflict; however, it is at the same time generic enough to suggest war in the broader sense. The film thus establishes internal indices of the generic violence of war on the one hand, and of a specific political refugee status for Isabelle and her companions on the other. (The three-episode version for Arte incorporates a scene immediately after the bombing sequence on a devastated landscape, with the plumes of smoke on the horizon, with Pierre leaning against the rock – an object of symbolic import in the novel and film – and joined by his mother. A less than joyous afterlife is thereby suggested for the characters.)

Although the originary world *precedes*, that does not necessarily mean that it is prior to individuation. Nor does it mean that this is a primordial world of equivalence. Rather there is *nothing but* differentiation here. The originary world is 'aformal', and unformed; in this sense it is 'prior' to character and to human subjectivity. The differentiation, however, is at a micrological level, and concerns gradations of light and dark, of levels of force and energy, degrees of intensity rather than intention. 'Il ne s'agit que de nous, ici et maintenant; mais ce qui est animal en nous, végétal, mineral ou humain n'est plus distinct' (Deleuze and Guattari 1991: 164–5).[22] Carax seems to have envisaged the figure of Isabelle less as a traditional character than as a zone of energies and intensities. She exists as an amalgam of speeds and slownesses; in her, rapid logorrhoea and mute catalepsy vie for position. Isabelle, Carax states, is as much Pierre's *part maudite* as she is his sister, but if she is accursed it is in the Bataillian sense, namely as irrecuperable and *in excess*. In Deleuze's conception, the originary world does not confront the constructions of humans with an opposing nature; rather it remains oblivious to such a distinction: the distinction is itself something at home only in derived milieux (Deleuze 1983; 1986). In this respect, Isabelle functions as locus of (and in a certain sense as equivalent to) the impulse which overwhelms Pierre, severing him from intentionality.

---

22 'It is a question only of ourselves, here and now; but what is animal, vegetable, mineral, or human in us is now indistinct' (Deleuze and Guattari 1994: 174).

## Analysis of key scenes

The scrutiny of two key scenes lends credence to the reading just proposed. The scene where Isabelle leads Pierre through a forest and recounts her strange tale is plunged into such obscurity that, as one commentator puts it, it almost looks like we are observing film printed on negative stock (Hoberman 2000). This scene was in fact filmed by Carax on Steadicam in broad daylight and digitally treated to resemble a scene shot at night. For Jean-Michel Frodon, the love scene between Pierre and Isabelle is, because it is mute ('L'union des sexes octroyés l'un et l'autre en un cérémonial doux et muet'),[23] but conducted in the same obscurity of their first encounter, the silent counterpart of that scene with its frenzy of Isabelle's monologue. That these scenes with Isabelle are so plunged into obscurity might lead some to reflect on their possible symbolism: perhaps, it might be argued, the darkness is there to evoke the unknown, even that which should not be 'known' in the biblical sense (the sister). However, these scenes must also be considered in the context provided by the previous films. The play of light and darkness according to the baroque economy associated with the Carax of the 1980s – but not necessarily, or not only in the context proposed by Bassan (see Chapter 1 for an outline of the baroque characteristics of Carax) – establishes the possibility of an alternative reading. These are beings of the 'clear-obscure' (Séguret is correct therefore when he writes that Isabelle is both 'le trou noir et le centre lumineux de *Pola X*' (Séguret 1999)); they exist part-plunged in the obscure, in the shadows. Such beings once more recall the seventeenth-century philosopher Leibniz, cinema's own dualist struggles in German expressionism, the baroque films of Werner Schroeter (*Der Rosen Koënig/King of Roses* (1984) in particular) and several of the films discussed in Chapter 1. In this respect, Higuinen is right to argue that the film 'résiste au binaire, aux oppositions faciles, entre la haute société et les réfugiés d'Europe de l'Est, l'art et la vie, l'effacement et la visibilitité, le paradis et l'enfer' (Higuinen 1999: 80).[24] Neither garden of earthly delights, nor inferno, this space, along with the film of which it forms part – as the added section in the television version suggests – is purgatorial.

23 'The union of her sex and his bestows on each a soft and mute ceremony.'
24 'resists binary, facile oppositions between high society and Eastern European refugees, art and life, erasure and visibility, heaven and hell.'

It is worth noting that the consummation of the incestuous desire between Pierre and Isabelle (for Séguret 'une scène d'amour qui comptera parmi les plus belles jamais filmées') is in no way presented as a transgressive act.[25] If the scene is central it is not primarily as a denouement of the subplot of incestuous desire as felt by two characters projecting forward according to a destiny or as determined by extraneous forces. Rather, there is a sense in which this scene embodies a crucial slowing down which creates the conditions for the two clusters of forces which the characters represent to be acted upon by a *fêlure*: what they produce in each other does not belong to them, although it reorients them in fundamental ways. It is worth noting the part played by the lack of artifice, of music, of a montage which would conform to soft- or hard-porn aesthetics and dynamics (not to mention hydraulics) in enabling this to take place (Higuinen comments that this is the anti-*Romance* film (Higuinen 1999: 80)). Decisions as to angle, framing, lighting and *mise en scène* facilitate, in addition to the attenuation of what might be called a normative pornographic gaze, the displacement of a psychoanalytic interpretation. These are bodies, communicating mutely and intensely at the edge of bifurcating and dissolving identities. Carax can be said, through his handling of this scene in particular, to approach the level of singularities, intensities, the 'aformal', or the figural.[26] Frodon in praising the director for certain of the risks taken by him in the film – effectively, its attempt to confront cinema with its own limits – points out also that these risks necessitate the film's weakness – and Carax himself is swift to agree with this general point. But, Frodon concludes by asking: 'combien de cinéastes aujourd'hui se lancent ainsi à corps perdu dans la matière même du cinéma, plongent dans les images et les sons chercher des perles nouvelles, certaines d'une exceptionnelle beauté?'[27]

Higuinen notes that at other key points the film's is a 'montage brutal, qui efface la transition, gomme le temps du voyage. On bondit d'un lieu à un autre, la route, lieu de nombreuses chevauchées à

25 'a love scene which will count among the most beautiful ever filmed'
26 In his book *Discours, figure* Jean-François Lyotard makes a distinction between the discursive and the figural wherein the *figural* is the name of a process of deformation that works against the *form* to which the discursive and the figurative respectively tend. See Lyotard (1971).
27 'how many filmmakers today throw themselves ... into the very matter of cinema, plunging into images and sounds to seek out new pearls, some of exceptional beauty?'

moto, étant moins ce qui relie deux endroits qu'un espace en soi'.[28]
This brusque editing complements that aspect of the film which
causes it to veer consistently towards dissonant conjunctions and
linkages (Carax clearly announces these intentions with his prefacing
note from *Hamlet* and Deleuze: the time is out of joint). Higuinen
concludes that despite what might at first sight appear to be its
totalising intentions, the film in fact is very much more focused on
sequences and on shots. 'Carax s'acharne, cruellement masochiste, à
mettre en danger tout ce qui, jusqu'à aujourd'hui, était emblématique
de son cinéma' (Higuinen 1999: 80).[29]

## Total fusion

Previous chapters have presented *amour fou* as manifest in Carax's
work through a form of what one might call 'total fusion'. In Caraxian
*amour fou*, there is a loss of identity through an impossible but desired
pact, or 'compacting'. Here in *Pola X* the quest for total fusion is
complexified and the world on-screen rendered all the more cata-
strophic by means of its incestuous aspect. Carax, then, intensifies the
claustrophobia of *Les Amants du Pont-Neuf* not by means of spatial
contraction (the space available to the characters could not after all
have become much smaller) but by reducing the 'time' of possibility.
Time is not only out of joint, but is coiled up, restricting the possibility
for action. Already sharing a 'time' or temporality – a familial one –
the protagonists, including Pierre's mother (they address each other
as 'sister' and 'brother'), consume it all at once. There is not enough
time for them to space themselves out one from the other. Hence the
descent into abjection and loss – a key element in naturalism in
literature and cinema – in this film is all the more precipitous and
rapid.

Pierre cannot respond to the normative demands made on him by
virtue of his status and that of his family because he partly dwells in a
universe of radical alterity, in the originary *and prior* world familiar to

28 'brutal montage which effaces transition, erases the journey-time. One leaps
   from one place to another, the road – site of numerous motorcycle rides – being
   less that which links two places than a space in itself.'
29 'Cruelly masochistic, Carax persists in putting in danger all that has been until
   now emblematic of his cinema.'

naturalist literature and cinema. Or, more precisely, the derived milieu is infiltrated by the originary world which rises up, as a spectral apparition fresh from the 'tombs', in the form of Isabelle (but Isabelle is that part of Pierre that belongs to the originary world). 'Le temps est hors de ses gonds' ('The time is out of joint'): Hamlet's words preface the film ('le siècle est détraqué' is another translation of the phrase usually rendered as 'le temps est hors de ces gonds'). One of the consequences of this unhinging is that the subject becomes un-moored from its anchor and, in the words of Rimbaud, implicitly utters 'Je est un autre' ('I is another' – Rimbaud [1871] 1966: 304). Consequently it is necessary, for both Carax and Pierre, to access the depths in a depersonalised fusion with the powers of the false, or 'the lies underneath everything' (the film's version of Melville's intriguing and self-reflexive passage on falsehood in *Pierre*).[30] It is crucial – and here Carax is decidedly aligned with Rimbaud – that the fusion be between a depersonalised amalgam of forces and intensities, and a set of forces called nature, rather than between a subject and an object. Just as he had done for Orson Welles through the character of the Confidence Man, Melville provides Carax with the perfect model. Pierre, with his ambiguities, has, like Hamlet, a constitutive weakness. If Hamlet is thwarted by self-doubt and hesitation in action, Pierre is absorbed in ambiguities and erupts into action without the presence of the guide-rails of intentionality or the superego, careering from one situation to the next in a sequence of irrational outbursts and alliances. Like Hamlet, however, Pierre is a being who alternates between the catatonic and the ecstatic.

One of Deleuze's best interpreters, François Zourabichvili, describes the nature of the interaction between such a subject and forces of speed and slowness in the following terms:

> The texture of the self is a membrane, not a thing but the capture of *another* thing, since a faculty exists only through the forces it captures, which sometimes captivate it (catatonia) and sometimes carry it away (fulguration). A writer does not therefore express lived experience, insofar as expression blurs into creation: the percept-affect reveals the intolerable, or with an intolerable force, reveals that which used to

30 'An overpowering sense of the world's downright positive falsity comes over him; the world seems to lie saturated and soaking with lies' (Melville [1852] 1996: 208).

remain enveloped within ordinary perceptions and affections (lived experience). (Zourabichvili 1996: 197)

Pierre, in Melville's novel and as transposed to the screen in Carax's version, is subject to the same play of centripetal and centrifugal forces as described by Zourabichvili in the preceding quotation. He is also a writer subject to the 'usurpings' referred to. Melville's majestic irony is that as well as giving us his author *en abîme* at precisely the locus of the conflict, and as host to the visitations, he lets us peer (as Carax also points out) over the shoulder of Pierre, but what is read is the clearly unformed and imperfect wild draft of a possible project. As for the issue of the intolerable and the limits of perception, there will be further discussion below (see also the chapter on *Les Amants du Pont-Neuf* above).

Lucretius's well-known concept of the clinamen, as glossed by the philosopher Michel Serres, provides further insight into the dynamism of *Pola X* in respect of its reflection on nature, and does so in a way which complements the approach of Deleuze, and which enables one to extrapolate further on the philosophical dimensions of the film. The first third of the film shows us a world governed by what Serres calls a 'thanatography'. Serres presents his argument in terms which closely mirror those of Lucretius, but which have an eye to more recent events on the world stage:

> There is nothing to be learned, to be discovered, to be invented, in this repetitive world, which falls in the parallel lines of identity. Nothing new under the sun of identity ... The chains of cause and effect, the fall of atoms, and the indefinite repetition of letters are the three necessary figures of science's nullity. You might very well think that the bloodied rulers were thrilled to find this world and to seize upon its laws of determination – their own, in fact – the very same ones as they had: the laws of extermination. Determination, identity, repetition, information-free, not a drop of knowledge: extermination, not even the shadow of a life, death at the end of entropy. (Serres 1982: 100)

The bombs falling at the start of *Pola X* describe such a world, a world where the fall of atoms is guaranteed. It is a sequence which finds a curious echo in Serres: 'the violence never stops, streaming the length of the thalweg; the atoms fall endlessly; reasons repeat indefinitely' (100). In this world, moreover, as Serres continues in his lyrical mode to delineate the devastating consequences of a universe ruled by the parallel lines of identity, 'Nature is put to death or is not allowed to be born' (100). When Pierre has decided to flee the estate, he takes a sledgehammer to the sealed room once occupied by Isabelle. He enters to find certain vestiges of a former inhabitant, but what he finds in another, philosophical sense, is a void, albeit a resonant one once it has been breached. However, remembering that Isabelle has, in a sense, not been allowed to be born – in being denied her membership of the family – his intervention also suggests a swerve against the dominant current or trajectory (or laminar flow) associated with the household. This is confirmed when the intervention in question comes back to him in a dream. In the dream-remembered version of the entry to the sealed room, the image shows that contact with a fluid turbulent space and matter has been severed by means of a founding act of exclusion. In his dream, Pierre sees turbulence of the oceanic through the window, which holds beyond it a maritime swirl which carries the doll mentioned by Isabelle in their nocturnal forest walk.

But the clinamen, the angle of inclination, in Lucretius is also that which 'cures the plague, breaks the chain of violence, interrupts the reign of the same, invents the new reason and the new law, *foedera naturae*, gives birth to nature as it really is' (100). The sprinklers of the opening section, with their linear and sequenced order, give way to the turbulent and the oceanic, or to 'The sweet vortices of the physics of Venus' (101) as Serres puts it. The computer-generated dream sequence in which Pierre is pulled into the bloodied cascading river can be thought of as representing his struggle between *thanatos* and the revolution of 'voluptuousness', 'Nature being born [in the words of Serres] in smiling voluptuousness' (Serres 1982: 102).

Pierre at the outset is falling – like the bombs – in a deterministic universe, but, already in advance, there is a *clinamen*, a swerve, directing him to the collision with Isabelle. Thus the film traces in part the re-enchantment of nature but in a world where *thanatos* ultimately holds sway. Nature, then, in the Lucretian sense, is killed, as Carax seems to underline by means of the after-life purgatorial image at the beginning of the television cut, which features a visual cipher for the magnificent rock on the Mount of Titans in Melville's novel.

Having established, then, that the paradigm of naturalism in various complementary guises provides a unique insight into the film's structural and thematic concerns, it is now time to turn to the novel, which, as we shall see below, itself belongs to this 'tradition'. The purpose of this section is to flesh out the intertextual horizons of the film with respect to its source, and to examine the shifts in emphasis, the elisions and the inventions which are brought to bear on the novel by Carax and his co-writers Lauren Sedofsky and Jean-Pol Fargeau.

### *Pierre, or The Ambiguities*

Melville's novel was first published in 1852 and can be seen, at least in part, as an attempt to restore a reputation in free-fall after the commercial disaster of *Moby Dick* (1850). The literary critic Lukács identified something of its specificity by calling it a novel of romantic disillusionment rather than one of abstract idealism. Or perhaps, given its deliberate foregrounding of the question of ambiguity and the lack of resolution of ambiguities which characterise it, the novel is best thought of as an unruly hybrid of the type identified by Lukács with Tolstoy. In part a contribution to a popular genre and in part a *roman-à-clef, Pierre* is also heavily in debt to the figure of Hamlet. There are many compelling parallels. In place of Hamlet's indecision, we have Pierre's ambiguities; in place of the apparition on the ramparts of the ghost of Hamlet's father we have the portrait of Pierre's father and the 'spectral' apparition of Isabel; in place of Hamlet's ambiguous relationships with his mother and Ophelia, Pierre has a brother–sister relationship with his mother and his half-sister (who herself in many respects is an Ophelia). Both texts have a protagonist who in some sense can be read as the 'expression of melancholy in a stricken world' (Jameson 1971: 70). Moreover, it is also true, and this move becomes clear as we move from *Hamlet* to *Pierre*, that 'the familiar context of baroque tragedy (that melancholy which we recognise from Hamlet) veers about strongly into a question of form, into the problem of objects, which is to say of allegory itself' (Jameson 1971: 71). If allegory is the mode of expression of a world in which things have been sundered from their meaning, then there arises the question of in what respects, if any, the allegorical work seeks a reconciliation and a suturing of these. The extent to which the novel's point of departure is a world thus riven is already suggested by its title, *Pierre, or The Ambiguities*. Ambiguity is a state of lack of clarity of meaning on the one hand (from the Latin *ambigiuus*) and a lack of certainty of form on the other. As a writer, Pierre perhaps seeks to *resolve*, but perhaps more properly he occupies precisely the space of allegory itself. There may be, as Jameson suggests, in the allegorical impulse, a will to the reconciliation of object and spirit, but it remains merely a will. The state of ruin, chaos and fragmentation (identified so often in Benjamin and not only in his book on the baroque) resists any attempt at such a reconciliation. In Melville's novel, it is nature and the forces of nature which are equivalent to this state:

> During this state of semi-consciousness, or rather trance, a remark-able dream or vision came to him. The actual artificial objects around him slid from him, and were replaced by a baseless yet most imposing spectacle of natural scenery. But though a baseless vision in itself, this airy spectacle assumed very familiar features to Pierre. It was the phantasmagoria of the Mount of the Titans, a singular height standing quite detached in a wide solitude not far from the grand range of dark blue hills encircling his ancestral manor. (Melville [1852] 1996: 342)

In the next paragraph, the narrator reflects that nature is but a puzzle which each interpreter deciphers according to his or her fancy. Nature is fundamentally ambiguous, as he goes on to explain by mentioning how one poet had named the Mount of Titans 'The Delectable Mountain', while irrespective of its nomenclature the form of the mountain itself was in continuous transformation: 'the annual displacements of huge rocks and gigantic trees were continually modifying its whole front and general contour' (Melville [1852] 1996: 342). Pierre continues to be defined by his ambiguities, to be in liaison with pre-personal forces, immersed, despite his late resolve to combat them, in the 'malady of his eyes, this new death-fiend of the trance, and this Inferno of his Titanic vision' (Melville [1852] 1996: 346). The problem lies at the heart of the structure of ambiguity, which, as Andrew Benjamin has argued, always entails an irreducible remainder (Benjamin 2001: 93).

In a move which could at one level be read as an attempt to resolve an especially nagging ambiguity, Melville undertakes in *Pierre* a lengthy meditation on American identity. One can see the appeal for Carax of this aspect of the novel, to judge by his incensed response to contemporary French ultra-right nationalism (Carax 1991a). Taken as a whole, Melville writes a great oeuvre part of the concern of which is to map the vast concept of American identity. In part it is a question of tradition: *Pierre* ponders the question of the relative depth of tradition available to an English as opposed to an American youth in the following terms: 'The monarchial world very generally imagines, that in demagoguical America the sacred Past hath no fixed statues erected to it, but all things irreverently seethe and boil in the vulgar cauldron of an everlasting uncrystalising Present' (Melville [1852] 1996: 8). Pierre himself – already in Melville as he would be in *Pola X* – however, is less a character than an amalgam of intensities. Pierre, after all, is equivalent, Melville's curious title informs us, to a series of ambiguities – ambiguities which in the end, in the final pages of the novel, come almost wholly to supplant him. In a manner to which the film closely adheres, as the novel progresses, the gradual effacement of Pierre as a 'character' is witnessed; it is an effacement which takes place through contact with ambiguities (possible worlds), a contact which is at once contaminatory and constitutive. In this respect, Melville is naturalist and Nietzschean: plurality holds sway within unitary identity; the multiple as multiple is presented. As the contact becomes more expansive, so does the space of self-identity decrease, until such point as that space is coterminous with an atrophied ego, seized up and incapable of intensity or affect.

Pierre, the novel's narrator declares (Melville [1852] 1996: 257), is very 'unarchitectural'. The narrator refers here to his inability to be architectural with the nature of which it is said that it has been a 'benediction' to him. One form of this nature is the magnificent rock on the Mount of Titans which we later read in the retrospective passage towards the end of the novel, his friends had attempted to dig beneath and failed to discover any of its mystery (the rock features in a scene in the film given a nineteenth-century flavour by Carax, with Pierre reaching the remote outpost on horseback). In fact, nature presents rather too much for this Pierre to project a hylomorphic form (by making it signify or symbolise something discernible) upon, which seems to be partly Melville's overall concern in this novel as elsewhere: the forces and energies of nature are in excess of human architecture's – what the philosopher Heidegger calls 'enframing' – capacities for form and formation.

The novel is much concerned to set out a cartography of points of access to that which is identified as 'nature'. It is instructive that many of these points entail, precisely, an architecture, a *dispositif*, and assemblage, a *techne*. Thus the portrait at Saddle Meadows ('unconsciously throwing himself open to all those ineffable hints and ambiguities, and undefined half-suggestions, which now and then people the soul's atmosphere': Melville [1852] 1996: 84); the paintings which occasion the bizarre communication between (and in a curious way not between, since the communication is incomplete) Isabel and Pierre in the concluding passages of the novel; Pierre's deranged book rejected by his publishers who go so far in their rejection as to take him for a swindler. The latter endeavour – Pierre's writing – is firmly linked in Melville's topography to nature, and to nature as *l'informe*: when at the end of each day's writing under the affliction which besets his eyes, Isabel proofreads, she discovers that '(T)hey were replete with errors; but preoccupied by the thronging, and undiluted, pure imaginings of things, he became impatient of such minute, gnat-like torments; he randomly corrected the worst, and let the rest go; jeering with himself at the rich harvest thus furnished to the entomological critics' (Melville [1852] 1996: 340). In *Pola X*, Pierre receives the verdict from a publisher in a letter which reads: 'vos cents pages forment une bouille délirante, qui de plus sent le plagiat'.[31]

The logic of error, here, is rejected by Pierre as an invalid judgement upon the work at hand. Harnessing the possible world of nature as excess, as that which names something which by definition exceeds, means a commitment to registering intensity. Access to excess (Brian Massumi's term) is suggested by the book in the following words: 'Probe, probe a little – see – there seems one little crack there, Pierre – a wedge a wedge' (Melville [1852] 1996: 84). Melville's perspectivism is gradually revealed in *Pierre* and comes to a dazzling conclusive statement in the chapter describing the visit to the exhibition. Here is an exhibition devoted to forgery, to poor copies of European paintings. A charade and a parade of false simulacra these copies may be, but, as Pierre attests, in the worst of these affronts there is, nonetheless, something of merit: in falsification a higher power to be discerned.

This moment comes after a crisis of perception for Pierre. Simultaneous with his desire to escape perception via 'the more secluded and deserted streets' is the beginning of his own loss of sight. Pierre flees then from perception by others and inadvertently from the ability to perceive: his own ability to perceive deserts him.

31 'your one hundred pages form a delirious figure which, in addition, reeks of plagiarism'

However he still has another 'third' vision, as testified to in the gallery scene.

Melville, then, as he does in *Moby Dick*, here presents us with perception at its limit. Frodon is alert to this aspect as it makes its way into the film:

> Au cours d'une séquence hallucinée, dans une obscurité presque complète, Isabelle parle, parle, parle; le cinéma est à l'extrême limite de ses possibilités, tandis qu'on se demande ce que c'est que cette œuvre au noir, cette danse de l'ombre et des mots, cette fille belle comme une morte, une Ophélie. (Frodon 1999)[32]

Pierre, in both the novel and film, liaises with a force, a flux, just as Isabel in the novel does on board the ferry when she declaims in ecstatic reverie about the oceanic maritime movement (in the film, Isabelle starts to hallucinate cadavers in the Seine and leaps in). These moments are equivalent to the emergence of what Gilles Deleuze calls the 'percept'. A 'percept' differs from a perception in so far as it is a mode of capture of the sensible world which lies either below or beyond a certain threshold (which would mark the moment of closure required for perceptions to form). Hence, 'les percepts peuvent être télescopiques ou microscopiques, ils donnent aux personnages et aux paysages des dimensions de géants, comme s'ils étaient gonflés par une vie à laquelle aucune perception vécue ne peut atteindre' (Deleuze and Guattari 1991: 162).[33] These are instances of Deleuzean 'sensibility', wherein literature succeeds in attaining the very limit of perception: 'ce moment-là, faisant éclater les perceptions vécues dans une sorte de cubisme, de simultanéisme, de lumière crue ou de crépuscule, de pourpre ou de bleu, qui n'ont plus d'autre objet ni sujet qu'eux-mêmes' (Deleuze and Guattari 1991: 162).[34] Here is the passage from the novel describing the breakdown in vision in the case of Pierre:

---

32 'At the heart of a hallucinatory sequence, in almost total darkness, Isabelle talks and talks and talks; cinema is at the extreme limit of its possibilities, while one asks oneself what is this black work, this dance of shadows and words, this beautiful girl like one of the dead, an Ophelia.'

33 'Percepts can be telescopic or microscopic, giving characters and landscapes giant dimensions as if they were swollen by a life that no lived perception can attain' (Deleuze and Guattari 1994: 171).

34 'That moment, shattering lived perceptions into a sort of cubism, a sort of simultaneism, of harsh or crepuscular light, of purple or blue, which have no other object or subject than themselves' (Deleuze and Guattari 1994: 171).

And as if all the leagued spiritual inveteracies and malices, combined with his general bodily exhaustion, were not enough, a special corporeal affliction now descended like a sky-hawk upon him. His incessant application told upon his eyes. They became so affected, that some days he wrote with the lids nearly closed, fearful of opening them wide to the light. Through the lashes he peered upon the paper, which so seemed fretted with wires. Sometimes he blindly wrote with his eyes turned away from the paper; – thus unconsciously symbolising the hostile necessity and distaste, the former whereof made of him this most unwilling states-prisoner of letters. (Melville [1852] 1996: 340)

Here vision is entrapped, constrained and tethered; its incapacitation is conceived in terms of a spatial contraction. Melville helpfully points to the metaphorical possibilities invited by his image – one of the many instances of another type of narrative excess in the novel (in that it, self-reflexively, prescribes a certain interpretation and robustly prefigures the imminent imprisonment of Pierre). But contraction and release imbue the novel and the film with a certain rhythm throughout. For Pierre himself, it is always a case of acceleration or deceleration, displacement or homecoming, and sometimes of dissipation and coalescence. The great atrophied space of Saddle Meadows/ the château with its arrest under the name of Glendenning/ Valombreuse contrasts with the fluid and labyrinthine spaces of the Apostles/the squat – his urban refuge – with its multiplicity of names and trades. Marriage to Lucy Tartan/Lucie would have marked a solidification, a coalescence, whereas the incestuous desire for Isabel(le) (on the family as social construct, see Melville [1852] 1996: 145) is indicative of a fluid transgression of propriety. In this novel, which is so concerned to speak of 'America', and which is caught up in a paranoid self-examination, Isabel is also linked to the fluid spaces of an unknown Europe, more ancient and primordial than the America of the settlers and their ancestors. The same contrast, this time looking eastwards from contemporary France, is evinced in the film. Isabel(le) is, moreover, also identified with fluidity. The following passage is indicative:

Now, unending as the wonderful rivers, which once bathed the feet of the primeval generations, and still remain to flow fast by the graves of all succeeding men, and by the beds of all now living; unending, ever-flowing, ran through the soul of Pierre, fresh and fresher, further and still further, thoughts of Isabel. (Melville [1852] 1996: 141)

This fluidity, however, this flux-like quality in Isabel, Pierre reflects in the same paragraph, is itself unchanging. Isabel and what she will bring to Pierre is fated, predestined: what will 'unravel' (Melville [1852] 1996: 141) will do so under the dictates inscribed in this destiny.

Writing is one of those releases for both the novel and the film, but in order to take flight through writing Pierre must go through the detour of catatonia, of being frozen both literally and metaphorically. Melville renders this as follows:

> With cheek rather pale, then, and lips rather blue, Pierre sits down to his plank ... Over his boots are his moccasins; over his ordinary coat is his surtout; and over that, a cloak of Isabel's. Now he is squared to his plank; and at his hint, the affectionate Isabel gently pushes his chair closer to it, for he is so muffled, he can hardly move of himself. (Melville [1852] 1996: 301)

In a remarkable *dispositif* to enable Pierre to write under these extremely unfavourable conditions, Melville anticipates the less than comfortable writing conditions under which Beckett's Malone would later labour (Beckett [1951] 1979):

> Is Pierre a shepherd, or a bishop, or a cripple? No, but he has in effect, reduced himself to the miserable condition of the last. With the crook-ended cane, Pierre – unable to rise without sadly impairing his manifold intrenchments, and admitting the cold air into their inner-most nooks, – Pierre, if in his solitude, he should chance to need any thing beyond the reach of his arm, then the crook-ended cane drags it to his immediate vicinity. (Melville [1852] 1996: 301)

*Pola X* features Pierre from behind bent over his writing desk, for, as Carax has said, every writer looks like a great writer when viewed from behind, and the scene opens all three episodes of the version for Arte. Writing, then, throughout *Pierre* and its Caraxian derivatives, is identified with a double bind: it releases, but at the price of a necessary entrapment as its precondition. It must be mentioned that the novel is in part a *roman-à-clef*, wherein Melville savages 'the assumptions, beliefs, and methods displayed by conventional novels of the sort that this one [*Pierre*] simultaneously imitates and lampoons' (Spengemann 1996: xi–xii). It is of course true that, once Pierre becomes relatively stationary in the Apostles, the novel itself settles down to an intro-spective mode of enquiry into the act of novel writing, and of the writing of this novel in particular (Melville scholars have evidence that shows that the sections of Pierre devoted to authorship were not 'organic to Melville's original idea and that they were penned out of anger and resentment at reviews and personal insults surrounding the reception on *Moby Dick*' (Haydock 2000: 80)). The flight then of the first half is partly away from the genre (what Melville called 'regular romance,' 'calculated for popularity' (cited in Haydock 2000: 81)) which Melville had to mimic in order to make his book saleable, a flight which terminates in a stasis within which it may be possible to access the fluid spaces of the *informe*. Carax does not attempt a translation of this synecdoche for his own artform, filmmaking: his Pierre could not really, after all, be a filmmaker in the same sense as Pierre in Melville can be a novelist. In this respect, then, Carax in *Pola X* continues to maintain a distance from both the Antonionian and Godardian lines of self-reflexivity. However, it is true that the cinema already furnishes ready-made clichés of suffering genius sufficient to enable the shorthand evocation of Pierre's dilemma in the film. Given that Pierre conducts his writing in the same building housing the composer played by Sharunas Bartas there is, however, an element of self-reflexivity, Bartas being the director whose work – and in particular *The House* in which Carax acted – is a kind of refuge for Carax (Higuinen 1999: 79). Moreover, by virtue of the emphasis on the collective – it is no accident that Carax's producer Albert Prévost is among the musicians – Carax enables a fleeting suggestion of a world not too far from that of cinema: Carax has on several occasions spoken of the centrality of collaboration to his method of filmmaking, stating that his sense of cinema is very close to making music. Be this as it may, however, for one critic, if we still see elements that foreground the concerns of the Carax of the 1980s, *Pola X* is not so much the putting into form of Carax's ideas as their being subject to a kind of deformation (Higuinen 1999: 80).

Naturalism, then, as defined by Deleuze and as discussed above in the expanded context offered by the thought of Serres, also goes some way to accounting for the trajectory of the novel's Pierre. We are never far, after all, from naturalism in the Lucretian sense in this novel of swerves, bends, forks and bifurcations. But, by the same token we are never far from 'nature' itself, but from a perspective which refuses to 'devalue Nature by taking away from it any virtuality or potentiality, any immanent power, any inherent being' (Deleuze 1990: 268). Nature is univocal in *Pierre* in a Spinozist sense: this nature is both univocal, in that it is the same force rumbling across as on a unique plane of immanence, and it is expressive of a generalised force of deformation:

> from out the infinite inhumanities of those profoundest forests, came a moaning, muttering, roaring, intermitted, changeful sound: rain-shakings of the palsied trees, slidings of rocks undermined, final crashings of long-riven boughs, and devilish gibberish of the forest-ghosts. (Melville [1852] 1996: 110)

It is through his repeated seeking out of liaison with these inhuman forces that Pierre succeeds in attaining the Icarian flight which will enable him, through its intensity, to forsake Saddle Meadows:

> the place is lost to him ... He knows it not, but his meditative route is sinuous; as if that moment his thought's stream was likewise serpentining: laterally obstructed by insinuated misgivings as to the ultimate utilitarian advisability of the enthusiastic resolution that was his. His steps decrease in quickness as he comes more nigh, and sees one feeble light struggling in the rustic double-casement. Infallibly he knows that his own voluntary steps are taking him forever from the brilliant chandeliers of the mansion of Saddle Meadows, to join company with the wretched rush-lights of poverty and woe. But his sublime intuitiveness also paints to him the sun-like glories of god-like truth and virtue; which though ever obscured by the dense fogs of earth, still shall shine eventually in unclouded radiance, casting illus-trative light upon the sapphire throne of God. (Melville [1852] 1996: 111)

Moving away from Saddle Meadows/the château entails here the loss of co-ordinates as such: if we read 'place' as being lost to him as opposed to or as well as '*the* place'. Place, position, lineage, inheritance and name: all these are lost to Pierre as he liaises with the profound depths (and virtual/potential) of nature and attends to its dissonant entreaties. One of the motifs suggesting these calls or lures is the music of Isabel's guitar (Carax has Isabelle play a concertina in the film): 'the music changed; and drooped and changed; and changed and changed; and lingeringly retreated as it changed; and at last was wholly gone' (Melville [1852] 1996: 127).

Tom Conley has evoked an aspect of Melville which he identifies in a short text 'I and my chimney' but which could equally describe the central question of *Pierre*, and as transposed to Europe and inverted, of *Pola X*:

The 'I' who settles into the American earth ... strives to obtain a mastery of its own insular space, its 'house', an isle and a kingdom in a western hemisphere. The narrator defends an I-land that resists European dominion. Yet, as the tale unfolds, the comparison itself seems to erode as the space encloses upon itself. The plot of the tale tells of a retreat from a whole and a drive towards metamorphosis by which the human becomes inorganic matter. A self-pulverising or self-triturating effect accompanies the move from a world-historical scene to another, or more modest measure, of self-dissemination. (Conley 2000: 277–8)

The latter part of this description remains entirely true of *Pola X*. There is both a retreat from the whole represented by Saddle Meadows/the château and a drive towards metamorphosis (one of the processes which can be identified with the structure of ambiguity), symbolised in the union with Isabel/Isabelle.

In his version of *Pierre* for the screen, Carax makes several key additions to the basic narrative. In the film, Pierre and Isabelle have the sexual relationship that is only hinted at in the novel's more circumspect approach to the question of incestuous desire (see Melville [1852] 1996: 192, although incest is foregrounded by means of numerous complex metaphors and extended metaphors). The source of the altered emphasis, however, remains a literary one, in this case Robert Musil's novel *The Man without Qualities*. Mysticism is replaced by a paramilitary cult, while the ravings of Plotinus Plinlimmon are transformed into the enigmatic performances of Sharunas Bartas at the baton. As in the novel, however, the final refuge of the central couple has denizens belonging both to the obscure arts and those who could be described, in Melville's own words, as children of 'the wretched rush-lights of poverty and woe'.

In Melville we learn that 'Pierre ... had read more novels than most persons of his years' (Melville [1852] 1996: 141). Carax of course combines a passion for reading with a cinephile's devotion to film history. However, from the point of view of the other films, one of the most notable aspects of *Pola X* is the abeyance of the characteristic cinephilia marked in the references and allusions packed into the first three films. The references are more oblique and cryptic in *Pola X*. Once unpacked, they leave us with quite a distinct set of co-ordinates and the manner in which one comes to overlay these upon the film generates quite a different map. Deneuve, Bartas: these names for one thing summon a past of cinema (Buñuel and naturalism perhaps) and a present refuge (for Carax in Bartas's work literally as an actor in *The House* (1997)). The other name summoned by the discordant opening montage sequence is Godard, and in particular the Godard of *Histoire(s) du cinéma*. These elements, however, are not the substance of the film – they do constitute part of the film's universe but not its core.

This question of tradition – both as it features as a theme in Melville and as it is raised in the question of Carax's cinephilia – demands further exploration. Pierre, in the novel, is an author mocked by the narrator for wasting his gift in soliciting flattery for superficial works. Of course, Carax is not a character in his *Pola X*, which renders the analogy at best partial, albeit tantalising. It is seductive to think that Carax uses Pierre as a cipher for himself in respect of his career – or as a way to meditate on the career to date.[35] By transposing but not translating the metonymic aspects of Melville's novel, Carax is enabled to evoke something of his own fate at the hands of certain critics who dismissed *Les Amants* as a folly and the work of a megalomaniac. It is difficult, moreover, in coming to the novel after the film, not to imagine that there must after all be a degree of mockery in Carax's presentation of Pierre. Carax, however, seems to rule out the latter reading when he asserts that he, unlike Melville, is not cut out for irony (Carax 1999a). However, there is a sense in which this is a red herring, as noted by Roussel when he states that 'ces deux mondes ne sont que clichés, ils sont volontairement caricaturés par un cinéaste qui ne croit ni à la réussite littéraire d'un écrivain-châtelain à la mode, ni à la rédemption de celui-ci dans la pauvreté la plus totale' (Roussel 2000: 12).[36] Carax draws attention to this himself in declaring himself so taken with Melville's 'peering' over the shoulder of Pierre to reveal the feeble nature of his work in progress.

If Melville's inhabitants of the Apostles are clearly portrayed as impostors and charlatans, then there is no reason as to why Carax's squat-dwellers should not be viewed in a similar light. This, perhaps,

35 One thinks for example of the ending disowned by Carax to *Les Amants*, and of his refusal to say that there is an influence of Vigo on that work (is this a way to deny 'ownership' of the Vigoesque ending?).

36 'These two worlds are nothing but clichés, they are deliberately caricatured by a cinéaste who believes neither in literary success of a fashionable squire-author, nor in the redemption of the latter in total poverty.'

helps to put into perspective several instances where Carax challenges
the audience by confronting them with scenes which it is difficult to
take seriously at the level of content (especially those featuring
Bartas), even if they have a serious formal purpose that overrides their
studied preposterousness. Although Carax asserts that he is incapable
of irony, it is inviting to read this as a piece of imposture on his part, in
other words as an ironic expression of an incapacity for irony.

   If Carax, as he had done in his three previous films, once more in
*Pola X* sets up the conditions for an encounter with the 'impossible' of
cinema, however, the approach this time is distinct. Here literature's
difference from film enables the latter to address problems specific to
it. This is registered in the fact that the act of adapting for screen
becomes part of the title of the resultant film. The film exists not so
much on its own as a completed artefact, but as a draft, even if a tenth
one, of a possible adaptation of the Melville novel. Frodon offers the
opinion that perhaps 'le gouffre entre l'abstraction lyrique du roman
et ce qu'il y a d'inévitablement figuratif dans un film était-il trop
grand, ou Carax n'a pas trouvé tous les ponts au-dessous de cet
abîme'.[37] However, this verdict perhaps does not take sufficient note
of the fact that *not* finding the bridges is surely part of Carax's aim, not
to mention the fact that the parodic elements in Melville's novel have
to remain specific to the novel, since they have an intertextual referent
specific to literature. That the internal dynamic of the novel in respect
of this element of its semantic register – that is, its 'discursivity' – is
distinct from the film should not hide the fact that in the novel itself
there is a *figural* element which comes to trouble the discourse.[38] The
figural eruption in *Pierre* is another way in which the originary world
– as a force of deformation – acts on the derived milieu. Literature,
then, becomes the difference of film; the figurative (image) propensities of the latter interact with the discursive (linguistic) elements of
the former, while in this interaction is sustained and maintained the
figural as reservoir of that difference itself.

37 'the gulf between the lyrical abstraction of the novel and that which is inevitably
   figurative in the film was too great, or Carax did not find all the bridges over this
   abyss.'
38 See Lyotard (1971) and the note on page 156 in this volume.

## Names

The title of *Pola X*, deriving from an acronym with an 'X' signalling the ten drafts that the script went through, and the name Leos Carax, an anagram, echo each other both by being invented and in ending with the same letter. In the film, as we have seen, the X proliferates, and finds itself in the many instances of identities forsaken and adopted, of places left behind or sought, of gaps, silences and absences. If the act of naming is the imposition of a signifier on a body, then Carax is interested in the state before naming, a state which can be identified both as ambiguous and as equivalent to the problem of allegory – the sundering of object and meaning. Pierre attempts to return to an elemental state prior to naming: a return to the figural body before it is subject to discursive policing.

The downfall of Pierre in the film is partly to do with the violence of the name. The act of naming – which belongs to the derived milieu – arrests the flux, arrests the force of his becoming other, of his simply becoming along the line of a vector without teleology. Celebrity is likewise a form of arrest, as the eloquent writer Pierre–Aladdin fails to utter more than a few stuttering words on his television appearance. In *Les Amants*, the appearance of the poster featuring Michèle puts an end to the fluid phase of her relationship with Alex, who responds characteristically by tipping over too far into deterritorialisation in a display of abject nihilism, setting fire to the bill poster. There, as in *Pola X*, naming and celebrity are on the side of thanatos.

For the *Cahiers* reviewer, Carax in *Pola X* uses Melville in order to 'attaquer son propre univers, défaire ses motifs, briser ses jouets, tordre les corps, faire dérailler ses romances, jusqu'à ce qu'il ne reste plus rien' (Higuinen 1999: 78).[39] He also suggests that the film is haunted by the possibility of failure, while *Sight and Sound* agrees that in the film's moments of testing 'Legibility and exposition to breaking point' there lies 'a metaphor for the contradictions in the director's uniquely self-defeating talent' (Smith 2000: 52). However, these claims require modification and qualification. Perhaps, given that this is a film that attempts to strain at the limits of the medium's own possibility, it would be more accurate to speak of the *necessity of failure* rather than failure per se. In the case of Leos Carax, it would therefore

39 'attack his own universe, undo its motifs, break its toys, twist its bodies, derail its romances, until nothing remains'

be less that his is a self-defeating talent, than that it is one which is capable of a performative defection from selfhood, making *Pola X* thereby the successful attainment of Carax's aim. Thus it is tempting to paraphrase Beckett, in suggesting that in his manner of transposing Pierre to the screen, Carax could not have failed better. The film is indeed the work of a great impostor.

## References

Baignères, Claude (1991), 'Zola congelé', *Le Figaro*, 16 October.

Baguley, David (1990), *Naturalist Fiction: The Entropic Vision*, Cambridge, Cambridge University Press.

Becker, Carole (1992), *Lire le réalisme et la naturalisme*, Paris, Dunod.

Beckett, Samuel [1951] 1979), *Malone Dies*, in *Molloy, Malone Dies, The Unnamable*, London, Picador.

Benjamin, Andrew (2001), *Philosophy's Literature*, Manchester, Clinamen Press.

Benjamin, Walter (1983), *Charles Baudelaire: A Lyric Poet in the Era of High Capitalism*, London, Verso.

—— (1985), *The Origin of German Tragic Drama*, trans. John Osborne, London, Verso.

Buci-Glucksmann, Christine (1994), *Baroque Reason: The Aesthetics of Modernity*, trans. Patrick Camiller, London, Sage.

Budd, Louis J. (1995), 'The American background', in Donald Pizer ed., *The Cambridge Companion to American Literary Naturalism: Howells to London*, Cambridge, Cambridge University Press, pp. 21–46.

Carax, Leos (1991), ed., *Cahiers du Cinéma, numéro spécial Les Amants du Pont-Neuf*.

—— (1991a), 'A l'impossible on est tenu', *Les Inrockuptibles*, no. 32, December. Available online at: *www.patoche.org/carax/interviews/inrocks.htm*

—— (1999), 'Nous dépasser ou sombrer' interview, *Libération*, 14 May.

—— (1999a), Interview by Pierre-André Boutang, *Métropolis*, Arte, 22 May. Available online at *www.patoche.org/carax/interviews/metropolis.htm*

—— (1999b), 'Interview FNAC', interview with Pierre-Andre Boutang, CanalWeb, 15 May.
Available online at *www.patoche.org/carax/interviews/fnac.htm*

—— (2000), Interview with Anthony Kaufmann, *Indiewire*, 13 September.

Conley, Tom (2000), 'I and my Deleuze', in Ian Buchanan and John Marks eds, *Deleuze and Literature*, Edinburgh, Edinburgh University Press, pp. 263–82.

Cormerais, Franck (1999), 'L'image mobile du temps', *http://www.regards.fr/archives/1999/199906creo8.htm*

Deleuze, Gilles (1969), *Logique du sens*, Paris, Minuit.

—— (1980), *Mille Plateaux. Capitalisme et schizophrénie*, Paris, Minuit .

—— (1983), *Cinéma 1. L'Image-mouvement*, Paris, Minuit.

—— (1986), *Cinema 1: The Movement Image*, trans. Hugh Tomlinson and Barbara Haberjam, London, Athlone.

—— (1987), *A Thousand Plateaus*, trans. Brian Massumi, London, Athlone.

—— (1990), *The Logic of Sense*, trans. Mark Lester with Charles Stivale, New York, Columbia University Press.

Deleuze, Gilles and Féliz Guattari (1991), *Qu'est-ce que la philosophie?*, Paris, Minuit.

— (1994), *What is Philosophy?*, trans. Graham Burchell, London, Verso.

Frodon, Jean-Michel (1999), 'L'œuvre au noir de Leos Carax', *Le Monde*, 26 May.

Fukker, Graham (2000), 'Leos Carax's bittersweet hereafter', *Village Voice*, 45:36, 9 December.

Hamon, Philippe (1983), *Le Personnel du roman: le système des personnages dans les Rougon-Macquart d'Emile Zola*, Geneva, Droz.

Haydock, John (2000), 'Melville and Balzac: Pierre's French model', *Leviathan: A Journal of Melville Studies* 2:1, 67–81.

Hertay, Alain (1999), '*Pola X*: la blessure et la beauté' (in 'courrier des lecteurs'), *Cahiers du Cinéma*, no. 536, 4.

Higuinen, E. (1999), 'Exorcisme', *Cahiers du Cinéma*, no. 535, 78–80.

Hoberman, J. (2000), 'Desperate remedies', *Village Voice*, 12 September.

Huysmans, J.-K. [1884] (1981), *A Rebours*, Paris, Imprimerie nationale.

—— (1969), *Against the Grain*, trans. Havelock Ellis, New York, Dover.

Jameson, Fredric (1971), *Marxism and Form: Twentieth Century Dialectical Theories of Literature*, Princeton, Princeton University Press.

Kaganski, Serge (1999), 'Pierre à part', *Les Inrockuptibles*, no. 198, 12–17 May.

Klawans, Stuart (1999), 'Bridge over Troubled Water', *Nation*, 19 July.

Kristeva, Julia (1989), *Etrangers à nous-mêmes*, Paris, Fayard.

Lagny, Michèle (1990), 'The fleeing gaze: Jean Renoir's *La Bête humaine* (1938)', in Susan Hayward and Ginette Vincendeau eds, *French Film: Texts and Contexts*, London, Routledge.

Léonardini, Jean-Pierre (1999), 'Leos Carax boxe à poings nus', *l'Humanité*, 14 May.

Leutrat, Jean-Louis (1997), 'L'horloge et la momie', in Oliver Fahle and Lorenz Engell eds, *Der Film bei Deleuze/Le Cinéma selon Deleuze*, Weimar, Verlag der Bauhaus-Universität Weimar/Presses de la Sorbonne Nouvelle, pp. 407–19.

—— (2000), 'The Power of Language: Notes on *Puissance de la parole, Le Dernier mot* and *On s'est tous défilé*, in Michael Temple and James S. Williams eds, *The Cinema Alone: Essays on the Work of Jean-Luc Godard 1985–2000*, Amsterdam, Amsterdam University Press, pp. 179–88.

Lucretius (1997), *De la nature/De Rerum Natura* (bilingual edition), trans. into French José Kany-Turpin, Paris, Flammarion.

Lyotard, Jean-François (1971), *Discours, figure*, Paris, Klincksieck.

Melville, Herman [1852] (1996), *Pierre or the Ambiguities*, Harmondsworth, Penguin.

Musil, Robert (1995), *The Man without Qualities*, trans. Sophie Wilkins, London, Picador.

Pizer, Donald ([1966] 1984), *Realism and Naturalism in Nineteenth-Century American Fiction*, Carbondale, South Illinois University Press.

Rimbaud, Arthur [1871] (1966), *Complete Works, Selected Letters* (bilingual edition), trans. Wallace Fowlie, Chicago, University of Chicago Press.

Roussel, Christophe (2000), 'Leos Carax', *http://chtiforce.com/carax/texte.htm* (accessed 31 February 2002).

Séguret, Olivier (1999), 'L'attraction de Pola', *Libération*, 14 May.

Seltzer, Mark (1992), *Bodies and Machines*, London, Routledge.

Serres, Michel (1982), 'Lucretius: science and religion', in *Hermes: Literature, Science, Philosophy*, Baltimore, Johns Hopkins University Press. Originally published as 'Conditions culturelles. Violence et contrat: Science et religion', in *La Naissance de la physique dans le texte de Lucrèce: Fleuves et turbulences*, Paris, Minuit, 1977.

Shakespeare, William (1980), *Hamlet*, The New Penguin Shakespeare, Harmondsworth, Penguin.

Smith, Gavin (2000), 'Pola X', *Sight and Sound* 10:6, 51.

Spengemann, William C. (1996), 'Introduction', in Melville ([1852] 1996), pp. vii–xx.

Sundquist, Eric (1982), 'The Country of the Blue', *American Realism: New Essays*, Baltimore, Johns Hopkins University Press.

*Vertigo* (Paris), 2001, numéro spécial hors-série, 'Projections baroques'.

Zourabichvili, François (1996), 'Six Notes on the Percept', in Paul Patton ed., *Deleuze: A Critical Reader*, Oxford, Blackwell, pp. 188–216.

# Filmography

### *Strangulation Blues* (1979) 16 min., b/w

Award at the Cinéma Internationale de Hyères 1981
Production: Les Films du Lagon Blue
Script: Léo Scarax
Director of photography: Bertrand Chatry
Principal actors: Eric Frey, Anne-Petit Lagrange

### *Boy Meets Girl* (1984) 100 min., b/w

Script:  Leos Carax
Production: Abilene Films
Producer: Alain Dahan
Director of photography: Jean-Yves Escoffier
Editing: Nelly Meunier, Francine Sandberg
Decor: Serge Marzolff, Jean Bauer
Sound: Jean Umansky, Francois Groult
Music: Jacques Pinault, Jo Lemaire/S. Gainsbourg, Dead Kennedys, David Bowie
Principal actors: Denis Lavant (Alex), Mireille Perrier (Mireille), Carroll Brooks, Maite Nahyr, Elie Pocard

### *Mauvais Sang (The Night is Young)* (1986) 125 min., col.

Script: Leos Carax
Production: Les Films Plain-chant, Soprofilms, FR3 Films production
Producers: Alain Dahan, Philippe Diaz
Photography: Jean-Yves Escoffier
Editor: Nelly Quettier
Decor: Michel Vandestien with Thomas Peckre and Jack Dubus
Sound: Hélène Muller
Music: Britten, Prokofiev, Chaplin

Songs: 'J'ai pas d'regrets' (Vian), performed by Serge Reggiani. 'Modern Love' (Bowie), performed by David Bowie

Film extract: *La Petite Lise* (Gremillon 1930)

Principal actors: Michel Piccoli (Marc), Denis Lavant (Alex), Juliette Binoche (Anna), Hans Meyer (Hans), Julie Delpy (Lise), Carroll Brooks (the American), Hugo Pratt, Mireille Perrier, Serge Reggiani

### *Les Amants du Pont-Neuf* (1991) 126 min., col.

Production company: Films Christian Fechner

Script: Leos Carax

Producer: Christian Fechner

Associate Producer: Alain Dahan

Director of photography: Jean-Yves Escoffier

Editor: Nelly Quettier

Sound editor: Nadine Muse

Art director: Michel Vandestien

Principal actors: Juliette Binoche (Michèle), Denis Lavant (Alex), Klaus-Michael Gruber (Hans)

### *Pola X* (1999) 134 min., col.

Production: Arena Films in association with Pola Production, Theo Films, Pandora Filmproduktion, Euro Space, Vega Film

Producer: Bruno Pesery

Screenplay: Leos Carax, Lauren Sedofsky, Jean-Pol Fargeau, after the novel *Pierre, or the Ambiguities* by Herman Melville

Director of photography: Eric Gautier

Editor: Nelly Quettier

Music: Scott Walker

Script supervisor: Elie Poicard

Sound: Jean-Louis Ughetto, Béatrice Wick, Jean-Pierre Laforce

Principal actors: Guillaume Depardieu (Pierre Valombreuse), Katarina Golubeva (Isabelle), Catherine Deneuve (Marie Valombreuse), Delphine Chuillot (Lucie de Boiseux)

### Television documentary on Carax

*Enquête sur un film au-dessous de tout soupçon* 1991

Production: Magic Films Productions

Director: Olivier Guiton

Text: André S. Labarthe

Images: Philippe Costantini

# Select bibliography

*The special number of* Cahiers du Cinéma *devoted to* Les Amants du Pont-Neuf *of which Carax was rédactuer en chef in 1991 is dominated by illustrations, and features drawings by Juliette Binoche, photographs of the set under construction, production stills and photographs of the cast by Marion Stalens and others, sketches and notes by Carax and extracts from works of literature.*

## Selected interviews with Leos Carax

(1984), 'Entretien' on France-Culture, November.
Available online at: *www.patoche.org/carax/interviews*

(1984), with Philippe Garrel, 'Dialogue en apesanteur', *Cahiers du Cinéma*, no. 365, November, 36–40.

(1984), 'Libé meets Carax', *Libération*, 17 May.
Available online at: *www.liberation.fr/cinema/cine25/carax.html*

(1986), 'La Beauté en revolte', *Cahiers du Cinéma*, no. 390, December, 24–32.

(1991), 'A l'impossible on est tenu', interview with Serge Kaganski, *Les Inrockuptibles*, no. 32, December.
Available online at: *www.patoche.org/carax/interviews/inrocks.htm*

(1992), 'Leos Carax', interview with David Thompson, *Sight and Sound*, 5:2 September, 10–11.

(1999), 'Nous dépasser, ou sombrer', interview with Laurent Rigoulet and Olivier Séguret, *Libération*, 14 May.

(1999), 'Interview FNAC' with Pierre-Andre Boutang, CanalWeb, 15 May.
Available online at: *www.patoche.org/carax/interviews/fnac.htm*

## Selected articles in journals, chapters in books and sections of books

Austin, Guy (1996), 'The *cinéma du look* and fantasy film', *Contemporary French Cinema: An Introduction*, Manchester, Manchester University Press, pp. 132–5. A brief discussion of Carax in relation to the *cinéma du look*.

Bassan, Raphaël (1989), 'Trois néobaroques français', *Revue du cinéma*, no. 449, 44–50. This important assessment of the films of Carax, Beineix and Besson, aside from the influential association of the three directors with the concept of the neo-baroque, contains highly enlightening statements about the genealogy of Carax's work.

Beugnet, Martine (2000), 'Filmer l'exclusion: *Les Amants du Pont-Neuf*', *Marginalité, sexualité, contrôle: Questions de représentation dans le cinéma français contemporain*, Paris, L'Harmattan, pp. 157–87. This 2000 assessment extols the film as a crucial moment in French cinema of the 1990s. Beugnet signals Carax's markedly alternative vision to that of Beineix and Patrice Leconte, mentioning in particular the tendency of these two directors towards the reification and objectification of (especially) the female body.

Cardinal, Serge (1997), 'L'espace dissonant. A propos d'un segment du film *Boy Meets Girl*', *Cinémas* 5:3 (*Cinelekta 1*), 77–98. This is a detailed analysis of one sequence wherein Cardinal exhaustively describes and analyses the disjunctive interplay of image and sound, making a convincing case for the innovations of Carax in this area.

Frodon, Jean-Michel (1995), 'Leos Carax, tous derrière et lui devant', *in L'Age Moderne du cinéma français: De la nouvelle vague à nos jours*, Paris, Flammarion, pp. 787–93. A diagnostic account of Carax's method. Citation or 'référence maniériste', both of which are required in order for Carax to declare his affiliations in *Boy Meets Girl* and *Mauvais Sang*, carries with it a certain danger – that of overidentification. Thus Frodon can situate *Les Amants du Pont-Neuf* in the context of a 'withdrawal from cinema' and from such identification.

Powrie, Phil (1997), '*Mauvais Sang*: the flight of the female', *French Cinema in the 1980s: Nostalgia and the Crisis of Masculinity*, Oxford, Oxford University Press. This study of *Mauvais Sang* begins with a listing of many of the intertextual references in the film. Coupling psychoanalytical concepts and Krutnik's study of *film noir*, the author explores the film in relation to questions of genre and the representation of masculinity.

Prédal, René (1996), *50 ans de cinéma français (1945–1995)*, Paris, Editions Nathan, pp. 546–51, 719–21. This overview begins by summarising and agreeing with Bassan's assessment of Carax. In terms of lineage, Prédal places Carax somewhere between the Rimbaudean poetry of Garrel and the freedom of expression of Godard.

Rosenbaum, Jonathan (1994), 'Leos Carax: the problem with poetry', *Film Comment*, May–June, 12–18, 22–3. An assessment of Carax's first three films which is notable for its stress on the emergence of Carax's vision in his early *Cahiers du Cinéma* reviews and the importance to Carax of the films of Philippe Garrel.

Udris, Raynalle (2000), 'Countryscape/cityscape and homelessness in Varda's *Sans toit ni loi* and Carax's *Les Amants du Pont-Neuf*', in Myro Konstantarakos ed., *Spaces in European Cinema*, London, Intellect Books, pp. 42–51. The author assesses the symbolic use of homelessness in both films and the degree to which this functions against the values of 'fixed settlement and security' associated with the city.

# Index

abjection 14, 22, 98, 123, 147, 157, 173
Alex
  *autiste-bavarde* 4-6, 11, 23
  *enfant-vieillard* 4-6, 11, 86, 93
  'orphan of chaos' 4, 6, 10–11, 133
allegory 21, 52, 124–5, 151, 161–2, 173
Allen, Woody 103–4
Alliez, Eric 131
ambiguity 5, 9, 57, 137–74 *passim*
*amour fou* 22, 74, 96, 113, 120, 128, 157
Andrew, Dudley 9
Andrews, Dana 84
Antonioni, Michelangelo 40–1, 63, 72, 168
Artaud, Antonin 71, 127n, 130
Assayas, Olivier 77–8, 120n
*L'Atalante* (1934) 126, 128
Augé, Marc 120, 126
Aumont, Jacques 9
Austin, Guy 107, 117n, 118

Baignères, Claude 149
Barbara 18, 19, 34
baroque/neo-baroque 5, 7, 10, 42–9, 96

Bartas, Sharunas 143, 168, 170, 172
'Bartleby the Scrivener' 133
Bassan, Raphäel 31, 42–3, 51–2, 155
Bataille, Georges 4n, 154
Baudelaire, Charles 19, 24, 52–3, 124–5
Bazin, André 7, 9
*Beau Travail* (1999) 89, 133
Beckett, Samuel 41, 55–6, 167, 174
Beineix, Jean-Jacques 57–60, 83–9
Bellour, Raymond 10
Belmondo, Jean-Paul 37, 86
Bene, Carmelo 47, 51
Benjamin, Andrew 138, 162
Benjamin, Walter 44, 52, 124–5, 151, 162
Bensmaïa, Réda 122–3
Bergala, Alain 13, 49, 60, 76
Bernini 46–7
Berry, David 120n
Besson, Luc 83–9
Beugnet, Martine 105n, 106, 115, 123–4
Binoche, Juliette 3, 36, 108, 115, 118, 128
Blanchot, Maurice 98

bodies 40–1, 72–8, 80–9, 115–16, 145, 156, 173
Bonitzer, Pascal 47, 55n, 75–7, 90
Bowie, David 9, 34–5, 69–70, 92, 95, 126
Bresson, Robert 7, 49, 76, 79, 117n
Buci-Glucksmann, Christine 44, 45, 60, 94–5, 103, 121
Budd, Louis J. 148n
Buñuel, Luis 146–7, 150, 171

Cache, Bernard 42, 124
*Cahiers du Cinéma* 1, 9, 11, 12, 16, 31, 42, 63, 66, 75, 140, 173
Carax, as critic 1, 9, 11–12
Cardinal, Serge 90–2, 97
Carpentier, Alejo 44, 46
Carroll, Lewis 121
Céline, Louis-Ferdinand 2, 19, 31, 38
centre/anchorage, loss of 18, 46, 49, 64, 66–7, 78, 120, 158
chance 3, 4, 37, 39, 66, 113–14, 146
Chaplin, Charles 58, 83, 104
Char, René 24
character, new type of 5, 38, 50, 67, 68, 80–3, 94, 113–14, 133
Charity, Tom 15
Chévrie, Marc 30–1, 81
Chion, Michel 79
*cinéma du look* 22–3, 51, 83–9, 105, 118, 123
Cocteau, Jean 6, 19, 21–2, 24, 37, 47, 61, 92, 127, 139
Cohen, Leonard 140
communication 22–3, 71–5, 80, 97, 156, 164
Conley, Tom 169
Conley, Verena Andermatt 120–1
cosmic forces 6, 58, 62, 66, 75, 93–4, 113
Courbet, Gustave 140

Daly, Fergus 41
dance 9, 18, 20, 37, 75–6, 132–3
Daney, Serge 1, 6, 30–1, 56, 76, 78, 90
Dead Kennedys 18, 19, 37
decadence/neo-decadence 52–7, 62, 82, 93
de Certeau, Michel 121, 126, 128
de Gregorio, Eduardo 61
Deleuze, Gilles 16–17, 41, 49, 53, 63–5, 69, 79, 82–3, 92, 122–3, 126–7, 130–3, 144–59 *passim*
Deleuze, Gilles and Guattari, Felix 71, 122, 128, 151, 154, 165
Delorme, Stéphane 55–6
Demy, Jacques 58, 83
Deneuve, Catherine 140, 170
Denis, Claire 6, 20, 84, 133
Depardieu, Gerard 84–9
Depardieu, Guillaume 140
Derrida, Jacques 116, 129
Descartes, René 45
destiny/fate 3, 39–40, 66, 75, 93, 97, 145, 167
*Diva* (1981) 57–9, 88
Dogme 95 111
doubling 9, 40, 42, 55–6, 103–4
Douchet, Jean 8, 50
Dowd, Garin 56n
Dreyer, Carl 20, 64, 74
Dulac, Germaine 127n
Dumont, Bruno 105, 120

*enfance* 7, 11, 13, 22, 40, 71
Epstein, Jean 17, 67
Escoffier, Jean-Yves 36, 97, 128

false, powers of 8–10, 49, 63, 147
Fargeau, Jean-Pol 161
Fellini, Federico 51
Ferrat, Jean 37
Ferré, Léo 18, 19, 54

*fille rêvée, La* 3
fireworks 18, 105, 116–18, 123, 125–7
*flânêrie* 33
Flot, Yonnick 16
flows/flux/fluidity 14, 19, 47, 68, 93, 121, 131, 160, 165–8, 173
Forbes, Jill 59, 65
Foucault, Michel 4n, 64
Franju, George 80
Frappat, Hélène 6, 61, 74–5
French, Philip 32
Frodon, Jean-Michel 107–9, 155–6, 165, 172
Fuller, Sam 36, 41, 74

Gabin, Jean 85–7
Gainsbourg, Serge 18
Garland, Judy 82
Gianvito, John 15n
Gance, Abel 17
Garrel, Philippe 1, 14–15, 51–2, 55–6, 73–4, 130
Gilloch, Graham 124
Godard, Jean-Luc 13, 36–9, 65–6, 76–8, 103–5, 140–1
Golubeva, Katarina 140
Gordon, Robert 67–8, 70
Grande, Maurizio 114
Gremillon, Jean 35
Griffith, D. W. 17
Gruber, Klaus-Michael 109
Guédiguian, Robert 105

Halley's Comet 19, 35, 73–4, 80, 82, 94, 149
*Hamlet* 95, 138, 140, 158, 161
Hamon, Philippe 146, 148
Hauser, Arnold 67
Haydock, John 139, 168
Hayes, Graeme 123, 127
Heidegger, Martin 163
Hendrix, Jimi 53

Heraclitus 104, 127
Hergé 121
Hermann, Bernard 57
Higuinen, E. 155–7, 168, 173
*Histoire(s) du Cinéma* (1988–98) 104, 141, 171
Hitchcock, Alfred 20, 57–8
Hoberman, J. 125, 155
Hocquenghem, Guy 44
*House, The* (Bartas) 168, 171
Huysmans, J.-K. 52–4, 147

image/reality 37, 62–7
imposture 139, 143, 172, 174
*inespéré/irredeemable*, concepts of 39, 108, 123, 130

Jacquot, Benoit 11n
Jameson, Frederic 149–50, 161
Jousse, Thierry 4n, 107

Kafka, Franz 96
Karina, Anna 37, 77
Keaton, Buster 41, 83, 104
Kierkegaard, Søren 86
Kiéslowski, Krzysztof 75
*King Lear* (Godard) 103–5
Klawans, Stuart 3, 107
Kramer, Robert 12
Kristeva, Julia 150
Kundera, Milan 81

Lacotte, Suzanne Heme de 78
Lagny, Michèle 146n
Lambert, Christophe 84–9
Langdon, Harry 83
Laurel, Stan 83
Lavant, Denis 4n, 21, 24, 30, 36, 71, 83–9, 107, 112, 128, 133–4
Léaud, Jean-Pierre 77
Leibniz, G. W. 16, 41, 44, 45, 46, 47, 56n, 92, 155
Leduc, Paul 44

Léonardini, Jean-Pierre 139, 142
Leutrat, Jean-Louis 145n
Lewis, Jerry 83
lightness, ontological 13–14, 39–40, 66–9, 96–7
literature 2, 19, 22–4, 30–1, 38, 137–74 *passim*
Lucretius 16, 47, 144–5, 159–60, 168
Lukács, Georg 161
Lynch, David 20
Lyotard, Jean-François 49, 118, 156n, 172n

Mailer, Norman 103–4
Mannerism 42–53 *passim*
Marais, Jean 21
Maravall, José 117
Marin, Louis 97
Martin, Adrian 10, 60, 74–5
Massumi, Brian 5, 133, 164
Mazabrard, Colette 24
McKibbin, Tony 84n
*Meet Me in St Louis* (1944) 82
Melville, Herman 2, 8, 17, 18, 20, 22, 133, 137–74 *passim*
Minnelli, Vincente 82
*mise-en-abyme* 21, 38, 48, 69, 104–5, 159
modernism 9, 40, 45, 48–9, 63, 68, 71–2, 83
modernity 52, 62, 125
'Modern Love' (Bowie) 75, 85, 93, 95
Monaco, James 77–8
movement 14, 39, 79–89, 93, 95–6, 115–16, 145
Murnau, F. W. 127, 140
music 18–20, 95–6, 125–6
Musil, Robert 2, 138, 170

naming 137–8, 173–4
Narboni, Jean 59, 72–3

naturalism 14, 17, 20–1, 24, 47, 52, 137–74 *passim*
Nico 54, 56
Nietzsche, Friedrich 22, 96–7, 163
*Night of the Hunter* (1955) 11, 140
Niney, François 115
Noé, Gaspar 105
Noguez, Dominique 52
*Nosferatu* (Murnau) 140

Oliveira, Manoel de 12
Ostria, Vincent 114, 116
Oudart, Thierry 116

Paris 3, 19, 117–21, 124, 149
Parmenides 144
Pasolini, Pier Paolo 38, 47, 51
Perrier, Mireille 9, 20, 36–7, 40–1, 80
Philippon, Alain 54, 84
*Pierre, ou Les Ambiguïtés* (Carax) 138, 141, 160
Pizer, Donald 146
Poicard, Elie 139
Pontormo 43
Pop, Iggy 125–6
Powrie, Phil 16, 70, 92, 123, 127
Prédal, René 107
*Première Nuit, La* (Franju) 80
Prévert, Jacques 19
Prigogine, Ilya 16
Proust, Marcel 74
Public Enemy 126

Quettier, Nelly 36

Rajchman, John 96–7
Ramuz, C.-F. 38
Reader, Keith 120n
Reggiani, Serge 18, 19
Rembrandt 119, 129
Renaud, Tristan 82
Renoir, Jean 146

Resnais, Alain 6, 75
Revault-d'Allonnes, Fabrice 6, 7,
    8, 14, 22, 33, 62, 81
Rimbaud, Arthur 24, 38, 69–70,
    85, 129, 158
Ringwald, Molly 104
Rita Mitsouko, Les 18
Rivette, Jacques 2, 6, 30, 32, 60–
    2, 66, 74–5, 77
Robbe-Grillet, Alain 17, 47, 52, 72
Rohdie, Sam 40
Rosenbaum, Jonathan 11, 14–15,
    30, 77, 120n
Roussel, Christophe 171
Rousset, Jean 47
Ruiz, Raoul 5,  8, 14, 38, 43, 48, 51,
    60, 90, 93, 96
Russell, David 32

Sabouraud, Frédéric 103
sampling 58
Sans titre (Carax) 11, 137, 140
Sarduy, Severo 44
Schefer, Jean-Louis 130
Schérer, René 44
Schneider, Alan 41
Schroeter, Werner 12, 44, 155
Sedofsky, Lauren 161
Séguret, Olivier 13, 143, 155–6
self-reflexivity 5, 9, 51, 63, 130, 137,
    141, 166, 168
Seltzer, Mark 146n, 148
selves/subjects 39, 41, 67–72, 97,
    113, 115, 158, 163
Serres, Michel 16, 44, 45, 47, 159–
    60, 168
Shakespeare, William 15, 17, 80,
    104, 137n, 138, 140
smile of speed 54, 96, 97–8
Smith, Gavin 173
Sonic Youth 18
sound, disjunctive use of 90–1,
    97, 129–30

space
    any-space-whatever 122–8
    election/exclusion 119–21
    fluid 166, 168
    heimlich/unheimlich 150
    inhabiting 77–80
    naturalist 148
    non-diegetic 18
    occupying 40
    purgatorial 155
Spengemann, William C. 167
Spinoza, Baruch de 88, 145, 168
Stallone, Sylvester 1, 9, 10, 11
Stengers, Isabelle 16
Sternberg, Joseph von 51
Strangulation Blues 3
Strauss, Frédéric 108, 113–14
Stroheim, Eric von 150
Sundquist, Eric 146
Sunset Boulevard (1950) 68
Syberberg, Hans-Jurgen 12

tableau vivants 47–8, 66, 68, 93
Taboulay, Camille 121, 128–9
Tarantino, Quentin 20, 65
Tati, Jacques 83
Téchiné, Andre 1, 12, 17, 51–2, 57–
    62, 65–6
Thomas l'imposteur (Cocteau) 139
Thomas l'Obscur (Blanchot) 98
Thompson, David 39
Thomson, David 84
thought 17, 40, 43, 59, 64, 71, 76,
    77, 127, 130–1
time 19, 40, 67, 69–70, 73–4, 94,
    124, 149
Tolstoy, Leo 161
'too late', concept of 52, 55, 57, 93–
    4
Trias, Jean-Philippe 73–4
'Trolley Song, The' 82
Truffaut, Francois 22, 86, 117n

van Sant, Gus 58
Varda, Agnès 120n
ventriloquism 22, 35, 57–8, 70–1,
    80, 91, 93, 133
*Vertigo* (French Film Journal)
    141
Viano, Maurizio 67
Vidor, King 17
Vigo, Jean 19, 109, 128, 171n
Vinterberg, Thomas 20, 150
Visconti, Luchino 51, 53
vision/the eye 21, 46, 116, 129–31,
    164–6
von Trier, Lars 15, 20–1

Walker, Scott 18, 141
Waugh, Katherine 41
Weil, Simone 76
Welles, Orson 47, 51, 64, 72, 158
Wiener, Jean 61
Willemen, Paul 15
Wölfflin, Heinrich 46
Wong kar-wai 75
Woolf, Virginia 104

Zanussi, K. 11
Zola, Emile 19, 52, 144–9, 152
Zonca, Eric 105
Zourabichvili, François 158–9